CW00471202

Macmillan Computer Science Series

Consulting Editor Professor F.H. Sumner, Universit

S.T. Allworth and R.N. Zobel, *Introduction to Real-time Software Design, second edition*

Ian O. Angell and Gareth Griffith, *High-resolution Computer Graphics Using FORTRAN 77*

Ian O. Angell and Gareth Griffith, *High-resolution Computer Graphics Using Pascal*

Ian O. Angell, *High-resolution Computer Graphics Using C*

M. Azmoodeh, *Abstract Data Types and Algorithms*

C. Bamford and P. Curran, *Data Structures, Files and Databases*

Philip Barker, *Author Languages for CAL*

A.N. Barrett and A.L. Mackay, *Spatial Structure and the Microcomputer*

R.E. Berry, B.A.E. Meekings and M.D. Soren, *A Book on C, second edition*

P. Beynon-Davies, *Information Systems Development*

G.M. Birtwistle, *Discrete Event Modelling on Simula*

B.G. Blundell, C.N. Daskalakis, N.A.E. Heyes and T.P. Hopkins, *An Introductory Guide to Silvar Lisco and Hilo Simulators*

B.G. Blundell and C.N. Daskalakis, *Using and Administering an Apollo Network*

T.B. Boffey, *Graph Theory in Operations Research*

Richard Bornat, *Understanding and Writing Compilers*

Linda E.M. Brackenbury, *Design of VLSI Systems – A Practical Introduction*

G.R. Brookes and A.J. Stewart, *Introduction to occam 2 on the Transputer*

J.K. Buckle, *Software Configuration Management*

W.D. Burnham and A.R. Hall, *Prolog Programming and Applications*

P.C. Capon and P.J. Jinks, *Compiler Engineering Using Pascal*

J.C. Cluley, *Interfacing to Microprocessors*

J.C. Cluley, *Introduction to Low-level Programming for Microprocessors*

Robert Cole, *Computer Communications, second edition*

Derek Coleman, *A Structured Programming Approach to Data*

Andrew J.T. Colin, *Fundamentals of Computer Science*

Andrew J.T. Colin, *Programming and Problem-solving in Algol 68*

S.M. Deen, *Fundamentals of Data Base Systems*

S.M. Deen, *Principles and Practice of Database Systems*

C. Delannoy, *Turbo Pascal Programming*

Tim Denvir, *Introduction to Discrete Mathematics for Software Engineering*

P.M. Dew and K.R. James, *Introduction to Numerical Computation in Pascal*

D. England et al., *A Sun User's Guide*

A.B. Fontaine and F. Barrand, *80286 and 80386 Microprocessors*

K.C.E. Gee, *Introduction to Local Area Computer Networks*

J.B. Gosling, *Design of Arithmetic Units for Digital Computers*

M.G. Hartley, M. Healey and P.G. Depledge, *Mini and Microcomputer Systems*

Roger Hutty, *Z80 Assembly Language Programming for Students*

Roland N. Ibbett and Nigel P. Topham, *Architecture of High Performance Computers, Volume I*

Roland N. Ibbett and Nigel P. Topham, *Architecture of High Performance Computers, Volume II*

Patrick Jaulent, *The 68000 – Hardware and Software*

P. Jaulent, L. Baticle and P. Pillot, *68020-30 Microprocessors and their Coprocessors*

J.M. King and J.P. Pardoe, *Program Design Using JSP – A Practical Introduction*

E.V. Krishnamurthy, *Introductory Theory of Computer Science*

continued overleaf

V.P. Lane, *Security of Computer-Based Information Systems*
Graham Lee, *From Hardware to Software – An Introduction To Computers*
A.M. Lister and R.D. Eager, *Fundamentals of Operating Systems*, fourth edition
Tom Manns and Michael Coleman, *Software Quality Assurance*
Brian Meek, *Fortran, PL/1 and the Algols*
A. Mével and T. Guéguen, *Smalltalk-80*
R.J. Mitchell, *Microcomputer Systems Using the STE Bus*
Y. Nishinuma and R. Espesser, *UNIX – First Contact*
Pim Oets, *MS-DOS and PC-DOS – A Practical Guide, second edition*
A.J. Pilavakis, *UNIX Workshop*
Christian Queinnec, *LISP*
E.J. Redfern, *Introduction to Pascal for Computational Mathematics*
Gordon Reece, *Microcomputer Modelling by Finite Differences*
W.P. Salman, O. Tisserand and B. Toulout, *FORTH*
L.E. Scales, *Introduction to Non-linear Optimization*
Peter S. Sell, *Expert Systems – A Practical Introduction*
A.G. Sutcliffe, *Human–Computer Interface Design*
Colin J. Theaker and Graham R. Brookes, *A Practical Course on Operating Systems*
M.R. Tolhurst et al., *Open Systems Interconnection*
J-M. Trio, *8086–8088 Architecture and Programming*
A.J. Tyrrell, *COBOL from Pascal*
M.J. Usher, *Information Theory for Information Technologists*
B.S. Walker, *Understanding Microprocessors*
Colin Walls, *Programming Dedicated Microprocessors*
I.R. Wilson and A.M. Addyman, *A Practical Introduction to Pascal – with BS6192, second edition*

Non-series
Roy Anderson, *Management, Information Systems and Computers*
I.O. Angell, *Advanced Graphics with the IBM Personal Computer*
J.E. Bingham and G.W.P Davies, *Planning for Data Communications*
B.V. Cordingley and D. Chamund, *Advanced BASIC Scientific Subroutines*
N. Frude, *A Guide to SPSS/PC+*
Barry Thomas, *A PostScript Cookbook*

Microcomputer Systems Using the STE Bus

R.J. Mitchell

Department of Cybernetics
The University of Reading

MACMILLAN

First published 1989

Published by
MACMILLAN EDUCATION LTD
Houndmills, Basingstoke, Hampshire RG21 2XS
and London
Companies and representatives
throughout the world

Laserset by
Ponting–Green Publishing Services, London

Printed in Great Britain by
Billings & Sons Ltd

British Library Cataloguing in Publication Data

Mitchell, R.J.
    Microcomputer Systems: using the STE Bus.-
    (Macmillan computer science series).
    1.   Microcomputer systems. Buses
    I.   Title
    004.6

ISBN 0-333-49649-3

Contents

Preface   *ix*

1   Introduction to bus systems   **1**
  1.1   Introduction   1
  1.2   Bus systems   2
  1.3   Data transfer protocols   7
  1.4   Arbitration   11
  1.5   Basic interfaces   13
  1.6   Bus systems with many processors   19
  1.7   Conclusion   21

2   Survey of microcomputer buses   **22**
  2.1   Processor independent bus systems   22
  2.2   S-100   23
  2.3   MUBUS   24
  2.4   CYBUS   25
  2.5   STD   26
  2.6   STE   27
  2.7   G64 and G96   28
  2.8   Multibus I   28
  2.9   VME   29
  2.10   Multibus II   30
  2.11   Futurebus   31
  2.12   The IEEE-488 instrument bus   32
  2.13   Conclusion   33

3   Interfacing slave devices   **34**
  3.1   Principles of interfacing simple devices   34
  3.2   STE bus signals   36
  3.3   Interfacing display and keypad   39
  3.4   Alternative design   43
  3.5   Software   45
  3.6   Interfacing many devices   46

3.7   Interface using a PLA   51
3.8   Interface to non-asynchronous buses   51
3.9   Interfacing EPROM   52
3.10 Interfacing static RAMs   55
3.11 Interfacing dynamic RAM   56
3.12 Analog-digital conversion   63
3.13 Attention requests   67
3.14 Multiple attention requests   72
3.15 Read-modify-write cycles   82
3.16 Burst transfer sequences   83
3.17 Conclusion   84

4   Other slave devices in STE systems   **85**
4.1   Serial communication   85
4.2   Parallel communication and Input/Output devices   95
4.3   Disks   97
4.4   Graphics   100

5   Bus masters on STE   **108**
5.1   Bus masters on STE   108
5.2   Transferring control between master devices   108
5.3   The design of microprocessor-based master devices   109
5.4   Design of direct memory access interfaces   148
5.5   'Intelligent' slaves   153
5.6   Conclusion   161

6   Software and testing   **162**
6.1   System development   162
6.2   Testing a slave module   164
6.3   Testing a master module   168
6.4   Other test equipment   169
6.5   Monitor program   170
6.6   Software development   171
6.7   Conclusion   174

7   Practical considerations   **175**
7.1   Logic elements   175
7.2   Power supplies   179
7.3   Buses   182
7.4   Interfacing to the 'real world'   186
7.5   Conclusion   190

Appendix 1   Asynchronous sequential logic design   **191**
  A1.1   Sequential logic   191
  A1.2   The design method   192
  A1.3   The DATACK* problem   196

Appendix 2   Synchronous sequential logic design   **200**
  A2.1   Synchronous sequential logic design method   201
  A2.2   PLA in keypad and displays circuit   205
  A2.3   6809 interface circuit   207
  A2.4   Dynamic RAM controller   209
  A2.5   Automatic design   211

  Bibliography   *213*
  Index   *215*

Preface

Computers are tools that help in the solution of problems. To do this, they must be given an appropriate set of instructions. If the computer is to be used in a 'real world' application, suitable interfaces are required for converting between the signals inside the computer and those needed outside. For any particular application an appropriate set of interfaces is required.

An ideal configuration which allows the connection of the necessary interfaces is a *bus* system. Here the computer consists of a number of modules which intercommunicate along a series of wires called a *bus*. These modules include microprocessors, memories and peripheral devices. For the particular application, the required interface modules are plugged into the bus.

Unfortunately, there is no standardisation among the manufacturers of microprocessors and their related devices as to the signals required for their interconnection. Hence interfacing these devices to the bus can be problematic. To remedy this a number of bus standards have been proposed. One of the most modern of these standards is the STE bus, now approved by the IEEE as the IEEE 1000 bus.

There are many outstanding features of the STE bus which make it eminently suitable for configuring computer systems.

First, STE was designed by a group of engineers independently of the manufacturers of microprocessors. Therefore, the products of most manufacturers can be connected easily to the bus.

Second, the bus contains a simple yet powerful set of well defined signals which make it very easy to design interfaces to the bus. Consequently, it is an excellent bus for use as the basis of teaching the principles of interfaces.

STE uses the reliable, standard 64-way connectors. One such connector is used for each board, so the system is much cheaper than, say, VME.

Also, STE uses the asynchronous protocol, so it is easy for different speed devices to communicate, and the system automatically allows the use of faster devices as and when they are produced.

In addition, the bus is very flexible. Systems can be produced with

ix

only one microprocessor, but multi-processor configurations are also possible. Thus STE can be used for parallel processing.

Also, the STE bus has IEEE approval. This means that the bus is defined formally and that manufacturers will adhere to the specification. Thus it should prove a very simple matter to interconnect the products from the various manufacturers.

Finally, many manufacturers offer products that connect to STE, so off-the-shelf modules are available with which to configure STE systems. In a period of 18 months STE has jumped from nowhere to being one of the most popular bus systems.

The aim of this book is to describe bus systems and interfacing to microprocessors in general and to describe the STE bus in particular. In the first chapter the principles of bus systems are introduced, showing many of the different schemes which can be used. In chapter 2 a survey is given of many of the bus systems that have been proposed. This shows the advantages of the STE bus. In the third chapter the interfacing of simple peripherals and memory devices to the bus is considered, and many practical circuits are given. Using the principles explained in this chapter, any other peripheral or memory can be connected to the bus. In chapter 4 some other peripherals are described showing how they can be used in systems, rather than giving detailed interfaces. In the fifth chapter circuits are provided showing how some microprocessors and other bus masters may be connected to the bus. This includes methods of handling multiprocessor systems. In chapter 6 the important topics of testing and programming are considered. Chapter 7 is devoted to the practical problems associated with computer systems in general and bus systems in particular. Technical requirements of the STE bus are also described. Finally, there are two appendices describing algorithms for designing sequential logic circuits.

This book is based on three courses given to second/third year students studying the various courses in Cybernetics at the University of Reading. It is assumed therefore that the reader knows about boolean logic and the operation of computers. Any reader without such knowledge is referred to the books listed in the bibliography. The subject matter covered by this short book is quite large, so it has not been possible to cover all the aspects in as great a detail as one might like. However, the book should give enough information to allow both the use of bus systems like STE and to allow readers to design and test their own modules. References are given where appropriate for the reader who requires more detailed information.

Inevitably, in a book about computers many jargon technical terms are used. Unfortunately, when such jargon is used continually it no longer appears as such (to the user), and so TLA*s will inevitably abound without

* Three Letter Abbreviation

the author being aware. It is hoped that all such occurrences are sufficiently explained for the reader.

The author wishes to thank the many people who have helped in the production of this book. These include various people in the Cybernetics Department – Professor Kevin Warwick and other colleagues; my fellow collaborators on *CYBUS*, Dr Andrew Findlay, Paul Minchinton and Chris Williams; Geoff Pearce and Shawn Frazer who helped produce some departmental STE bus systems; thanks also to Dick Zobel for his comments on the manuscript, to Malcolm Stewart for agreeing to the suggestion for the book, to family and friends for encouragement, and to many Cybernetics students, who as part of their projects tested some of the circuits given in this book, or who attended the lectures where this material was tried out.

Reading 1989

1 Introduction to Bus Systems

1.1 Introduction

The computer is a tool – a device to aid in the solution of problems. It does this by processing information; under instruction, it performs logical operations on binary data. At the heart of a computer, therefore, is a central processing unit which can perform these operations: in practice this is often a microprocessor. Also required is memory from which the processor acquires the instructions and which is also used for the storage of data. To serve a useful purpose, the computer must be able to communicate with the 'real world', so an input/output unit is needed also. A general block diagram of a computer is shown in figure 1.1. Here there are the three blocks, the central processing unit (CPU), the memory and the input/output (I/O) unit, and these are connected together by a series of wires called a *bus*.

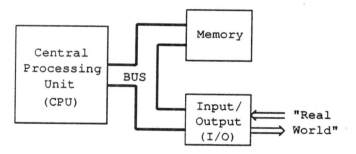

Figure 1.1 Structure of a computer

Alan Turing, one of the founding fathers of modern computing, described the computer as the all purpose processing machine: if given a different set of instructions, the computer will perform a different task. The Turing model of a computer has information fed into the processor, and the results of the processing are output. However, to interact with the 'real world', the signals required externally must be converted by a suitable transducer into those required inside the computer: the reverse process is required for

1

output. As many different types of signal are needed externally, so various transducers are required. For a particular task, the appropriate transducers must be selected, just as the correct set of instructions are needed. A bus system provides a structure which allows the connection of those devices which are required for the given task.

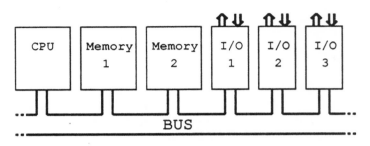

Figure 1.2 Modular bus system

1.2   Bus systems

Modular bus systems

Figure 1.2 shows the structure of a simple microprocessor bus system. As in figure 1.1, there are the basic blocks, CPU, memory and I/O, but these are implemented in separate modules so that it is possible to have a number of different memories (thus reflecting the variety of memory available) and many I/O devices (there are also many possible transducers). It is also possible to have many CPUs. This modular structure allows the user to configure the most appropriate system for any particular task. Consider the following examples.

In a personal computer, the I/O devices required include a keyboard (to allow input from the user), a VDU (visual display unit, on which the computer puts messages to the user), a printer port (so the user can get 'hardcopy' of his program, his word-processed document, or the data in a database, etc.) and disk drives (for storing programs and data). Thus a PC could contain these modules: CPU, memory, disk, keyboard, VDU and printer interface.

The computer based controller of a washing machine receives commands from the switches and dials manipulated by the user, it affects valves which control the flow of water into the machine and it controls the speed of the motor which drives the revolving drum (this may require output signals to command the motor and input signals of measurement of the speed of the motor), etc. Again these could be implemented in a bus structure.

Master/slave concept

In a computer system the CPU is the controller: to fulfil its function it must read its instructions and obey them. Therefore, these instructions must be transferred from the memory to the CPU. When the instructions are obeyed, information may be read from or written to memory, or it may be input from or output to the 'real word'. On a bus system some mechanism is required so that data can be transferred between one device and another, and some device must cause this transfer to happen. The sequence of operations by which the transfer occurs is called a *cycle*.

In a bus system the device which does this is called the *master* and this is often the microprocessor. The device, whether it is a memory or an I/O port, with which the master communicates is called a *slave*. In a bus system there is usually only one master, but there can be many slaves, though usually only one is accessed at a time. (Where there are many masters, which is allowed sometimes, only one instigates data transfer on the bus at any one time.)

Data transfers

When the master device wishes to read data from or write data to a slave device, it must inform the slave of this intention. The first piece of information needed must identify the one slave to be accessed. Each slave is allocated a unique number or *address*; thus when the master instigates the transfer, it first outputs the appropriate address. The address is put on those lines of the bus which are called the *address bus*. The one device whose allocated address matches the values on the address bus is the device with which the master is communicating.

In some systems there is no distinction between memory and I/O devices, they are just given different addresses; the I/O devices are said to be *memory mapped*. In other systems there are separate memory and peripheral addresses. The size of the address bus, that is, the number of unique items that can be accessed, varies with different microprocessors. There are normally at least 16 address lines or bits (that is 2^{16} or 65536 unique items can be accessed) and on some systems there can be as many as 32 lines.

In a bus system there are a number of physical positions in which the modules can be connected. It is sometimes possible to address a module by its position in the system rather than by the allocated number. This is called *geographical* addressing. However, recognition of a module irrespective of its physical position can offer alternative advantages.

Another section of the bus, the *data bus*, is used for transferring the data. If the master is reading the data from the slave, the slave should output the data on to the data bus to be read by the master. However, if a write operation occurs, the master should put the data on to the data bus and the slave will then read the data. The width of the data bus can also vary, normally it is 8, 16 or 32 lines wide; early processors had an 8-bit data bus, the most modern high power processors have 32 lines. The wider the bus, the more data can be transferred at one time and the faster the system can operate. When a processor has a 32 line bus it can usually transfer 8, 16, 24 or 32 items of data depending on requirements: memory devices usually have the same width as the processor, but most peripherals are only 8-bit devices.

The address and data buses together can require many wires. One way of reducing the number of wires is to use the same wires for both address and data, but at different times: address and data are said to be *multiplexed*. At the start of the transfer (or cycle) the lines contain the address, and there is a signal indicating this; for the rest of the cycle they contain data, and another control signal indicates this. One potential problem with multiplexing is that the cycle may take longer than if two separate buses were used. Another problem is that the address may still be required when data are on the bus, so the address will have to be stored in a latch.

Clearly, other information is required as well; for instance, whether data are to be read or written or when address or data are on a multiplexed bus. Thus there is another section of the bus, the *control bus*, along which such signals are passed. There are two parts to the control bus, those which clarify the data transfer and those which provide synchronisation between the master and the slave. As with the address and data buses, the signals on the control bus vary according to the particular microprocessor or bus system being used.

In the first part of the control bus are signals which indicate the direction of data travel (read or write), or signals for handling multiplexed address and data, signals that indicate if a memory or an I/O device is being accessed (in systems which distinguish between the two), and also the size of the data bus (for processors which have a data bus wider than 8 lines), etc. Advanced systems allow the memory to be divided into areas which can be used only by the operating system (the program which supervises the operation of the computer) and others which are used by the application program. This is achieved using other clarification signals on the control bus.

The second part of the control bus, which provides synchronisation between the master and the slave, is needed because of the finite time that it takes for signals to reach their required state and for them to propagate along the bus and through the devices. Thus the slave needs to know that the address and control buses have reached the required state, and the master needs to know that the slave has stored the data being written or output the data on to the data bus for the processor to read. Three synchronisation methods (or protocols) are used for this purpose: these are described in more detail in section 1.3.

Accordingly thus the bus, as shown in figure 1.2, consists of separate parts: the address bus that indicates the slave device with which the master device is communicating, the data bus that contains the data being transferred, and the control bus that determines how and when the transfer occurs. These three parts are usually of different size.

Interrupts

One of the tasks that a computer might perform is to process data entered by the user on a keyboard. When a key is pressed, the computer should read the keyboard to find out which key has been pressed. This can be achieved by *polling*, whereby the computer periodically reads the keyboard interface to test if a key has been pressed. This is a potential waste of the computer's time. Alternatively, the keyboard interface could tell the computer that a key has been pressed and that the computer should read the value of that key. That is, the interface should *interrupt* the processor so that it stops obeying its current program when it has finished the current instruction, then obeys another part of the program which causes the keyboard to be read, and then returns to the program. The action of reading the keyboard is termed *servicing* the interrupt: the instructions needed to do this are said to be in an interrupt service routine, which is similar to a normal subroutine. The advantage of interrupts over polling is that the peripheral is serviced almost immediately rather than only when the processor notices that it needs servicing, although this is not significant if the processor is polling one peripheral continuously and just waiting for it to have data. There is the time penalty, however, in that to run the service routine the processor must push some of its registers on to the stack, and retrieve them again at the end of the routine.

Note that most processors have both *maskable* and *non-maskable* interrupts. A maskable interrupt is one which the processor will ignore unless it specifically enables the interrupt. Typically the processor initialises any pertinent details, such as what to do in response to an interrupt, before enabling it. A non-maskable interrupt, or NMI, cannot be disabled, it is always serviced immediately the processor detects it. NMI is often used for very urgent tasks, such as when the system detects that the power supply is about to fail. Then, it is often possible to store important data in a *non volatile memory*, that is, a device whose contents remain even when the power is removed.

Thus if a slave device wants to attract the attention of the master it must assert an interrupt which it does by signalling one of the lines of the control bus. In response to this the processor, if the interrupt is not masked, will service the interrupt, part of the action of which will cause the interrupt request to be removed. Thus another part of the control bus is used for handling interrupts.

The situation is complicated when there are many potential sources of interrupt. Which should be serviced first? If another interrupt occurs while the processor is obeying a service routine, should this second interrupt be serviced immediately or when the first routine has finished? Methods for solving these problems are considered in section 1.4.

Direct memory access

When a peripheral has new data available, these data are often stored in memory for later processing. This can be done by the processor; when it notices that there are new data or is told so by an interrupt, it reads the data and then stores them in memory. This can be slow: first the polling or interrupt can take time, then two transfer cycles are needed, one to read from the peripheral into the processor and the other to write from the processor to the memory. A better method is to have the peripheral write the data to memory directly: this is termed *direct memory access* or DMA.

To achieve this, the DMA circuitry must instigate a data transfer cycle, that is, the circuit must output addresses, data (in a write cycle) and relevant control information. This it cannot do if the bus master is issuing its own transfer cycles. Thus the DMA circuit must first request control of the bus. The master then stops accessing the bus and sends an acknowledgement to the DMA circuit. Then, and only then, does the DMA circuit instigate its own transfer cycle or cycles. When all the data have been transferred, the circuit removes the request signal and the master carries on with its program.

Again, priority schemes are required for when a number of potential masters simultaneously request control of the bus. This scheme is a faster method than one using the processor, as the actual data transfer takes less time (one cycle only is needed) and the requesting and granting of the bus is usually very fast: often the bus is granted as soon as the current cycle is complete, whereas for an interrupt the acknowledge is not generated until after the current instruction has been obeyed (which may take many cycles).

1.3 Data transfer protocols

As mentioned earlier, a suitable protocol is required for synchronising the master and the slave with which it is communicating. Three such protocols are used in microprocessor based systems: synchronous, semi-synchronous and asynchronous. There are many microprocessors and the exact method by which it implements the protocol(s) that it uses depends on the processor. In this section an arbitrary simple collection of signals are used which, it is hoped, illustrate the principles of the three protocols.

Synchronous transfers

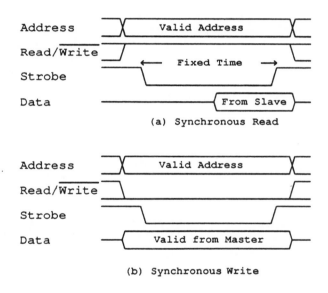

(a) Synchronous Read

(b) Synchronous Write

Figure 1.3 Synchronous data transfers

In the synchronous protocol all transfers take a fixed length of time: the master instigates the transfer cycle and, after a fixed period, it terminates the cycle. The sequence of events for a typical read cycle, also shown in figure 1.3a, is as follows:

Master outputs address on to the bus, specifies a read operation and size of data bus, etc.
When these are stable, the master asserts a strobe signal.
The addressed slave finds the data and puts them on to the bus.
The master, a fixed time after the strobe was asserted, reads the data from the bus and releases the strobe signal.

A similar sequence is used for a write cycle (see figure 1.3b).

> *Master outputs the address, specifies write, data bus size, etc., and puts the data on the data bus.*
> *When these are stable, the master asserts the strobe signal.*
> *The master releases the strobe a fixed time later.*
> *The addressed slave reads the data bus and stores the data when this occurs.*
> *The master then releases the other signals.*

The above assumes that the slave device is fast enough. It is possible, however, that the master will read the data bus before the slave has found the data, or that the slave will not have stored the data before the master terminates the cycle. This problem could be solved by ensuring that the length of the cycle is as long as that needed by the slowest slave device in the system. This is clearly wasteful, and does not allow the system to be improved by the addition of a faster device. Also, in a bus system where different devices are connected depending on the application, the length of the cycle should adapt to fit the current slowest device.

Therefore, a system which allows variable length cycles would be advantageous. This can be achieved by an extension to the above: the semi-synchronous protocol.

Semi-synchronous transfers

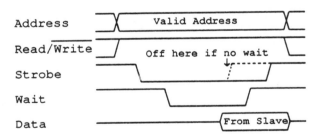

Figure 1.4 Semi-synchronous read cycle

This protocol is the same as for synchronous transfers, unless the slave device is too slow. If this is the case, the slave issues a signal requesting the master to 'wait' so that the master does not end the cycle after the fixed period, but continues it until the 'wait' signal is removed. In figure 1.4 a read cycle is shown with the wait signal being used to extend the cycle. For a fast enough slave the cycle ends after the fixed time, but for a slower slave the end occurs when the slave is ready.

Note that 'wait' should not be used to interface a very slow slave to the processor: typically, 'wait' should not be asserted for more than a few normal cycle times. This is because the processor cannot do anything else during this period, so interrupts are not handled or DMA requests acknowledged. Thus the interface to a very slow device should provide a status line which can be tested by software: the processor should test this line continually until it notices that the device is ready.

This semi-synchronous protocol is used with many different processors, but it is not infallible. A very fast master may terminate the cycle before the slave has asserted the wait signal, thus it will not extend the cycle and data will be incorrect. Also, if a slave circuit has been designed to work with a slow master, there may be no 'wait generator'. Thus the circuit may not work correctly with a faster master unless a wait generator circuit is added. In practice this is often not possible as the circuit, following the well-known law, will have expanded to fill the complete circuit board!

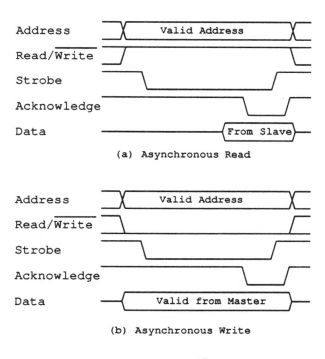

Figure 1.5 Asynchronous data cycles

Asynchronous transfers

An even better protocol would be to have the master and slave talk to each other: this is often termed *handshake*. The master instigates the cycle, but this is terminated only when the slave device has transferred the data. This requires an extra line, asserted by the slave, which 'acknowledges' the transfer. Thus the length of the cycle will vary depending on the speed of the slave device: it will be short for a fast device and longer for a slow device. A typical sequence of operations for a read operation in this asynchronous protocol, illustrated in figure 1.5a, is as follows:

Master outputs address, read signal, etc.
When these are stable, the master asserts the strobe.
The slave, when it has found the data, puts them on the data bus and then asserts the acknowledge signal.
The master detects this, reads the data and then removes the strobe.
The slave releases the acknowledge signal.

For a write operation, a similar sequence occurs: see figure 1.5b:

Master outputs address, write signal, etc., and the data.
When these are stable, master asserts the strobe signal.
The slave, when it is ready, stores the data and then asserts the acknowledge signal.
The master detects this and then removes the strobe, etc.
The slave then releases the acknowledge signal.

Thus with the asynchronous protocol, the cycle adapts automatically with the speed of the slave device: the cycle is short with a fast slave and it is long with a slow slave. If a new faster master is added to the system, it will still work with existing hardware, although the full potential of the faster device will not be utilised.

A problem with the asynchronous protocol occurs when the master tries to access a slave that does not exist. No acknowledge is returned, so the cycle continues indefinitely. However, this problem can be cured, and to advantage. If a program causes the master to access a non-existent slave, it is likely that the program is in error and this should be reported. The error can be detected if it is noticed that an acknowledgement has not been generated within, say, 20 cycle times after the strobe has been asserted: this can be achieved by a simple circuit whose output terminates the cycle and issues an interrupt or similar to the processor telling it of the error.

Having the master and slave handshake can have other advantages. On the 68020, a 32-bit microprocessor, the processor can instigate a cycle in which 32 bits of data are transferred, but if the slave can handle only 8 bits of data it can send back a suitable acknowledgement. The result of this is that the processor can tell that 8 bits have been transferred correctly and that it must transfer the other 24 bits in separate cycles.

It is sometimes said that the asynchronous protocol is slower than the others because of the time it takes for the signals to propagate through the strobe and acknowledgement generator circuitry. However, the propagation delays through modern circuits are small, though the delay is dependent on the length of the bus, so this is a minor problem. The advantages of the method outweigh this disadvantage.

There is an additional logic cost associated with asynchronous systems, but this is also incurred in semi-synchronous systems which assert WAIT states, to deal with slow memories, for example.

Thus the asynchronous protocol seems to be the best method of providing synchronisation between the master and the slave device. It is interesting to note that many of the more modern microprocessors and bus systems (including STE) use the asynchronous method.

1.4 Arbitration

When a slave attracts the attention of a master, by issuing an interrupt or a DMA request, the master responds suitably. However, when many devices issue a request at the same time, there are problems, in determining which device issued the request, which should be serviced and whether a higher priority request should override one currently being serviced.

Multiple request lines

One method of handling multiple requests is to have one line per requesting device. The processor can therefore tell which device issued the request by which line was asserted. If many lines are asserted at once, some scheme is required for determining the priority of which should be serviced first.

This can be achieved with a fixed priority scheme: line 1 has the highest priority, then line 2, etc. Thus, if both lines 3 and 6 are asserted, line 3 will be serviced first and line 6 afterwards (assuming that no higher priority line is asserted by then). The problem with this is that the lowest priority device may never be serviced.

An alternative, often called *round-robin*, is a rotating priority scheme. Once a line has been serviced, it automatically becomes the lowest priority line. This is generally more fair, but can be more complicated to operate.

Single lines with vectors and daisy-chain priority

One problem with the above is that there may not be enough request lines if there are many I/O devices. To surmount this problem a single request line can be used, which any device can assert. In response to such an assertion the master issues an acknowledgement which is passed down the bus to the requesting device. If it is necessary for the master to know which device issued the request, the interruptor must return some form of identification to the master. (With interrupts this is often required, because the master must obey the code in the appropriate service routine, although with DMA requests it may not be necessary). This identification is called a *vector*, and when the slave receives the acknowledgement, it puts the vector on to the data bus. Such a transfer is called a *vector fetch* cycle. In some systems the vector is a number which is used to calculate the address of the service routine to be obeyed: if vector V is returned, the service routine is the 'Vth' one in a list. In other systems the vector is an instruction which is to be obeyed by the master: it might tell the master to jump to a particular address for example.

There is a problem if many devices issue a request simultaneously: they will all receive the acknowledgement and so may all try to put their vector on to the data bus. A solution to this lies in the way that the acknowledgment is propagated down the bus. Figure 1.6a shows a *daisy-chain* connection for the acknowledgement where for each module there is an input from the previous one and an output to the next. Normally, the input of the module is passed directly to the output, but if the particular module issued the request, that module does not pass the signal on. Thus the device which issued a request and is nearest the master is the only one that receives the acknow- ledgement and outputs its vector.

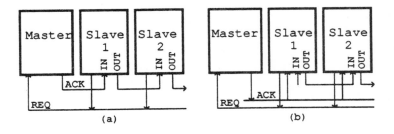

Figure 1.6 Daisy-chain methods

An alternative daisy-chain priority scheme is shown in figure 1.6b. Here the acknowledge line is global to all devices, so they will all receive it, but only one will respond to it. That one device is determined by the daisy-chain lines, which can be thought of as enable lines. Each module has an 'in' and an 'out' line. Normally the 'out' line has the same value as the 'in' line, but if a module is asserting a request, it forces the 'out' line to be off and so disables all devices further down the chain. Thus one device only which issued a request will have its 'in' line in the on state, and that is the device which should accept the acknowledgement and output the vector.

There are problems with both of these schemes. First, the priority is fixed and is based on the physical location of the boards, which can be problematic. Second, if there is a gap in the bus, the signal will not propagate further down the chain. Third, it takes time for the acknowledge signal to propagate through each module, so the operation might be slow, though this is applicable to the first scheme only. Also, care is needed to ensure that a higher priority device does not interrupt the chain part way through an acknowledge cycle, as then the requesting device further down the chain may only receive a part cycle, and thus be serviced inadequately.

Polling after interrupt

Another method that can be used to discover which device issued the request is to have the master test each potential device. This is done in a series of transfer cycles: the master reads from each slave until it discovers one which issued an interrupt. This method is not very satisfactory as it can be slow, but suitable algorithms can be used to select the priority for handling the various devices.

1.5 Basic interfaces

The constituent parts of a bus system, the microprocessor(s), the memories, the I/O devices and the bus, must all be connected together. That is, interfaces are needed between the processor(s) and the bus, and between the other devices and the bus. In some computer systems the processor can be connected directly to the bus, but in a modular bus system, where signals have to travel significant distances, buffers are needed as the processors do not have the necessary capacity to drive the signals. Also, the signals from the processor may not be those required for the bus; a different transfer protocol may be needed for example, so the interface will need to convert those signals from the processor into those required on the bus. As regards the slave devices, interface circuitry is required to check that the correct address is on the bus and to handle the protocol, and buffers may be needed because these devices also may not be able to drive signals along the bus.

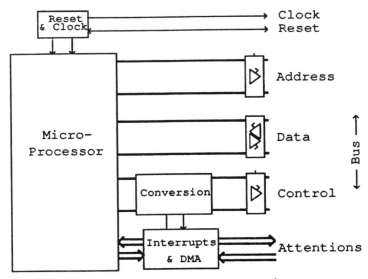

Figure 1.7 Basic processor interface

Interfacing microprocessors to a bus

Figure 1.7 shows a block diagram of a board with a microprocessor and its interface to a bus. The constituent parts are the microprocessor itself, the clock and reset circuit, buffers to drive the address and data bus, a circuit to convert the control signals from the processor into those required on the bus and the block to handle interrupt and DMA requests.

Microprocessors need a continuous train of pulses at regular intervals, termed a clock. This clock signal is used to provide regular timing and for synchronisation of events, both internal to the processor and externally. This signal is normally generated using a quartz crystal and it is often output to the bus as well, being used for timing purposes in other modules. A reset signal is needed to ensure that the processor starts correctly when the system is first switched on, and to allow the user to restart the program when something has gone drastically wrong. Thus the reset circuit is in two halves: one provides a 'power-up' reset and the other interfaces a reset switch to the processor.

The address and data bus buffers provide two facilities, extra driving capability for signals, and they allow different devices to drive the bus at different times. This latter mode is clearly needed on the data bus: during read cycles the one addressed slave must output data on to the bus, while all other slaves must not and, during write cycles, the processor must drive the bus. This is achieved by buffers with *tristate* outputs.

Normally, the outputs of logic circuits can take one of two states, logic '1' or logic '0', but tristate outputs have a third state: high impedance. In this last state the output is turned off, it does not drive the bus at all, so that effectively the output is disconnected. Thus it is possible to connect a number of tristate outputs together, provided that at most only one has its output in the non-high impedance state: the one turned on has a low impedance, while all the other outputs have a high impedance, so that these others have a negligible effect. Thus, tristate buffers have a series of inputs and corresponding outputs, and a control signal which enables or disables the outputs. Other circuits, including latches, can also have tristate outputs.

For the data bus, where data can travel in either direction, a bidirectional tristate buffer is usually used. This contains two sets of buffer circuits, one able to pass data from the processor to the bus, the second able to pass data in the opposite direction. Two control signals are needed: one is an enable, which if asserted causes outputs of one set of buffers to be turned on; the other control signal, direction, is used to select which set of buffers is enabled.

For the address bus it is not so obvious at first that tristate buffers are needed. If the microprocessor is the only master in the system, they are not needed, but if there are other processors or DMA control circuitry, then these devices may want to drive the bus and so output addresses, data and control signals. Thus buffers are needed for the address bus and their outputs are disabled when a bus request is acknowledged. Another device is then allowed to drive the bus.

For the control signals, conversion is required from those which are used by the microprocessor to those needed for the bus. Some of these signals will also have tristate outputs. The conversion is needed because there is no standardisation between manufacturers of microprocessors as to what control signals are needed. In addition to the different protocols, some processors have a signal specifying read or write and a separate strobe (as in the system described in section 1.3), whereas others have separate strobes for reading and writing. Also there is the handling of memory and I/O devices, bus width, etc.

For interrupts, some processors have a number of interrupt request lines, whereas others have just one or two (one being NMI). Some processors understand the concept of vectors and can use them directly, whereas others cannot. Most processors can handle one bus request and generate a suitable acknowledge, though the exact requirements for the processor varies between the different devices.

For systems containing multiple processors, the basic block diagram for a processor board is appropriate, though extra circuitry may be needed. This is covered in more detail in section 1.6. It is also possible, and often desirable, to have some memory and I/O devices on the same board as the processor.

Interfacing slave devices

A block diagram for connecting a simple slave board to a bus is shown in figure 1.8. This board contains three slave devices on it and does not generate interrupts or DMA requests. Here the basic blocks are a valid signal circuit, which checks that the correct valid address is on the bus, the select circuit which selects the one of many possible devices that may be on the board, and finally a bidirectional buffer to drive the data bus.

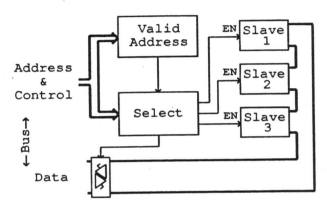

Figure 1.8 Basic slave interface

The valid signal circuit compares the address on the bus with the one allocated to the module (normally set by switches) and also ensures that the strobe signal(s) are active. It also generates the acknowledge or wait signal for handling the transfer protocol.

The select circuit determines which device of many is accessed when a valid address has been detected. The selection is usually determined by some address lines and sometimes the read/write signal: some devices can only be read from, others only written to, and some both. The simple device that is selected is the one which accepts data during a write cycle or which outputs its data during a read cycle.

Often the various devices have tristate outputs themselves, but they are not powerful enough to drive the bus directly even though they can be used within the board. This means that outputs of each device can be connected together (so long as one set at most is enabled at any time), and the combined bus is connected to the system bus via a bidirectional buffer whose control signals are generated appropriately from the valid address block.

A slave with interrupts

The interface of a slave device which can also generate interrupts is the same as that in figure 1.8, except for an extra block to handle the interrupt. This extra block contains circuitry to generate the interrupt request, handle the acknowledgement (potentially returning a vector on the data bus and clearing the request) and process any daisy-chain priority lines.

As regards the interrupt request signal, as any slave in the system may generate this signal, some means is needed so that one or many can do so. This can be achieved by an open-collector (or open-drain) output of a device. This is illustrated by figure 1.9.

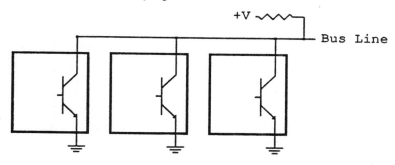

Figure 1.9 Open collector outputs

The output stage of the device is a transistor whose collector (or drain for an FET) is open circuit (hence 'open collector'). To operate correctly, an external resistor is required between the output and the power supply. If the transistor is turned on, current flows through the resistor and the transistor, so a voltage is dropped across the resistor and the output is a logic '0'. If the transistor is off, no current flows, so the output is a logic '1'. The advantage of this type of output is that many such outputs can be connected together (as in figure 1.9). If any of these transistors is turned on, current flows, so the output is a logic '0': it is a logic '1' only if all the output transistors are off. This is exactly what is required. The interrupt request line is common to all slaves, and any one of them can assert the line, thus requesting an interrupt. Note that open-collector lines are also used for generating wait or acknowledge signals (again any slave can issue these signals).

When the interrupt acknowledge signal is returned, the device (if enabled) should clear the request signal and, if appropriate, output the vector on to the data bus. The slave can assert the request line when it has data for the master or wishes for data from the master. In systems with daisy-chain lines the slave must handle these lines. Care is needed with these lines during an acknowledge cycle not to disable a device further down the chain part way through the cycle, as the interrupt may not be serviced correctly if this occurs.

Slave with DMA interface

A slave which is capable of direct memory access has a slightly more complicated interface: this is shown in figure 1.10. Again the basic interface shown in figure 1.8 will probably be required because normal processor instigated data transfers with the board will be needed for programming the interface. However, extra circutry is needed for requesting the bus and for driving the bus when this has been given.

As regards the request signal, this will be similar to that for issuing interrupts. Again an open collector signal is often used. When the acknowledge signal is returned to the slave (and it is enabled by priority lines), the slave can take control of the bus. Now it must issue the address, data (during a write operation) and the appropriate control signals, handle the protocol of the bus and, for a read operation, store the data returned to the circuit. This part of the circuit is similar to that required for the microprocessor interface. In fact, most of the circuit is normally achieved by a DMA controller device, which is a preprogrammed microprocessor able to generate addresses and suitable control signals.

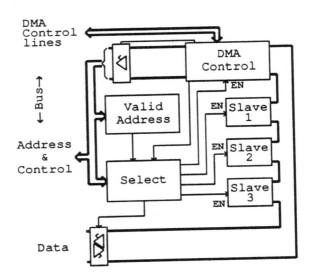

Figure 1.10 DMA slave interface

1.6   Bus systems with many processors

In a modular bus system there is no reason why there should not be many master devices as well as many slaves, although this requires some special handling. The advantage of such multiple processor systems is that many programs, or many parts of a program, can be run at the same time. This is known as *parallel processing* and is becoming more common with the increasing variety and availablity of microprocessors. In a parallel processing system the various processors are each solving part of the problem and need to communicate with each other to pass results obtained by each part.

Although the same structure can be used for single processor systems as for those with many processors, there is the problem that only one device can control the bus at any one time. Thus, for example, if two processors want to use the bus, one has to wait until the other has finished using the bus before it can continue. There is then no great advantage in having the second processor.

This problem can be obviated by ensuring that each processor uses the bus only infrequently. This can be achieved by having memory and I/O devices on the same board as the processor: normally each processor reads its own program from its own memory and accesses its own I/O ports. The bus is used only for transferring data between the processors and for accessing devices that are shared. A suitable method is needed for controlling such a system.

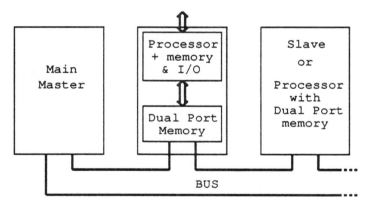

Figure 1.11 A multi-processor bus system

One way this can be done, illustrated in figure 1.11, is to have a master processor which is the only one that drives the bus directly: it is therefore the device which controls all the memory and I/O devices on the bus. The other processors, often called *intelligent slaves*, are self contained, having their own memory and I/O devices and a suitable interface allowing them to send messages to or receive messages from the master processor. Often this interface is a memory device which can be accessed both by the on-board processor and by the master processor: this is called a *dual-port memory*. When the processor wants to send data to the master, it loads the memory with the data. When the master detects this, it can read the data. Alternatively, the processor could issue an interrupt when the data have been loaded. The reverse process could be used for sending data to the on-board processor. It is a good idea if the master processor is also able to send data to all other processors at the same time, because in some applications these other processors operate on the same data, and so the master processor has only to transfer the data once.

Another method is to have a slave memory module on the bus which each device can use for transmitting messages to other devices. When one master wishes to send a message, it checks that no other device is using the memory and then marks it available and loads the message which can then be read. If another device is already sending data, the first device must wait. If the amount of message passing is small, this system can be quite effective.

For faster transmission of messages, block transfers can be used. In these the data being sent are stored in successive addresses. Thus as soon as one byte is sent the address of the next byte is known; there is therefore no point in transmitting the address, hence the cycle can take less time.

One problem with shared memories is that two devices might examine the memory to check that it is available, both find that it is, and so both mark the memory as unavailable. This problem can be overcome by an uninterruptible cycle in which the memory is read and a new value written: this is called a *read-modify-write* cycle. Thus the second device will not be able to read the memory before the first has read it and marked it. An alternative method is to *lock* the bus: that is, a device takes control of the bus and does not allow another to instigate transfers until the bus has been unlocked.

Another scheme for message passing is by interrupt cycles. These are another form of data transfer cycles. Here the address contains both the address of the device to which the message is sent and that of the sender, and the data contains the message. When such a cycle is detected, the data are passed to the appropriate processor immediately.

A better approach is some method which allows each processor to have access to all other resources: then the programmer of the processor does not need to worry about how the data are acquired or where they are stored; that is done by hardware. This method can be achieved by a buffer or *cache* memory for each processor which contains the data needed and the processor accesses its own cache. This basic idea is utilised in the advanced Futurebus system: more information on this is available in the literature and in chapter 2.

1.7 Conclusion

A modular bus system provides a suitable structure for configuring a computer with the devices needed for a given application. Many such devices are available but the signals required for their interconnection are also varied: different-sized buses are needed, various transfer protocols are used, etc. To solve this problem a number of standard buses have been designed to allow the connection of the devices and some of these are described and contrasted in the next chapter.

2 Survey Of Microcomputer Buses

2.1 Processor independent bus systems

It has been shown that a modular bus system is an ideal configuration for constructing a computer to help solve a problem: those devices which are best suited to the problem are plugged into the bus, just as the appropriate instructions are selected. The description 'devices' includes not only memory and peripherals, but also the microprocessor. The devices need to be connected together, but there is no standardisation between manufacturers as to the signals required for the connection; hence a number of bus systems have been proposed. Some systems were designed by the manufacturers and so are based around their own products, which can make connecting other devices to these buses problematic. Other systems were proposed by independent bodies with the requirement that any device could be connected easily, regardless of manufacturer or product: these systems are described as *processor independent*. Some of the proposals have been adopted formally by bodies such as the IEEE: the advantage of these is that a standard is provided to which designers adhere. Where this has not occurred, there tend to be variations in the standard, making it awkward to connect devices from different manufacturers.

In this chapter a number of these bus systems are described and contrasted. The survey is not exhaustive, for there are many different bus systems; but significant early systems and many of the more modern systems are given. Also included in the survey is the IEEE 488 instrument bus, as this provides a comparison between a microcomputer bus system and an instrumentation bus. Note that the section on each bus must, of necessity, be short: for more information the reader should refer to the literature. Suitable references are given in the appropriate sections.

In the survey the characteristics of the buses are given, including the size of the bus, the type of transfers, handling of interrupts and multiple processors, the edge connector used (specifically indicating if the 64 or 96-way DIN 41612 type connector is used, as these are considered to be very reliable) and an indication of speed. This last figure is given as the time for a read cycle and the amount of data transferred (8, 16 or 32 bits); it is based on information in *Microcomputer Buses and Links* by Del Corso, Kirrman and Nicoud. This time is chosen because most transfer cycles are read operations. A system which has a wide data bus (say 32 bits) can obviously transfer more data at one time than a system whose data bus is only 8 bits wide. Note that the time considers only bus and protocol delays; it does not include those due to memory or logic, nor does it show the advantages of block transfers. In the reference given above these buses, and others, are contrasted and the results given in tabular form.

2.2   S-100

The S-100 bus was one of the first to be accepted widely. It was introduced by MITS Inc in the USA in 1975 as part of an 8080 based system. Thus the signals on S-100 largely follow the 8080 bus. The bus is so named because it uses a 100-line gold-plated edge connector. Under the original specification, 19 of these lines were undefined, and the timing of other lines was not fixed, so it could not be guaranteed that any S-100 board would work with any other. Thus the IEEE proposed a tighter specification to ensure compatibility. As a result of this S-100 became one of the most widely used buses.

There are a number of oddities in the bus. First, rather than having a single bidirectional data bus, on S-100 there are two unidirectional buses. This was done because of the then lack of bidirectional buffers: clearly there is no advantage these days. Also, most S-100 boards recombine the two buses into one! There was one advantage to this system: when 16-bit processors became available, requiring a 16-bit data bus, the two S-100 data buses were combined to form one bidirectional 16-bit bus. Two handshake lines were introduced also, so that the master device could find out from the slave whether it could accept a 16-bit transfer of data. In the revised S-100 standard there are 24 address lines.

The semi-synchronous bus protocol is used on S-100, so there are 'wait' signals on the bus: two in fact. There are also a number of signals indicating memory or peripheral accesses, reading or writing, etc. There are more signals than are necessary which makes designing a processor board for a device other than an 8080 more difficult. This makes the bus somewhat unsatisfactory. Designers of more modern buses have thought more carefully!

Also provided are 4 DMA request lines, 8 vector interrupt lines and a non-maskable interrupt, as well as the appropriate acknowledge signals. Thus the S-100 is quite flexible.

Another feature of S-100 is the power supply. Rather than providing regulated supplies, unregulated +8 V and +/-16 V are supplied. Thus each board requires a regulator to generate the required voltages. This can be useful in reducing noise, but bad layout on the bus defeats this: fast moving clock signals are placed next to slower lines and this can induce noise into these slower lines.

The speed rating is 1000 ns for a 16-bit transfer (2 Mbytes/s).

In summary, the S-100 is not a very good bus. It has too many lines which are specific to the 8080 and often more than one signal for producing the same function. Also the layout of signals is not ideal and, by modern standards, it is slow. However, the S-100 did prove to be very successful. It was superseded by the Multibus (see section 2.8). More information on the bus is given in *The S-100 and other MicroBuses* by Poe and Goodwin.

2.3   MUBUS

In 1977, J.D. Nicoud designed one of the first processor-independent bus systems: it was called MUBUS. The object of MUBUS was to provide a simple yet powerful set of signals allowing the design of modular micro-processor systems with the ability to accept microprocessors of various manufacturers. Also, a minimal number of signals would be needed in the design of an interface to the bus. Also provided are interrupt and DMA request lines. It uses a double sided, 37 way connector.

On MUBUS there are 16 address lines and 16 data lines, although it is not required that all these lines be used. The address bus is only 7 bits wide during peripheral or refresh cycles (see chapter 3 regarding refresh of dynamic memory). There is no way of determining whether 8 or 16 bits of data are transferred. The control signals for simple transfers are like those postulated in chapter 1 for a semi-synchronous bus: a single line indicating read or write, three strobes (one for memory access, one for I/O and the third for memory refresh), and a wait signal. The appropriate strobe signal is asserted only after the address lines and the read/write signal are stable. These lines and the data remain valid until after the strobe is released. Another signal is used to indicate when the data bus contains valid data, though this is not strictly needed as the data are on the bus when the strobe signal is released and that is a the best time for the addressed slave to store the data.

For interrupts, there is one interrupt request line and a corresponding acknowledge line in response to which the interrupting device should put an identifying vector on the bus. To determine priority, two daisy-chain lines are used. Identification of interruptor can also be achieved by polling. A non-maskable interrupt is also provided.

As regards DMA, there is a corresponding set of signals: a bus request, acknowledge and two daisy-chain lines. A potential master asserts the request line and can take the bus when the acknowledge is returned and the input priority line is true. There is a separate request line for another processor to request the bus.

The power supply on the bus is well defined and well provided. This is divided into three sections, for digital signals, analog signals and external opto-isolated signals. For digital signals there are a GND, +5 V, +12 V, −5 V and −12 V regulated supplies. For analog signals there is a separate GND as well as +15 V and −15 V supplies: this is a good idea as digital signals can affect high resolution analog-digital converters; these extra supplies help to reduce interference on the analog signals. For opto-isolated circuits there is another GND and a +5 V supply.

The speed rating is 200 ns for 16-bit data (10 Mbytes/s).

In conclusion, MUBUS provided an early truly processor independent bus. It was well designed, and provided a good set of signals for small microcomputer systems. However, its use was largely restricted to Europe, particularly Switzerland. For more information, see *Microscope* − special edition on the MUBUS standard, Vol 1. No 8. April 1977.

2.4 CYBUS

In 1980 in the Department of Cybernetics at the University of Reading another bus was designed (as part of an undergraduate project) based largely on MUBUS with some improvements. At that time various micro-computer systems were being designed and, to save time, the students doing the projects agreed to produce interfaces to a standard bus so that they could share peripheral boards. The resulting bus, CYBUS, which was subsequently enhanced by postgraduates (including the author), became the standard bus in the department for 8 years. CYBUS has been used as the basis for teaching the principles of interfacing and for various projects during this time and is only now being replaced by the STE bus.

The basic principle on CYBUS is that the signals on the bus should be those which make it very easy to interface slave devices. This means that CYBUS can be used for teaching the principles without having to worry about the idiosyncrasies and complexities required when interfacing to real processors. MUBUS almost did just that, but it was felt that some slight changes were needed, and that the DIN 41612 edge connector should be used.

On CYBUS there are 16 address lines (though 8 only are significant for peripheral transfers), and 16 data lines, the bottom 8 of which are used for byte transfers. An extra signal is used to distinguish between 8-bit and 16-bit transfers: it has the same timings as the read/write signal. Another difference from MUBUS is that during write cycles the data are output before the strobe is asserted. Thus there is no need for another signal indicating when valid data are on the bus: the strobe signal does that.

Also provided is a signal which indicates whether an instruction is being fetched by the current data transfer cycle. This can be useful when bus analysers are connected to the system, particularly devices which are able to record and process instructions, as this signal tells the analyser that an instruction is on the bus.

As regards interrupts and DMA requests, the same signals are used as with MUBUS, though only one bus request signal is used for both DMA controllers and other processors.

A late extension to the standard allowed for extra address lines by multiplexing the upper 16 lines on to the data bus at the start of a cycle.

Speed rating: 200 ns for 16-bits (10 Mbytes/s).

Philosophically, CYBUS provides an ideal set of signals for a semi-synchronous bus for small systems. However, as explained in chapter 1, an asynchronous bus is better, which is why the department has adopted the STE bus. The internal departmental reference is *The CYBUS Book*, Dept of Cybernetics, University of Reading.

2.5   STD

Another early semi-synchronous bus is the STD or IEEE 961 bus, proposed in 1976. STD is short for STandarD, and in some respects it is the forerunner of STE. It has been one of the more popular 8-bit buses. Although originally designed as a peripheral bus, it has been used in medium performance systems, often in industrial control and instrumentation.

STD provides 16 address lines, although the latest version has extended this to 24 (the extra 8 are multiplexed on the data bus, so new boards may not be compatible with the old). The data bus is only 8-bit wide. There are separate strobes for memory and peripherals and for read and write cycles, and vector fetch and refresh cycles are also supported. STD also has status lines, one of which indicates an instruction fetch cycle.

Again there are bus and interrupt request and acknowledge lines, but only one pair of daisy-chain priority lines (this can be configured for either bus requests or interrupts, but not both). There is also an NMI line.

Speed rating: 500 ns for 8-bit transfer (2 Mbytes/s).

It is largely because of the extensions and various options on the bus, which make the interworking of products from different vendors problematic, that the STE bus has been adopted by the IEEE as a replacement for STD. Also, a double 28 way edge connecter is used in STD.

2.6 STE

The STE or IEEE 1000 bus was first proposed in 1982 and the standard approved by the IEEE in 1988. STE stands for STandard Eurocard bus. It is an asynchronous bus designed for small bus applications and which has gained much support in its particular niche in the market. There are currently many manufacturers of STE products, making it a truly processor-independent bus.

STE has 20 address lines, though 12 only are significant during I/O cycles, but only 8 data lines. It provides read, write, indivisible read-modify-write and multiple (block) data transfers, and the cycles are classified as memory, peripheral or vector fetch. These options are specified by codes on three command lines (three of the eight codes are unused but reserved for expansion purposes). There is an address strobe; which when active indicates a valid address on the address lines, and a data strobe, when this is activated the command lines (and data during a write cycle) are stable. The addressed device responds to the cycle, when it is ready, by issuing an acknowledge signal; if no such signal occurs within a suitable time, a bus error signal is activated by the system controller.

There are 8 attention request lines, which can be configured by the user for interrupts, DMA requests, or any other purpose non-specific to a par-ticular processor. In response to an attention request, the bus master can identify the requesting device by issuing a vector fetch cycle (the address output is in the range 0..7 corresponding to the number of the request line) or by polling. There are no daisy-chain lines, so one board only should assert any particular request line.

As regards bus requests, in addition to the above there are two sets of specific bus request and acknowledge signals. Thus there can be a default master and up to two potential bus masters. The handling of these is performed by a central arbiter which is normally on the same board as a microprocessor and the system controller. This controller also provides the reset and clock signals.

A two way DIN 41612 edge connector is used.

The speed rating is 200 ns for 8-bit transfers (5 Mbytes/s).

STE was designed in collaboration with the IEEE group working on the VME bus (section 2.9), so there are similarities between them: STE has been described as the 'little brother of VME'. Both buses have been used in the same system, with the STE bus being used for peripherals (where the 8-bit bus is no great limitation) with larger memory cards on VME. A 16 or 32-bit processor can be put on the bus with no disadvantage if 16 or 32-bit wide memory is on the same board as the processor. This book is a reference to the STE bus, but the full specification is available from the

IEEE in the USA or, in the UK, from the STEMUG, the STE manufacturers and users group.

2.7   G64 and G96

G64 was designed in 1981 by GESPAC and has gained quite wide acceptance in Europe. G96 is an updated version providing either more address lines or data lines (it is interpreted variously by different groups). The buses do not have IEEE support. G64 uses a two way DIN 41612 connector; G96 uses the three row version.

G64 has 16 address lines, G96 has 24, and 16 data lines (though the upper byte is sometimes interpreted as extra address lines). During peripheral cycles, 10 address lines are used. The transfer cycles accepted are read, write, read-modify-write and vector fetch. Two timing protocols are provided: asynchronous and semi-synchronous. The timings are in fact rather like those of the 68000 (see chapter 5), so G64 is not as processor independent as STE.

On G64 there are 3 interrupt request lines (like those of the 6809) and 5 on G96, and an interrupt acknowledge signal. Daisy-chain priority lines are available, though these can be used for interrupts only if they are not required for bus requests. The three lines needed for bus requests are again like those needed with the 68000. G96 has 6 lines which can be used to handle priorities for potential bus masters.

Speed rating: for semi-synchronous mode, 1000 ns (2 Mbytes/s), for asynchronous mode, 200 ns (10 Mbytes/s), for 16-bit transfers.

The applications for G64 and G96 are the same as for STE. However, although the buses are quite widely used, they are not as good as STE for example, because of the uncertainty of some of the lines in G96, and the too great a resemblance to signals required for the 68000. Also they do not have the support of the IEEE to maintain the standard rigidly. More information about the buses can be acquired from GESPAC.

2.8   Multibus I

Multibus was proposed by INTEL in 1976 and standardised as IEEE 796. It was the first fully specified systems bus, and so became very popular. Although introduced to support the INTEL 8080, 8085 and 8086 families of processors, products from other manufacturers can be used. Multibus provides many features allowing the systems to be expanded to meet new specifications. In particular, it has many facilities specifically for handling multiple processors on the bus. It uses an 86-pin connector.

Multibus can support 20 address lines (16 for peripherals) and 16 or 8 data lines (it has a signal indicating bus width). Read, write and vector fetch cycles only can be generated, and the asynchronous protocol is used.

It has 8 interrupt request lines and various responses to these are allowed, including vector fetch. The variety reflects the properties of the different INTEL processors.

As regards multiprocessing, there can be many potential masters on the bus, but one is the default master. Other devices may request the bus and the arbitration can be provided by daisy-chain priority or specific request-grant operations. For handling a shared resource, a master can issue a lock signal which remains active for many transfer cycles, thus preventing any other device from accessing the bus.

Speed rating: 200 ns for 16-bits (10 Mbytes/s).

Although produced by INTEL for their products, Multibus I became a most popular microprocessor bus with a great many boards being available. It has now been superseded by Multibus II (see section 2.10). More information is available from INTEL.

2.9   VME

VME was developed by Motorola with Philips and Signetics for their 68000 processor in 1980, and it has been adopted as IEEE 1014. The bus was first called VERSABUS and, because most of the development was in Europe, boards produced were referred to as VERSA modules – Europe; this became VME.

There are 32 address lines on the latest version of VME and 6 address modifier bits which can be used for specifying operating system memory, etc. The data bus is up to 32 bits wide and the bus determines dynamically whether 8, 16 or 32 bits are transferred. Peripherals are memory mapped, although this can be done using one of the modifier bits.

Read, write, read-modify-write and vector fetch cycles are provided and the asynchronous protocol is used. There are separate address and data strobes, and acknowledge and bus error signals are used to terminate cycles.

VME has 7 interrupt request lines with an interrupt acknowledge and daisy-chain priority lines. As regards multiprocessors, there are 4 bus request lines, and these are processed by the arbiter which allocates the bus appropriately. There are 4 daisy-chain lines: a bus grant signal propagates from the arbiter through the various boards until it reaches the board which issued the request. When the device has received the grant signal, it asserts the bus busy line to inform the arbiter that it has control of the bus. If a higher priority device then wants the bus, the arbiter can inform the current master by issuing the bus clear signal. The master, at an appropriate moment (which may be when it has finished with the bus), then relinquishes the bus by releasing the bus busy line.

The VME speed rating is 210 ns for 32-bit transfers (19 Mbytes/s).

VME is widely used and popular and it uses DIN 41612 connectors. It is a more powerful bus and more expensive than say STE, so it fits into a different niche in the market: for example, many high performance work stations use the bus. Although it is claimed that VME is processor independent, it is optimised for the 68000 family of processors. For more information, see *The VMEbus Specification* by HTE.

2.10   Multibus II

Multibus II was developed by INTEL in 1983 to improve on Multibus I. It provides enhanced multiprocessor support, better reliability (it uses a DIN 41612 connector), easy configuration and maintenance and a higher bus bandwidth than Multibus I. It has been accepted as standard IEEE 1296.

Multibus II has 32 lines multiplexed to provide address and data: not all addresses are required for some transfers, for example, only 24 are significant regarding peripherals. The four classes of addressing are memory, peripherals, messages and interconnect; the first two are common to most buses, but the others require comment. Interconnect cycles are used to discover information about any board: its test status, self tests, dual-port memory configuration, etc. Message cycles are used for interrupts (see below). Geographical addressing is provided: a particular physical position on the bus can be specified. Transfer cycles are read, write, sequential read or write and locked (for shared resources). The protocol used in the bus is synchronous: the speed is 10 MHz. This allows easy design currently, but it may be a limitation in the future.

Also provided is some error checking: some lines on the bus provide 'parity'. For example, associated with 8 of the address/data lines there is a parity bit which is set or reset so that there is an even number of '1's in the 9 lines. There are 6 such parity lines. Many ground lines are included in the bus also to improve reliability (see chapter 7).

In a simple system, with one master processor, interrupts are used so that a slave can attract the attention of the processor. Most buses provide between 1 and 8 lines for the purpose. In a multiprocessor system, each processor may want to attract any of the others; thus more interrupt lines are needed or a different strategy is employed. In Multibus II a different strategy is used: interrupt message cycles. These are like normal transfers except that the address output is 16 bits and this contains information on the destination and the source of the 'interrupt': the message sent by this method is on the data lines.

The speed rating for 32-bit data is 300 ns (13 Mbytes/s) for single read operations, and 150 ns bits (27 Mbytes/s) in sequential transfers.

Clearly Multibus II is a more powerful type of bus than those described so far. It is designed for multiprocessor systems, and has special features to maximise the speed of data transfer between the processors. Although only recently introduced it is likely that it will have a significant effect in the market, but it will probably be outperformed by Futurebus. Again, more information is available from INTEL.

2.11 Futurebus

In 1978 the IEEE recognised the need for a new high performance bus that was processor, manufacturer and architecture independent, which would support 32-bit processors and provide a reliable multiprocessor enviroment. After many years' work, the IEEE 896.1 Futurebus has been adopted as a formal standard. It provides the basis of high performance multiprocessor systems, but it is likely to be enhanced: a working party already exists for IEEE 896.2!

Futurebus has 32 multiplexed address and data lines, with parity check. Read, write, read-modify-write and sequential transfers are allowed, and these can be with a single target or broadcast to all targets. It uses an asynchronous protocol with acknowledges to both the address and data parts of the cycle. There are no interrupts as such, only data transfers between processors.

Futurebus is designed for multiprocessor systems, so appropriate facilities are provided. Bus arbitration is performed by a self-selection mechanism with 7 priority lines and 3 handshake lines. Nominally each processor has access to all memory, so the programmer does not have to worry about where the data are stored. This would make the system slow if all processors wanted to access the memories of other processors, so a cache-memory system is used. Each processor has a local memory which has copies of the required data: these are acquired at suitable moments when the bus is free, so the processor is not delayed. There is the *cache-coherency* problem though that the cache may not contain the most up-to-date data.

There are other interesting points on Futurebus. The working group found that traditional chips were not ideally suited for driving the bus at speed, so special chips have been produced for the purpose. Also, it is possible to insert or remove boards from the system at any time: there are means to detect the presence or absence of a board. Geographical addressing is also provided; that is, any slot on the bus can be addressed.

The speed rating for 32-bit data is 160 ns for single transfers (25 Mbytes/s), and 80 ns for sequential transfers (50 Mbytes/s).

Futurebus is the most powerful of the buses described here. For high performance systems, it is probably the obvious choice. It is a true standard: there are no options at all. Provision is also made for expansion for extra features. For more information, the specification is available from the IEEE, or in the UK contact FMUG, the Futurebus manufacturers and users group.

2.12   The IEEE-488 instrument bus

This is a different type of bus: rather than connecting microprocessors and related devices, it is used to connect pieces of equipment, for example, computers, oscilloscopes, voltmeters, function generators, etc., that is, instrumentation devices. The object of the bus is to provide the means whereby a piece of equipment can be tested, usually under computer control, and the results processed and presented. The bus was developed by Hewlett-Packard and subsequently submitted to the IEEE, it is now known as IEEE-488, replacing the earlier name GP-IB (general purpose instrument bus).

A device on the bus is classified as a talker (which outputs data when addressed), a listener (which accepts data) or a controller (which both outputs and inputs data). There can be only one controller, but several talkers and listeners. At any time one device only can be talking, though many devices may listen.

The bus has 8 data lines, 5 of which are multiplexed as address lines (for this there is a strobe signal). A handshake protocol is adopted for data transfer. When all devices are ready, the controller activates the data valid line. The 'acceptor' acknowledges this, when ready, by asserting the data accepted line. Standard logic signals are used and the strobe signals are open-collector.

The other lines on the bus include a reset line, a service request line (interrupt), a line to enable or disable manual control of the instruments, and an indicator that a complete message has been transferred.

Many instruments are provided with an IEEE-488 interface, and suitable controller cards are available for various buses and computers. Special purpose chips have also been designed.

The speed rating for the IEEE 488 bus is 5000 ns for 8-bit transfers (0.2 Mbytes/s). An instrumentation bus is much slower than a microcomputer system bus.

The instrument bus, as can be seen, is a different type of bus, though some of the principles are the same as for the other buses.

2.13 Conclusion

The buses surveyed in this chapter are varied: the earlier buses are now quite old and not worth using, but the later ones are worth examining. There are some 50 buses available, though only a few can be regarded as standard or have the support of more than one manufacturer and thus have a suitable range of products. Most support is given to those buses which have become international standards, the most prominent of which are STE, VME, Multibus II and Futurebus.

These four buses have their own areas of applications. STE is at the low end: low cost, but relatively low performance, though it has been well designed. VME is a more powerful system, and is used widely. For higher performance systems, VME will be replaced by Multibus II as more cards become available. Futurebus is the most powerful bus, and is designed for the top of the range.

We return to STE, the subject of this book. For small systems it seems ideal: it has the asynchronous protocol, so it will adapt to faster devices, though its clock speed of only 16 MHz may be a limitation, and it uses the reliable DIN 41612 connector. It is a good choice in many circumstances. First, it is widely used in various process control applications. It is also applicable in industry and research departments where computers are needed with various peripheral devices. Also, for use in a university department, where the principles of interfacing are to be taught, where small interfacing projects are undertaken by students and where small control and instrumentation systems are required, the STE bus is very suitable. STE is well defined, cheap and many boards are available. In a period of about 18 months, STE has become one of the most popular low-cost buses, with many manufacturers and distributors providing a good range of projects.

3 Interfacing Slave Devices

In this chapter the interfacing of various memory and peripheral devices to the STE bus will be described. In the course of this, the principles of interfacing as well as a description of typical devices will be given. All the examples use chips currently available, but these examples have been chosen to illustrate the principles involved and so should be modifiable to meet the requirements of more modern devices. In any practical design it is essential to consult the appropriate data sheets.

3.1 Principles of interfacing simple devices

Instead of jumping into the detail of the STE specification, a simple example will be considered first: interfacing a 7-segment display and a numerical keypad. First, the signals required in the interface will be described and then methods for their generation using the STE bus will be considered. A block diagram of the interface is shown in figure 3.1.

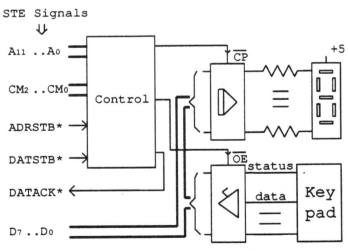

Figure 3.1 Simple interface to STE

Interfacing a 7-segment display

A 7-segment display consists of seven rectangular light-emitting (or liquid crystal) devices arranged in the shape of an 8. To display a particular number, the appropriate segments must be illuminated: if all segments are on, an '8' appears, if the two displays on the right side only are on, a '1' appears, etc. To illuminate any segment on an LED display, a circuit is required where the anode of the segment is connected to +5 V and the cathode to an output of a logic gate via a voltage dropping resistor: if this logic output is '0', current flows through the resistor and segment and it is illuminated, but the segment remains dark if the output is '1'. A 7-segment display has 7 segments and one dot, so it needs 8 resistors and to be connected to 8 logic gates and, for a *common anode* display, the anodes of each segment are connected together and so to +5 V. Note that the interface to liquid crystal displays is similar, though the pull-up resistors are not needed because such displays are voltage-driven devices.

To interface such a display to a computer, the logic '0's have to be provided. This cannot be done by simply connecting the devices to the data bus as no clear value will appear on the display because the data bus is changing continually. Instead, an octal latch circuit is used, the inputs of which are connected to the data bus, and the outputs control the display. Such a latch contains 8 edge-triggered, D-type flip-flops, with a common clock on the rising edge of which the state of each input is transferred to the corresponding output. Note that these chips require the data to be present for a short time before (the *set-up time*), and a short time after (the *hold time*), the clock edge. Set-up times of the order of 20 ns are typical; hold times however can be only 0 ns.

Interfacing a display to a computer therefore requires that a latch be interfaced to the bus. The interface circuit must generate the clock signal for the latch and also, for the case of an asynchronous bus like STE, the acknowledge signal. These should be generated if the following are true:

The valid address on the address bus is the address of the latch.
A peripheral write cycle is in operation.
Valid data are on the data bus.

Note that each device must be at a unique address because a great variety of different devices may be connected to the system and each address must be identifiable.

Interfacing a simple keypad

The following properties for the numerical keypad will be assumed; it has four data outputs indicating the value of the key pressed, and a status signal which tests whether a key is pressed. In practice this can be achieved by a keypad with contacts arranged in a matrix and an encoder chip which deduces if a key is pressed, which key it is, and provides a 'debounce' circuit (when a key is pressed, the mechanical contact will make, break, make, etc., a number of times before reaching a steady state, this also happens when you release the key; the debounce circuit 'hides' this from the user). If no debounce circuit is available, the debouncing must be done in software: when doing this it should be remembered that in the time taken before the switch has settled to a steady value, the microprocessor could have performed of the order of 1000 operations.

To interface such a keypad, one needs to connect the data and status outputs to the data bus via a tristate buffer. A typical octal tristate buffer will have eight data inputs, eight outputs and an enable input: when the enable is active (usually this is low), the outputs are turned on (non HI-Z) and each output has the value of its corresponding input. These outputs should be turned on (and an acknowledge signal generated) under the following conditions only:

The valid address on the address bus is that of the keypad.
A peripheral read cycle is in operation.

Clearly the circuitry needed to interface the latch is similar to that needed for the keypad. Both must check that the address is correct and that a peripheral cycle is in operation, and both must generate an acknowledge signal. Thus the interface will be implemented in one circuit. Note that they can both have the same address: when a read cycle at that address occurs the keypad is read, but a write cycle at that address causes data to be written to the display.

3.2 STE signals

To implement the block diagram of figure 3.1, particularly the block which generates the clock signal for the latch, the enable signal for the buffer and the acknowledge signal, the signals on the STE bus must be known. Full details about STE can be found in the STE bus specification, but here a brief summary is given.

There are five types of data transfer which can occur on the bus between the current master and a slave device. These are a read or write cycle with a memory slave, read or write to a peripheral slave, or a vector fetch (where the master is acknowledging an attention request, an interrupt, for example).

The address bus contains values which specify the address of the slave to be accessed. The number of valid address lines depends on the transfer:

In a memory transfer, all of the 20 lines $A_{19}..A_0$ are used.

In an I/O transfer, the 12 lines $A_{11}..A_0$ only are used.

In a vector fetch, the 3 lines $A_2..A_0$ only are used.

When the *address strobe* signal **ADRSTB*** is active (the * indicates that it is active *low*), the address lines contain valid signals.

The type of transfer is determined by the command signals CM_2, CM_1 and CM_0, according to the following truth table:

CM_2	CM_1	CM_0	Transfer type
0	0	0	Reserved
0	0	1	Reserved
0	1	0	Reserved
0	1	1	Vector fetch
1	0	0	I/O write
1	0	1	I/O read
1	1	0	Memory write
1	1	1	Memory read

The reserved types should be ignored by any interface, to maintain compatibility with any future enhancements of the specification.

The command signals are valid only when the *data strobe* signal **DATSTB*** is active (low). Also, when data are being read (during a read cycle or vector fetch), an active **DATSTB*** means that the addressed slave can put data on to the data bus; during a write cycle, an active **DATSTB*** means that the master has put valid data on the data bus which the slave can read.

The bidirectional data bus is 8 bits wide: the signals are $D_7..D_0$.

DATACK* is the open-collector (or open-drain) acknowledge signal generated by the slave. It is pulled low when the data have been put on the bus (during a read cycle), or when the slave has stored the data (during a write cycle).

TFRERR* may be asserted by any slave if there is an error during the transfer. No slave should issue both **DATACK*** and **TFRERR***.

SYSCLK is the system clock. It is not synchronised with the other signals on the bus and it can be used for timing the **DATACK*** signal, for example. The frequency of the clock is 16 MHz, its period is thus 62.5 ns +/-1 ns. The clock waveform need not be square: the time when it is '0' and when it is '1' must be between 21 ns and 41 ns.

SYSRST* is the reset signal. It can be used to initialise any device which needs setting up when the system is first switched on.

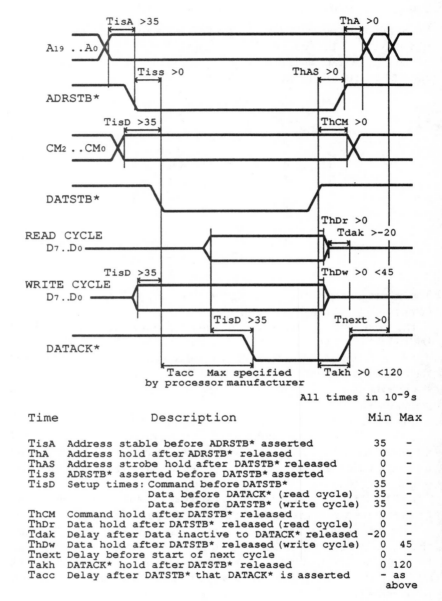

Time	Description	Min	Max
TisA	Address stable before ADRSTB* asserted	35	-
ThA	Address hold after ADRSTB* released	0	-
ThAS	Address strobe hold after DATSTB* released	0	-
Tiss	ADRSTB* asserted before DATSTB* asserted	0	-
TisD	Setup times: Command before DATSTB*	35	-
	Data before DATACK* (read cycle)	35	-
	Data before DATSTB* (write cycle)	35	-
ThCM	Command hold after DATSTB* released	0	-
ThDr	Data hold after DATSTB* released (read cycle)	0	-
Tdak	Delay after Data inactive to DATACK* released	-20	-
ThDw	Data hold after DATSTB* released (write cycle)	0	45
Tnext	Delay before start of next cycle	0	-
Takh	DATACK* hold after DATSTB* released	0	120
Tacc	Delay after DATSTB* that DATACK* is asserted	-	as above

Figure 3.2 STE bus timings

The timing diagrams for a read cycle and a write cycle are given in figure 3.2: both cycles are combined in one diagram as the only difference between the two is the state of the data lines. This is an unusual timing diagram as all the information is on one sheet. In most data sheets there is the diagram and all the values of times are labelled in the form t_{as}, and the actual value for t_{as} is to be found on another page. Thus, when designing hardware, one is constantly turning the page back and forth. Clearly, an important requirement of the hardware designer is a photo-copier!

From these diagrams (and the full STE specification) one can deduce the following salient points:

A master shall not activate **DATSTB*** if **ADRSTB*** is inactive.

A slave shall not respond to **DATSTB*** if **ADRSTB*** is inactive.

All address lines are valid when **ADRSTB*** is asserted and they remain valid until **ADRSTB*** is released.

All commands are valid when **DATSTB*** is asserted and they remain valid until **DATSTB*** goes inactive.

During read transfers, all the data lines are valid when **DATACK*** is asserted, and they remain valid until **DATSTB*** is released. The data must be output on the data bus before **DATACK*** is asserted.

During write transfers, all the data lines are valid when **DATSTB*** is asserted and they remain valid until **DATSTB*** is released. As there is no guaranteed hold time after **DATSTB*** is released, the data should be written before **DATACK*** is asserted.

The command line CM_0 indicates if data are being read or written: this is true for memory and peripheral accesses and for the vector fetch cycle.

It is recommended that the logic inputs connected to the bus should have Schmitt trigger inputs, thereby reducing the effects of noise, and this is mandatory for the signals **ADRSTB***, **DATSTB***, **DATACK***, **TFRERR*** and **SYSCLK**.

3.3 Interfacing display and keypad

The design of the interface of the display and keypad, introduced in section 3.1, can now be completed. This requires that the signals for the clock input to the latch, the enable of the buffer and the acknowledge signal, must be generated. A few properties of typical latches and buffers are needed:

The latch stores the data when the clock goes from '0' to '1'.
Set-up and hold times on the latch are 20 ns and 0 ns, respectively.
The outputs of the buffer are non-tristate when the enable input is '0'.

The maximum time to turn the outputs on from tristate is 30 ns.
The time for a data signal to propagate through the chip is < 18 ns.

To meet the STE specification, the data must be put on the data bus at least 35 ns before **DATACK*** is asserted; that is, **DATACK*** must not be asserted until at least 65 ns after the enable on the buffer has been asserted.

For a write cycle, the data bus will contain the data for at least 35 ns before **DATSTB*** is asserted, so the set up times will be met. Hence, in this case, the data can be latched when **DATSTB*** is asserted and then **DATACK*** turned on immediately.

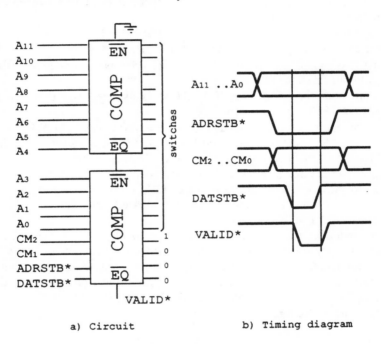

a) Circuit   b) Timing diagram

Figure 3.3 Valid address detection circuit

The enable, clock and acknowledge signals should be generated only if the valid peripheral address on the address bus is the address of the display and keypad; that is, the address lines $A_{11}..A_0$ must be correct, CM_2 must be '1', CM_1 must be '0', and **ADRSTB*** and **DATSTB*** must both be '0'. On a flexible bus system it is a good idea to be able to change the address of any device, so it is recommended that the address detect circuit compares the actual address on the bus with a set of switches; this is achieved by a comparator chip. A typical comparator has two sets of eight inputs and one active low enable input, and generates a '0' on the output if the enable input in '0' and each pair of inputs is the same. Note that some comparators have Schmitt trigger inputs: these are just right for the STE bus. The circuit shown in figure 3.3, which consists of two such comparators, gives a '0' output on the line marked **VALID*** if the above conditions are met: the timings of this signal, relative to the signals on the bus, are also shown in the figure. Note that the comparator is also used to check the command lines CM_2, CM_1, and the strobes **ADRSTB*** and **DATSTB***. *A comparator whose inputs have the required Schmitt trigger characteristics must be used, otherwise* **ADRSTB*** *and* **DATSTB*** *must be connected to the comparator via a device with such inputs.* Also, the output of the first comparator enables the second one; address lines only are put in the first chip as the address lines are stable *before* the other signals are asserted.

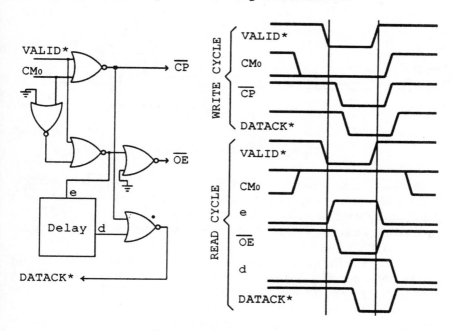

Figure 3.4 Decode circuit

The signal **VALID*** is then used in the rest of the interface circuit. The buffer should be enabled if **VALID*** is '0' and CM_0 is '1' and **DATACK*** asserted at least 65 ns later. The latch should be enabled if **VALID*** and CM_0 are both '0'. As data can be stored immediately, the clock signal must go from '0' to '1' and **DATACK*** asserted at the same time. Note that **DATACK*** is an open collector circuit. Figure 3.4 shows a circuit for this part of the interface, and the timings of the associated signals. The 'blob' on the NOR gate indicates that it is an open-collector output.

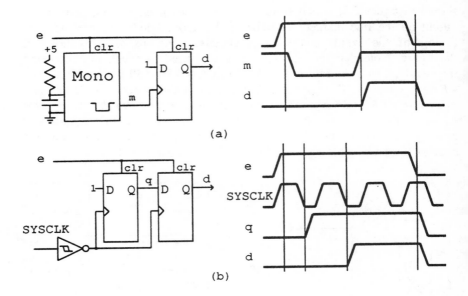

Figure 3.5 Delay circuits

The delay before asserting **DATACK*** for the read cycle can be achieved in many ways. The simplest is to use a monostable: the circuit for this is shown in figure 3.5a with the associated timing diagram. Normally, the input labelled e is '0', so the output of the monostable is '1' and that of the flip-flop is '0'. When e goes to '1', the output of the D-type remains at '0', but the monostable output goes to '0' for a period determined by the resistor and capacitor. When this returns to a '1', the output of the D-type goes to '1' and this can be used to generate **DATACK*** via the open collector NOR gate (in figure 3.4). Note that a retriggerable monostable should be used, as there might be 'glitches' on the bus, and that suitable values for the external components are 5 kΩ and 6.8 pF.

Timings using monostables will not be very accurate, because of tolerances and working variations of these components, so a reasonable margin should be allowed to ensure that the specification is maintained.

Alternatively, a different form of delay can be used. Given that the delay must be 65 ns, which is about the period of the system clock, **SYSCLK**, two flip-flops configured as a two-bit shift register could be used. This is shown in figure 3.5b with suitable timings. When e is '0', the outputs of the flip-flops are both '0'. On the first rising clock edge after e has gone to '1', the output of the first flip-flop will go to '1', and on the next rising edge, the second output will go to '1', and this output is used to generate **DATACK***.

The disadvantage of this is that **DATACK*** will be asserted between one and two clock periods after e goes to '1', that is (given a clock period of 62 ns and typical delays through a flip-flop and open-collector inverter of 13 ns and 15 ns) between 90 and 152 ns. Unfortunately, the minimum delay through the flip-flop and inverter are not given, so the required delay of 65 ns is not guaranteed, but these values should give sufficient time for the data to be on the bus before the acknowledge is asserted.

To reduce the variation in delay, a circuit could be designed with the following specification:

> if the clock is '0' when e is asserted, **DATACK*** is generated on the second rising edge of clock after e is asserted.
>
> otherwise, **DATACK*** is generated on the second falling edge of clock after e is asserted.

Such a circuit, which can be designed using the asynchronous sequential logic design technique, is given in Appendix 1. For more information on this design method, see *Design of Logic Systems*, by D. Lewin. Another advantage of such a circuit is that it can be implemented directly in a programmable logic array (**PLA**). Given the limited size of Eurocards, it is often important to minimise the number of components on a board, so the use of PLAs is recommended where feasible.

A fourth possibility is to use a delay line. This has one input and many outputs, each output being a particular delayed version of the input.

3.4 Alternative design

Another design philosophy for write cycles, and one which must be used for devices requiring a set-up time greater than 35 ns, is to generate signals similar to the buffer enable and **DATACK*** used above for read cycles, but to turn the 'enable' signal off when **DATACK*** is asserted (i.e to write the data then). It is important to write the data just before **DATACK*** is asserted, not at the end of the cycle when **DATSTB*** is released, as there is no guaranteed hold time on the data lines. The advantage of this method is that the circuitry for read and write cycles is more symmetrical, which will prove useful when connecting many devices (as shown in section 3.6).

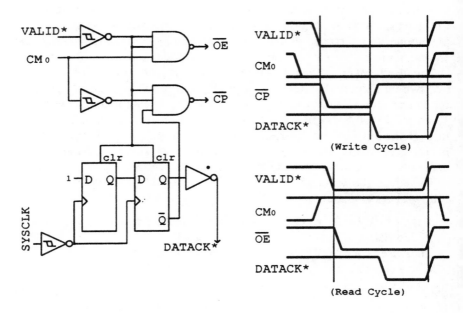

Figure 3.6 Decode circuit

A circuit employing this method, and the associated timings, are given in figure 3.6. For a read cycle the output enable signal remains active as long as **VALID*** is asserted, but for a write cycle the clock signal for the latch is released when **DATACK*** is asserted. Note the use of the Schmitt trigger inverter for **SYSCLK** (which is mandatory) and, as there are six such inverters in one chip, the use of the other inverters elsewhere in the circuit. An inverter with open-collector outputs is used to drive **DATACK***, but if this is the only open-collector gate used in the circuit, it might be better to use a suitable transistor to drive this line.

Note that there might be a problem with signals at the end of the cycle, that is, when **DATSTB*** is released, because there is no guaranteed hold time for the command signals or address lines after that time. Thus it is possible that CM_0 may change when **DATSTB*** changes and, as there will be a delay through the comparator, **VALID*** may change *after* CM_0 does and this may cause a glitch on the buffer output enable or the latch clock signal. One solution to this is to latch CM_0 around this time, that is, when **DATACK*** is asserted. This can be achieved using a transparent latch: CM_0 is connected to the data input and the output is passed to the circuit (of figure 3.6), and the latch is controlled by **DATACK***. Before **DATACK***

is asserted, the input is passed directly to the output, but when **DATACK***
is turned on the output is held at the state CM_0 was during the main part of
the cycle.

3.5 Software

In this section software which might be used to access the above circuit is
described. The necessary instructions are given in a general form, rather
than being those of a specific microprocessor. Some microprocessors have
special instructions for accessing peripherals: IN and OUT, rather than
LOAD or STORE for memory. Other processors do not distinguish between
memory and I/O, so the same instructions are used for both.

When reading from the keypad it will be assumed that the least significant
4 bits, $D_3..D_0$, will contain the value of the key pressed, and that bit 7 will
be a '1' if a key has been pressed.

A routine for reading the keypad is given below:

```
readkey: read keypad into ACC      ;keep reading until key is pressed

         test bit 7 of ACC
         jump if zero to readkey
                                    ;lower four bits have value of key
         and ACC with 15           ;rest are now set to 0
         push ACC on to stack      ;save ACC
release: read keypad into ACC      ;now wait until key released
         test bit 7 of ACC
         jump if non zero to  release
         restore ACC from stack ;restore value of key
         return
```

The above assumes a register called ACC which can be loaded with a
value for subsequent processing. The instruction to read the keypad, which
will cause the microprocessor to output the bus signals which specify a
peripheral read cycle, could be something like

```
       IN A, keypad           ;on a micro with i/o instructions
or     LDA keypad
or     MOVE A, keypad
```

The above routine reads a value in the range 0..9 and stores it in the ACC register. To show the suitable pattern on the display, this value must be converted to the appropriate code. For example, the number 1 requires bits 2 and 1 only to be illuminated, so to show a 1 the binary number 11111001 must be output to the latch (note that a '0' is written if a segment is to be on). The conversion is best done by having a table of values and indexing into the table using an index or pointer register: the address of the required pattern is at the start address of the table plus the 0..9 value. The following routine will display the value input on the keypad. As is good practice, the routine returns without (apparently) changing any registers.

```
output:   push ACC and INDEXreg on to stack
          load INDEXreg with start of table  ;load ACC with pattern
          add ACC to INDEXreg                ;needed for display
          load ACC with data pointed to by INDEXreg
                                             ;ACC now has pattern
          write ACC to display               ;output value
          pop ACC and INDEXreg from stack
          return
table:    DefineBytes  %11000000, %11111001, %10100100, etc.
```

The DefineByte statement stores a series of bytes in sequential locations. In this case these bytes are specified in binary, which best shows the bits that should be on.

The write ACC to display instruction could be like

```
          OUT display, A
or        STA display
or        MOVE display, A
```

3.6   Interfacing many devices

There is a considerable overhead in an interface like that given above: the board itself and edge connector, as well as the circuits for address comparison, acknowledge generation, etc., are all needed. The overhead becomes less significant if a number of devices are interfaced, because much is common. To illustrate this the interface of one keypad and four displays will be considered. The complete circuit is shown in figure 3.7.

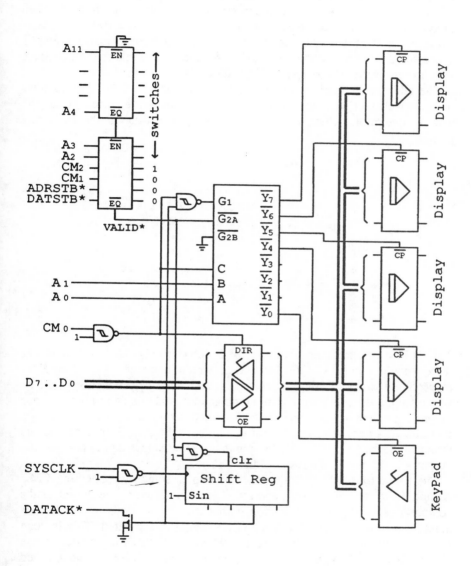

Figure 3.7 Interface of four displays and a keypad

The four displays can either have their own latch or be multiplexed: that is, each display is written to for a short period, then the next one. The four latch method is simpler, and illustrates better the design method.

Each display has its own latch and attendant resistors, and it has its own unique address. The addresses are chosen to be consecutive from some base value so that for these addresses the lines $A_{11}..A_2$ are common, for example, addresses 0,1,2,3 or 64,65,66,67. Lines A_1 and A_0 determine the one latch which is accessed. The keypad will be at one of these addresses.

The address comparison circuit thus checks the upper 10 address lines only, as well as CM_2, etc. Assuming that these lines are correct, CM_0, A_1 and A_0 determine which device is accessed, according to the following table:

CM_0	A_1	A_0	required action
0	0	0	clock on latch 0 set to 0
0	0	1	clock on latch 1 set to 0
0	1	0	clock on latch 2 set to 0
0	1	1	clock on latch 3 set to 0
1	0	0	enable on buffer set to 0
1	0	1	no action required
1	1	0	no action required
1	1	1	no action required

This is best implemented using a 1 of 8 decoder chip. One such chip has three enable inputs, G_1, $\overline{G}_{2a}$ and $\overline{G}_{2b}$, which must be '1', '0' and '0' respectively to enable the device, and it has three select inputs C, B, A, which form a three-bit number in the range 0..7, and this determines the one output $\overline{Y}_n$, where n is between 0 and 7, which is on (active low); if the chip is disabled, all outputs are '1'. For example, if the chip is enabled and the select inputs are '0', '1', '1', the number on the select inputs is 3, so the output $\overline{Y}_3$ will be '0', the rest will be '1'.

The above truth table can therefore be implemented by connecting CM_0, A_1 and A_0 to the select lines, and the $\overline{G}_{2a}$ enable input to the output of the comparators. A slight complication is that the clock signals for the latches must be turned off when the **DATACK*** signal is generated. This is done by connecting the **DATACK*** signal 'NANDed' with CM_0 inverted to the G_1 enable input: CM_0 is low if a write cycle is in operation, so the asserted **DATACK*** signal turns off the latch clock signal. As usual, all other inputs should be connected to a suitable value. Note that the inverted version of

CM_0 is connected to select input C of the decoder, as this means that the command line is connected to one gate only and so there is minimal loading on the line. It is a good idea to do this.

Connecting four latches and one buffer to the data bus is providing a significant load on the bus. To reduce this load it is recommended that a protective tristate buffer is connected between the bus and these chips. This must be a bidirectional buffer as data must be able to travel in either direction. Such a buffer has an enable input and a direction input and two sets of 8 data input/outputs; again these data lines have Schmitt trigger inputs. If the enable input is '0' then the outputs of one set of data lines are enabled, which one being determined by the direction input, and the data are passed from the other set of data lines. The direction is determined by CM_0, that is, whether data are being read or written. Hence, the inverse of this command line is connected to the direction input of the buffer. The maximum propagation delay through the buffer is typically 12 ns. This value should be taken into account when designing the circuit to delay DATACK* until after the keypad data have been put on the bus.

Note that because of the bidirectional buffer, whose maximum output enable time is 40 ns, the set-up time on the data for the latch is not guaranteed, so the data cannot be written when DATSTB* is asserted, and the design philosophy described in section 3.4 must be adopted.

The timing of DATACK* needs consideration. For a read cycle, DATACK* must not be asserted until after the delays due to the decoder (35 ns max), the keypad buffer (30 ns max), propagation through the bidirectional buffer (12 ns max) and the required set-up time on the bus (35 ns): the total delay must be at least 107 ns. As the bidirectional buffer is turned on when the correct valid peripheral address is detected, the delay in turning on the buffer (40 ns max) need not be considered in the timing of DATACK* because this value is less than the maximum combined delay through the decoder and keypad buffer. For a write cycle, the required delay before asserting DATACK* is determined by the propagation delay through the buffer and the set-up time for the latch: this is less than the delay required for a read cycle. Thus, in figure 3.7, the delay is achieved using three stages of a four bit shift register: the delay is at least two clock cycles (125 ns).

Note also the use of a MOSFET to drive DATACK* rather than using an open-collector inverter. The MOSFET is used instead of a normal transistor as a MOSFET can be connected directly to the output of a logic gate, whereas a transistor requires a series resistor between the base and the output of the gate.

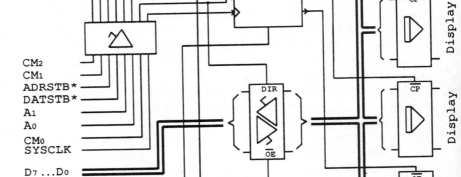

a) Circuit

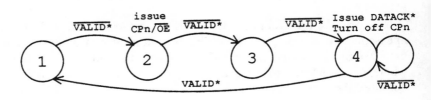

b) State Diagram

Figure 3.8 Interface using a PLA

3.7   Interface using a PLA

The number of components in a circuit can often be reduced by using a PLA. Figure 3.8a shows a circuit which interfaces the same devices as shown in figure 3.7, but which has fewer components. In this case the decoder, the shift register and some logic have been replaced by a PLA. Also included in this circuit is an extra buffer which is used to provide the required Schmitt trigger characteristics for some of the STE signals: this shows how comparators without such inputs can be used in interfacing to STE.

The PLA receives as input **VALID***, CM_0, A_1, A_0 and **SYSCLK** which is used for timing purposes. It generates the clock signals for the latches, the enable signal for the keypad buffer and the **DATACK*** signal. This is accomplished by a sequential logic circuit implemented within the PLA. The initial design for the circuit is given here, but the final implementation is described in appendix 2. The delay before asserting **DATACK*** must be at least two clock cycles, thus the circuit is implemented as a *synchronous* sequential logic circuit controlled by the clock signal **SYSCLK**.

The basic idea of a synchronous sequential logic circuit is that all actions occur on the rising edge of the clock signal only. At that time the inputs and any internal states are sampled; then, and only then, the outputs and these internal states are changed. The actions of the PLA for this circuit are described by the state diagram shown in figure 3.8b.

Normally the circuit is in state 1, where all the outputs are inactive. If **VALID*** is asserted, on the next clock cycle the circuit enters state 2, and the clock signal on one of the latches is asserted or the keypad buffer enabled (depending on the state of A_1, A_0 and CM_0). On the following clock cycle state 3 is entered, but the outputs remain the same. On the next clock cycle, which is at least two clock cycles after **VALID*** was asserted, **DATACK*** should be asserted and, if data are being written, the appropriate latch clock signal should be released. The circuit is now in state 4, and will remain so until **VALID*** is released (which will happen when the bus master removes **DATSTB*** in response to the assertion of **DATACK***). Then the circuit will return to state 1 and all outputs will be inactive. The final implementation of this circuit is in appendix 2.

3.8   Interface to non-asynchronous buses

The interface to a synchronous or semi-synchronous bus is very similar to that given above. Assuming that the buffers and latches are fast enough, so no wait signal is needed, the required circuit is the same as in figure 3.7, except that there is no acknowledge circuit and the clock inputs to the latches are not turned off early (there being no signal to do this!). This assumes the existence of signals similar to **ADRSTB***, **DATSTB***, CM_2, etc.

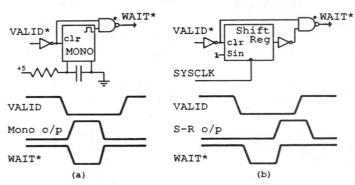

Figure 3.9 Wait generators

If a wait signal is needed, the requirements are similar to the acknowledge generator: a delay is required until the data have been written, or the data have been put on the data bus. In particular, the wait signal, **WAIT***, should be asserted as soon as a valid address is detected, and released after the required delay. Again there are many ways of generating the delay using methods similar to those for producing an acknowledge signal; two of these methods are given in figure 3.9 with associated timing diagrams. The first uses a monostable, the second a shift-register. Note that with the monostable, **WAIT*** can be asserted only if **VALID*** is active: there will be no problem due to a false triggering of the monostable (because of noise) when another slave is being accessed.

3.9   Interfacing EPROM

The interface of memory devices is achieved using similar methods to those described above. There are a number of types of memory whose interfaces are of varying complexity. The first to be discussed, EPROM, has the simplest interface, then static RAMs and finally dynamic RAMs will be considered.

EPROM, erasable programmable read only memory, comes in various sizes, but the principles of interfacing are the same for each type. Larger EPROMs require more address lines than smaller chips because they have more locations to be accessed. Most modern EPROMs have 28 pins (in the normal dual-in-line package), although some chips have only 24 pins. The JEDEC standard for EPROMs, conformed to by most manufacturers, means that almost any size EPROM from 2k bytes to 64k bytes can be put into a standard 28-pin socket (including 24 pin EPROMs), so a design can be made for any standard EPROM, and the actual chip placed in the socket chosen for the particular requirement. Note that static RAMs can be put in such sockets with only minor modification to the interface. The very latest EPROMs have 32 pins, but this is just an extension to the JEDEC standard.

Essentially, an EPROM has a number of address inputs which specify the one location to be accessed, eight tristatable data outputs, and at least two control inputs, chip enable, $\overline{CE}$, and output enable, $\overline{OE}$. When $\overline{CE}$ is asserted (it is low), the data are extracted from the location specified by the address lines, but they do not appear on the external data lines until $\overline{OE}$ is low. Note that both control inputs must be asserted before the outputs become non-tristate. The *access time*, that is, the time after the EPROM is accessed when the data appear on the bus, is the longest of the

1) time after the address lines are stable,
2) time after $\overline{CE}$ is asserted,
3) time after $\overline{OE}$ is asserted.

Normally, the access times due to 1) and 2) are comparable and longer than that due to 3). This is reasonable: the delay after $\overline{OE}$ is due only to the time taken to turn the tristate outputs on. Typical values of access time are of the order of 250 ns from address and $\overline{CE}$, and 100 ns from $\overline{OE}$, though faster devices are available.

The interface to an EPROM is in principle similar to that of a buffer: the differences are that two signals must be generated ($\overline{CE}$ and $\overline{OE}$), the address decode does not specify just the one address, and it must be verified that a memory cycle, not a peripheral cycle, is in operation. If possible, one should try to turn $\overline{CE}$ on before $\overline{OE}$, but it is not necessary to do so. One could turn $\overline{CE}$ on when a valid address is detected on the bus, but there is no great advantage to this as there is no guaranteed delay between **ADRSTB*** being asserted and **DATSTB***. Also, when **ADRSTB*** is asserted, it is not known whether the cycle is memory, I/O or vector fetch.

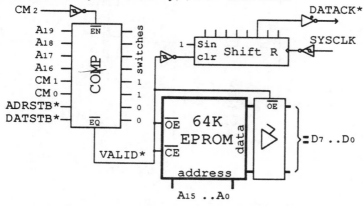

Figure 3.10 Interface of one 64K EPROM to STE

An interface for one 64K byte EPROM is given in figure 3.10. The valid address detect circuit checks that the upper 4 address lines ($A_{19}..A_{16}$) are correct, that **ADRSTB*** is asserted, that the command lines specify a memory read (they are all '1'), and that **DATSTB*** is on. This is accomplished using an octal comparator again: as nine inputs are required the enable input is used, and CM_2 inverted provides the enable (neither **ADRSTB*** nor **DATSTB*** could be used as the enable inputs of comparators do not have Schmitt trigger inputs). The output of the comparator, **VALID***, enables the EPROM and also the tristate buffer (which is required because MOS EPROMs are not powerful enough to drive the bus). The acknowledge circuit generates **DATACK*** at least 310 ns after the memory is enabled (this being the memory access time plus the delay through the buffer and the set-up time on the bus). This time is at least 5 clock cycles: so output six of an 8-bit shift register is used. One advantage of using a shift register is that, if a faster EPROM is used, a shorter delay before asserting **DATACK*** can be achieved by using an earlier output from the shift register.

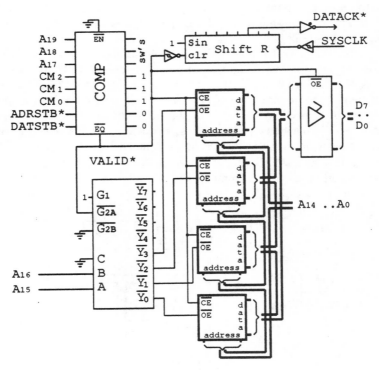

Figure 3.11 Interface of four EPROMs to STE

A circuit for four 32K EPROMs is shown in figure 3.11. This is similar to that shown in figure 3.10. Four EPROMs are needed (obviously), and the one to be enabled is determined by the two address lines A_{16} and A_{15} (which are not included in the comparator circuit). Here all the EPROMs are enabled when the correct valid memory address is on the bus, but the outputs of one only are enabled (by the decoder). Thus the timing of the acknowledge is the same as for the circuit in figure 3.10.

Note that it might be better to connect the address lines to the EPROM via buffers which have Schmitt trigger inputs. Also it might be advisable to latch the address and command lines when **DATACK*** is active so that these signals do not change just after **DATSTB*** is released (see section 3.4).

3.10 Interfacing static RAMs

Static RAMs are very similar to EPROMs, and they also come in various forms. The RAM which will be considered here is an 8K * 8 RAM: that is, it has 13 address line inputs, eight data input/output lines and three control inputs, being chip enable, $\overline{CE}$, output enable, $\overline{OE}$, and write enable, $\overline{WE}$. To read from the device, both $\overline{CE}$ and $\overline{OE}$ must be low, and the addressed data will appear on the data lines; to write to the device, the data to be written must be put on the data lines and both $\overline{CE}$ and $\overline{WE}$ must be low, the data being written when either of these is removed. For many RAMs the access times for reading are similar to those for an EPROM; for writing, the time after the address is stable and the chip enabled so that data can be written is usually about 20% less than the read access time from $\overline{CE}$, and the data set-up time before $\overline{WE}$ is removed is again about 20% less than the read access time from $\overline{OE}$. However, some modern static RAMs are available which are much faster having access times of the order of 40 ns.

The interface is therefore similar to that involving both read and write peripherals. For peripherals, the clock input to a latch was generated during write cycles, and a buffer enabled for read cycles. For the memory, the equivalent signals are the $\overline{WE}$ and $\overline{OE}$ inputs to the RAM. The strategy for write cycles is (again) to turn the enable signal off when **DATACK*** is generated. A circuit which interfaces four RAMs is shown in figure 3.12. Note that all RAMs are enabled, but the $\overline{WE}$ or $\overline{OE}$ of one only is asserted.

As the access time for write cycles is less than that for read cycles, the circuit could be modified to give an earlier **DATACK***, but this would complicate the generation of **DATACK***. Again the circuit could be improved by buffering of the address lines and latching the address and control lines when **DATACK*** is active.

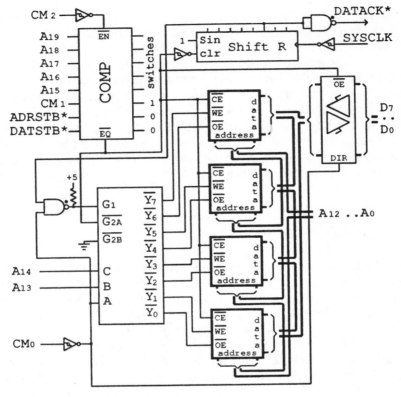

Figure 3.12 Four static RAM interface to STE

Not all static RAMs are 8-bits wide, some are single bit, some four bit, etc. When considering any particular chip, it is important to refer to the data sheets for exact signal requirements and timings.

3.11   Interfacing dynamic RAM

The actual memory element in dynamic RAMs is simpler than that in static RAMs, so that more elements can be put on a given area of silicon. However, in consequence, the interface to dynamic RAMs is more complicated. There are two problems to overcome: the method for accessing an element and the refreshing of the elements. The latter is required because of the simplicity of each memory element so that it forgets its contents and so needs to be reminded. Essentially, the RAM contains a number of capacitors which discharge and refreshing is required to recharge the capacitors.

The memory device is arranged in a matrix which has a number of rows and columns. To access an element, the row in which that element is to be found is copied from the matrix into a buffer, then the particular column in that buffer is accessed. At the end of the cycle the buffer is written back into the matrix. The action of rewriting the row refreshes that row.

An interface to a dynamic RAM must specify the row address (by putting the row address on the address lines and asserting the Row Address Strobe, $\overline{RAS}$), and then specify the column address (by putting the column address on the address lines and asserting the Column Address Strobe, $\overline{CAS}$).

For a read cycle, the $\overline{WE}$ (write enable) input is held high, and the specified bit of data appears on the output data line. For a write cycle, the bit to be written is put on the input data line and $\overline{WE}$ taken low.

One of the advantages of specifying the address in two halves is that the number of address lines on the memory is half what one might expect. A typical 256K by 1 memory chip has 16 pins only: 9 address lines, 2 data lines (one in, one out), 3 control signals ($\overline{RAS}$, $\overline{CAS}$ and $\overline{WE}$) and two power supply lines. These chips operate very quickly: the complete cycle time to read or write data is no worse and can be better than most common static RAMs, though they are much slower than the very fast static RAMs.

For most applications on STE, eight RAMs are connected in parallel: one for each bit. Some dynamic RAMs are 4 bits wide. It has been noted (chapter 2) that an 8-bit bus, like STE, slows down a 16-bit or 32-bit microprocessor because it can read only 8 bits at once. This problem can be circumvented by having wider memory on the processor board itself and using the bus for peripherals only.

Timing diagrams (with typical values on the *same* sheet) for read and write cycles are shown in figure 3.13. Points to consider are set-up and hold times on addresses, the maximum time $\overline{RAS}$ or $\overline{CAS}$ can be on (the row-buffer also forgets its contents), and the minimum time $\overline{RAS}$ must be inactive (the precharge time when the row is being written back into the matrix).

Each row in the matrix must be refreshed every 2 ms, at least that is the worst case quoted in the data sheets (that is, it is the figure which relates to the operation of the device at high temperatures). A friend built a Z80 system which required him to enter (in binary, using switches) a three-byte jump instruction into dynamic RAM. He took much longer than 2 ms to enter these 24 bits and then set the machine to run but, as his program worked, the memory must have retained its contents for longer than the stated refresh time. However, to guarantee data retention each row should be refreshed every 2 ms.

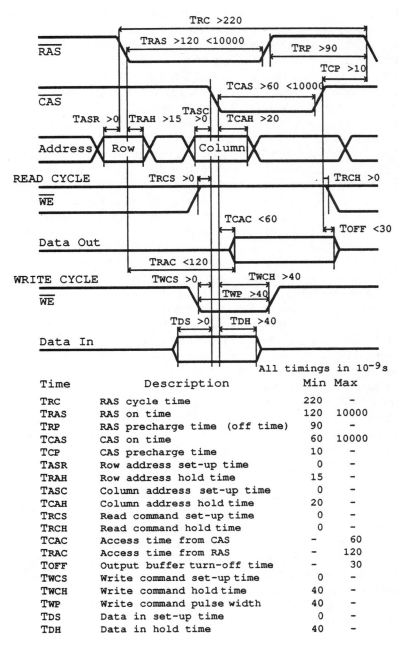

Time	Description	Min	Max
TRC	RAS cycle time	220	-
TRAS	RAS on time	120	10000
TRP	RAS precharge time (off time)	90	-
TCAS	CAS on time	60	10000
TCP	CAS precharge time	10	-
TASR	Row address set-up time	0	-
TRAH	Row address hold time	15	-
TASC	Column address set-up time	0	-
TCAH	Column address hold time	20	-
TRCS	Read command set-up time	0	-
TRCH	Read command hold time	0	-
TCAC	Access time from CAS	-	60
TRAC	Access time from RAS	-	120
TOFF	Output buffer turn-off time	-	30
TWCS	Write command set-up time	0	-
TWCH	Write command hold time	40	-
TWP	Write command pulse width	40	-
TDS	Data in set-up time	0	-
TDH	Data in hold time	40	-

Figure 3.13 Typical dynamic RAM timings

There are many ways in which a row can be refreshed. The obvious method, as a row is refreshed when $\overline{\text{RAS}}$ is released, is the *RAS-only-Refresh*: the row address of the row to be refreshed is given, but no column address is given. This requires circuitry to remember which row needs refreshing next. Some more modern RAMs have *CAS-before-RAS* refresh. Here the $\overline{\text{CAS}}$ signal is asserted *before* $\overline{\text{RAS}}$ is turned on. These RAMs have a built-in counter which determines the row to be refreshed, so a circuit using this method need only generate the two address strobes. Timings for the latter method of refresh are given in figure 3.14.

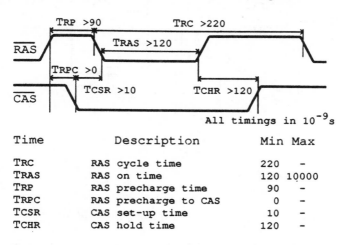

Time	Description	Min	Max
TRC	RAS cycle time	220	-
TRAS	RAS on time	120	10000
TRP	RAS precharge time	90	-
TRPC	RAS precharge to CAS	0	-
TCSR	CAS set-up time	10	-
TCHR	CAS hold time	120	-

Figure 3.14 Typical CAS before RAS refresh timings

It is also possible to access a number of bits in one row by specifying the row address once only but the column address many times; this is termed *Page mode* operation. Also, one can read one bit and write a different value in the same cycle: this is called a *Read-Modified-Write* cycle. STE can support such operations: they are described in sections 3.15 and 3.16. *Dual-port* video RAMs are also available: these allow the data to be accessed in the method described above as well as providing serial access using a built-in shift register. One application for these is in graphics systems (see chapter 4).

Figure 3.15 shows a block diagram of an interface allowing only the more straightforward access to the memory. Eight 256K dynamic RAMs are shown; thus the two most significant address lines specify the area in memory where the chips are accessible. Again a comparator is used to check for a valid memory address; the output of this enables the controller which selects the appropriate addresses using multiplexors, and generates the strobes. The block marked *Refresh Control* issues a signal (REQ)

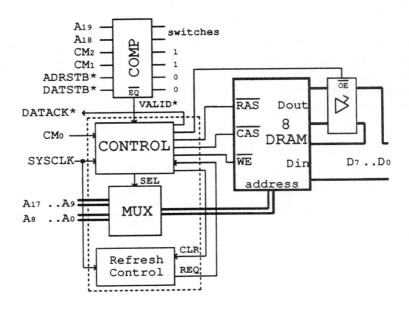

Figure 3.15 Block diagram of dynamic RAM interface

whenever a row should be refreshed; 512 rows must be refreshed every 2 ms so a request is issued about every 3.9 μs. A signal (CLR) is issued by the control circuit to clear this request signal: it acknowledges REQ. A tristate buffer is used for the output data lines because the memory chips are not sufficiently powerful to drive the bus.

The controller can be implemented using a special purpose dynamic-RAM controller chip: a number of these are available for RAMs up to 64K, but fewer for the larger chips. Another approach is to design a synchronous sequential logic circuit. This is quite straightforward and can be implemented easily using registered PLAs. Again, the initial design for this is given here, but the final circuit is given in appendix 2.

In this case, $\overline{\text{RAS}}$ is asserted on the first rising clock edge after a valid address is detected, the **SELect** line changes on the next clock, $\overline{\text{CAS}}$ is asserted on the following clock, etc. Given the 62.5 ns period of the system clock, the timings of addresses and strobes easily conform to the required specification for the memory. The idealised timing diagrams for a read cycle, a write cycle and refresh are given in figure 3.16. CAS before RAS refresh is used, as this does not need a row address to be specified.

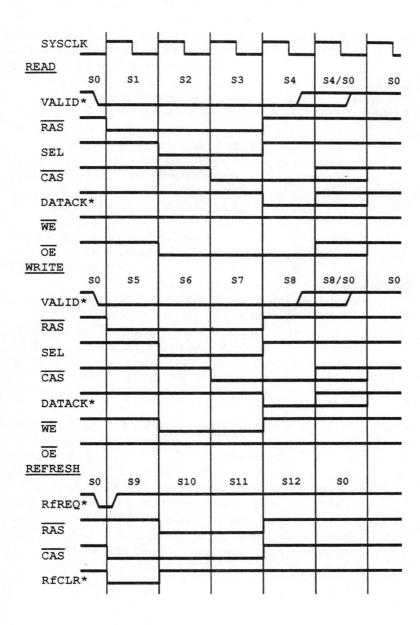

Fig 3.16 Synchronised timings for dynamic RAM interface

The circuit is in the inactive state until a refresh or a memory access cycle is required; these are indicated by **RfREQ*** and **VALID*** respectively (see figure 3.16). If **RfREQ*** is asserted, which has priority over **VALID***, a refresh cycle occurs. Otherwise, if **VALID*** is asserted, a normal memory cycle occurs and CM_0 determines whether it is a read or a write operation. The cycle will not end until after **VALID*** is released: many clock cycles may occur before this happens, hence the uncertainty shown in figure 3.16. Once one cycle has started, it continues to the end whatever the state of **VALID*** and **RfREQ***. Thus a longer memory access will occur if a refresh cycle is in operation, but this is no problem with an asynchronous bus provided that the refresh cycle is not so long that the watch-dog circuit is activated: there should be no problem as the refresh cycle lasts four clock periods only. The refresh request will be delayed if a memory cycle is in operation: this will be a problem only if the memory cycle lasts more than 3.9 µs. **RfREQ*** is cleared by the signal **RfCLR** as soon as a refresh cycle begins.

From the timing diagram and the above description, a *state diagram* can be drawn showing the operation of the controller: the states S0, S1, etc., are shown in figure 3.16. This is then processed using the design method described fully in Lewin and briefly in appendix 2.

Note that one could in principle pull the select input low a short time after $\overline{RAS}$ is asserted, rather than waiting for the next clock cycle. A memory cycle would then be one clock cycle shorter, and the number of states in the sequential machine reduced thus simplifying the design method. The obvious method of creating the delay is to change **SEL** on the falling edge of clock. A simple logic expression for this is:

$$SEL = \overline{RAS} + \overline{CAS}\ SYSCLK$$

Unfortunately, the address lines through the multiplexor must be stable before $\overline{CAS}$ is asserted: the maximum delay through the multiplexor is 27 ns which is greater than the minimum 'half' clock cycle. The row address hold time is 10 ns, so **SEL** cannot change within 10 ns of $\overline{RAS}$ being asserted. Given the delay through the multiplexor, **SEL** must change during the 35 ns period after $\overline{RAS}$ has been asserted. As the minimum propagation delay through a TTL chip is not specified, it is very difficult to guarantee a valid delay for **SEL**, so it is best to use the timing diagram of figure 3.16, especially as the work of the circuit is being done by a PLA anyway.

3.12   Analog-digital conversion

An analog-to-digital converter (**ADC**) transforms an analog voltage into an equivalent digital number. A digital-to-analog converter (**DAC**) is the opposite. In each case the analog voltage which can be represented digitally in the computer is limited in range, but the range can be selected. If the range is purely positive the operation is termed *unipolar*, but if the limits are a positive and a negative voltage it is *bipolar*. The smallest voltage which can be distinguished by the transducer is determined by this range and by the number of bits (the *resolution*) used to make up the digital number. For example, for a unipolar voltage range of 0 V to 5 V and an 8-bit converter, the smallest voltage which can be resolved is 5/256 volts, that is 1.98 mV; for a bipolar voltage range of −5 V to +5 V and a 12-bit converter the voltage is 10/4096 volts.

The principles of the conversion are well known (R-2R ladders, dual ramp, successive approximation, etc.), so only the methods of interfacing will be described here. There are two sides to this: the digital interface to the bus and the analog buffering and scaling circuitry.

Digital interface

The bus interface is quite straightforward. To operate a DAC, the digital number to be converted is written into the data inputs. Some DACs have a built-in latch, but others require the data to be latched externally. Thus the digital interface to a DAC is the same as that for a latch. This is made more complicated if the resolution of the converter is more than 8-bits on an 8-bit system (like STE): some converters allow the digital data to be written in separate parts (usually two parts), but others require that all the data are written at one time. In the former case, the two bytes are distinguished by being written to two different addresses: the least significant address line is usually connected to the converter to specify which byte is being written. In the latter case, the interface must store one byte in a latch, and then pass this latched value to the converter with the second byte when that is written.

An ADC has a *start convert* input which tells the device to convert the analog input signal; it has a *busy* output, which is used to indicate when the conversion is complete; and it has a number of data outputs, how many depends on the resolution of the converter. These data outputs are tristate on some devices, but a buffer is needed for other devices so connecting to the bus is just like interfacing a buffer. The busy signal usually has a totem-pole output, so this has to be buffered on to the data bus. Some converters also require a clock signal. If the conversion time is less than 1 µs, it might be worth issuing a start convert at the start of the cycle and not issuing DATACK* until after the conversion is complete. Otherwise, the start convert should be issued in one cycle, using one instruction, then the processor should keep reading the busy line and testing it until the conversion is done, and then it can read the data. Again the interface is made more complicated if the resolution of the device is greater than the bus width of the system.

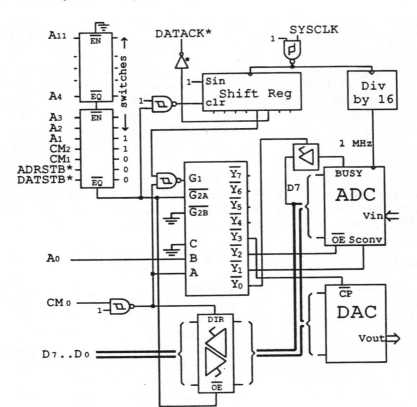

Fig 3.17 Analog-digital conversion interface

The digital interface for a circuit with one 8-bit DAC (with built-in latch) and one 8-bit ADC (with tristate outputs) is shown in figure 3.17. The circuit requires two addresses distinguished by A_0. The read and write cycles for the board are defined by the following truth table:

A_0	CM_0	Operation
0	0	issue start convert
0	1	read busy line
1	0	write data to DAC
1	1	read data from ADC

The following typical parameters are used in the design:

Data set-up and hold times for the DAC are 150 ns and 10 ns.
Minimum width of start convert pulse is 200 ns.
Access time of converted data to ADC output is 250 ns.
Maximum clock frequency for the ADC is 1 MHz.

The bidirectional buffer is used because the ADC is not powerful enough to drive the data bus, and to provide the Schmitt trigger inputs for when writing to the DAC. The ADC busy line is buffered on to the internal data bus, but the ADC data appear on tristate outputs. The (admittedly small) hold time is achieved by disabling the 1 of 8 decoder using the fourth output of the shift register and generating **DATACK*** using the fifth output. Using the earlier input is in practice unnecessary, as there will undoubtedly be delays between asserting **DATACK*** and the cycle being terminated, but by using this method, which requires no extra hardware, one can be confident that the circuit will work. The 1 MHz clock signal is generated by feeding the 16 MHz system clock, **SYSCLK**, into a 4-bit binary counter, that is the input clock is divided by 16.

Analog interface

Most ADCs convert voltages in the range of 0 to 2.5 V, and DACs generate voltages in this range. To process voltages in a greater range than this, or to provide *bipolar* ranges, some analog scaling circuitry is required. Some more modern converters have such circuits in built. Reference voltages are also required.

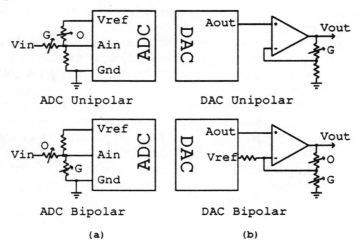

(a)   (b)

Figure 3.18 Analog interface to ADCs and DACs

In figure 3.18a are shown the scaling circuits used on the ADC for unipolar and bipolar operation. The values of components required will depend on the particular chip and the required voltage range: refer to specific data sheets. The potentiometers provide fine control of the range (in the figure, O is the offset adjust, G is the gain adjust); setting these is a somewhat tedious process best given to someone else! The procedure is to apply the voltage equivalent of half a bit to the analog input and to adjust the offset adjust pot until the data output is sometimes the lowest digital value and sometimes the next one. Then the maximum voltage minus one half bit is applied and the gain adjust pot is set so that the converted output is sometimes the full scale value and sometimes that value minus 1. Setting the second pot may have upset the first one, so that has to be checked, etc. I said it was tedious!

An alternative (better but more expensive) method of scaling the input is to use op-amp circuitry where the two adjustments do not interact. This is particularly recommended for mass produced systems where significant time spent in setting up the device is expensive. Incorporated in such circuitry there can be automatically controlled gain amplifiers and sample-and-hold circuits. The latter is needed to latch the analog signal being measured if it is likely that the signal will change during the conversion period.

For some ADCs, a small negative voltage is required in the circuit which is not required elsewhere; this can be achieved by a *diode pump* circuit: again refer to data sheets.

If many analog sources are to be converted, rather than having many (relatively expensive) ADCs, an analog multiplexor can be connected so that one source only is fed to the ADC and then converted. Selecting the source is achieved by writing the appropriate select pattern to a latch in the multiplexor. Some ADCs have multiplexors in-built.

For the DAC, the scaling is achieved using an operational amplifier, and this also provides some protective buffering. Circuits to achieve unipolar and bipolar outputs are given in figure 3.18b. Again, setting the potentiometers is a little tedious.

It is essential that good noise immunity is provided in these circuits. The power supply should be well decoupled, and it is a good idea to connect the analog earth to the digital earth at one point only. Earth planes are also recommended. Other factors which need consideration when using these devices are the length of time taken to convert an analog signal, the rate at which the analog signal is sampled and the problem of aliasing. These factors are discussed in more detail in chapter 7.

3.13   Attention requests

To use the ADC in the above example, a signal is issued telling the ADC to start conversion, and then the processor tests the BUSY signal until the conversion has been completed when the digital number can be read. This method of finding out when the conversion is complete is termed *polling*.

The alternative to polling is to get the ADC to tell the processor when the conversion is complete: the ADC should issue a signal which interrupts the action of the processor and which gets the processor to read the converted value. In general, a device which wants attention issues an interrupt signal, and the processor stops its current action and services the request.

Interrupts are straightforward: their salient points can be illustrated by analogy. Suppose you are reading this book and the phone rings. You will probably finish the current sentence, mark the position in the book and answer the phone. At the end of the conversation, you may well return to the book and carry on reading from where you were.

On being interrupted, a microprocessor will finish obeying the current instruction, remember the address of the next instruction (typically it pushes the program counter on to the stack) and then obey a *service routine*, which is a series of instructions which handles the interrupt. At the end of the service routine the processor reloads the program counter (from the stack) and obeys the next instruction: it carries on from where it was.

To continue the analogy: suppose you find this book so absorbing that you do not want to be disturbed. In this case you will ignore the phone.

Similarly, a microprocessor can be set so that it ignores interrupts: they are said to be masked. Usually, interrupts are masked unless they are specifically enabled.

However, the book will not be so absorbing that you would carry on reading in the event that your house caught fire.

Most microprocessors have a non-maskable interrupt which is always serviced. A typical use of such is when the power supply is about to turn off: it may be possible to store the contents of RAM on to disk or other non-volataile memory, for example.

Most processors respond to different types of interrupt. Similarly, a computer system may well have many slave devices which are capable of issuing interrupts, for example, keyboards, UARTs, timers, etc. Interrupts are often used for irregular events, like the pressing of a key on a keyboard: effectively interrupts provide a method of synchronising the (fast) computer and the (slow) peripheral. Another use is for regular events like precise timing. Many computer systems provide a clock for telling the time; this is often achieved by having the time stored in memory, and an interrupt issued, say, every tenth of a second; the action of the associated service' routine is to increment the stored value of time. For accurate control of a system, the computer should measure the state of that system and output appropriate control information at regular intervals: interrupts provide a good method of doing this. Some computers refresh dynamic RAM by interrupt: every 2 ms an interrupt occurs and the action of the service routine is to refresh every row in the RAM (typically by a series of read operations). Woe betide the programmer who disables interrupts in such a system: his program will fade away!

Another circumstance where a slave might want to attract attention is a request for *Direct Memory Access* (DMA). Here a device wants to take control of the bus from the master so that the slave can access the memory directly. Interfaces to floppy and hard disks often use DMA.

These different attention requests must be handled somehow. As many devices may issue a request at the same time, a priority system is needed to determine the order in which they are serviced, and some means is required whereby the master can identify the device issuing the request. Normally there is a defined priority for different types of interrupt: non-maskable interrupt having the highest. Daisy-chain techniques provide another method: the device nearest the master has the highest priority. Identification of the interruptor is often achieved by the master issuing an *acknowledgement* cycle as a result of which the interruptor returns an identifying number: this number is often called a vector.

Attention requests on STE

On STE, there are 8 attention request lines, $ATNRQ_7*..ATNRQ_0*$, and these can be used for interrupts, DMA (although there are also two other request lines for DMA), and any other type of attention request as long as the use is not to implement a function which is specific to a particular microprocessor. Essentially, the idea is to make the system flexible, although the limit of eight lines may be a problem.

$ATNRQ_0*$ has the highest priority. All signals are level triggered: they are on if their level is '0', rather than being on when they go to state '0'. The attention request signals are open-collector (or open-drain).

A master can acknowledge an attention request by issuing a *vector fetch* cycle. This is just like a read cycle, except the command lines, CM_2, CM_1 and CM_0 are '0', '1', '1', respectively (note that CM_0 is again '1' when data are being read), and the three least significant address lines only are issued: these have a number in the range 0 to 7, thereby specifying the particular request line being acknowledged. In response to this cycle, the device issuing the attention request should clear the request and put its identification vector on to the bus. The STE specification calls this action an *explicit response*.

Alternatively, the master can obtain the same information by using normal read and write cycles: these cycles should read any relevant data and clear the request signal. In other words, a circuit capable of issuing an attention request should also be usable by *polling*. This is called an *implicit response*.

A board which issues an attention request should be able to respond to an implicit response, but it need not be able to respond to an explicit (vector fetch cycle) response. The advantage of vector fetch cycles is that a microprocessor which uses them may be able to respond to an interrupt more quickly than a processor which does not.

Any device can listen to an attention request: the power failure request can be acted on by a variety of devices, for example. Such actions are termed *local action responses*. However, the master only can respond to the request by issuing signals on to the bus, and only the device which issued the request can, when accessed, put its vector on to the data bus.

It should be possible to prevent the issuing of attention requests. As a processor should not be interrupted until it has set up any necessary parameters (for example, setting the stack pointer to point to RAM), it is best that these requests are prevented from occurring when the system is first powered up and enabled only when the master is ready. It should also be possible to select the particular ATNRQ* line used by any given device because there can be many devices in the system capable of issuing requests. It is recommended in the STE specification that, in systems with both interrupt and DMA attention requests, the interrupts should be connected to the four highest priority lines ($ATNRQ_0*..ATNRQ_3*$).

ADC and DAC board with interrupts

The circuit shown in figure 3.17 will now be extended so that an interrupt can be issued when the ADC has finished the conversion. The complete diagram is shown in figure 3.19. Note that the extra facilities are provided by an extension of the circuit of figure 3.17.

When the BUSY output of the ADC goes from '0' to '1', an attention request is issued, provided that requests have been enabled. This action is achieved by the two D-type flip-flops at the bottom of the figure. If the output of the first flip-flop is a '1', the Q output of the second device will become '1' on the rising edge of BUSY and so generate an attention request. However, if the output of the first flip-flop is a '0', no request will

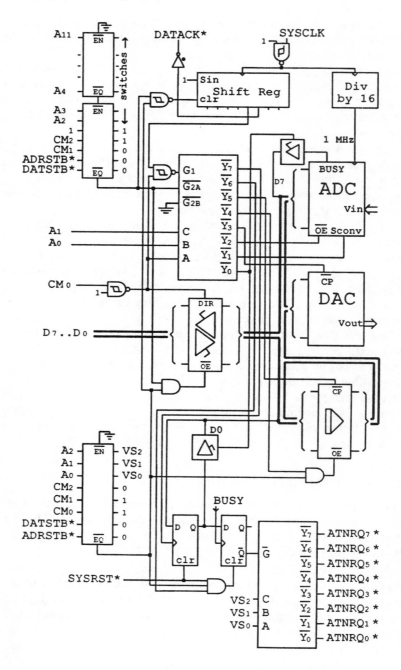

Figure 3.19 Analog-digital interface with interrupts

be generated. When the system is first switched on, the reset signal **SYSRST*** is asserted; as this signal is connected via an AND gate to the **clr** inputs of the flip-flops, the flip-flops will be cleared initially and so requests are disabled on power-up. To enable attention requests, a '1' has to be written into the first flip-flop. This is achieved during a normal peripheral write cycle when bit 0 on the data bus should be a '1' if requests are to be enabled. Note that this requires another address line into the 1 of 8 decoder chip. For flexibility, it is arranged that the state of this flip-flop can be read at the same time that the BUSY line is polled: BUSY is on bit 7, the enable signal is on bit 0 of the bus.

The inverting output of the second flip-flop is fed into the active low enable input of a 1 of 8 decoder circuit with open-collector outputs. Three switches, VS_2, VS_1 and VS_0, are the select inputs of this chip. This circuit selects the one attention request line which is asserted by the circuit.

In response to a vector fetch cycle (acknowledging an interrupt from this circuit), the identification vector should be put on the bus and the attention request cleared. This is achieved by having a latch in which the vector is stored; during the vector fetch cycle, the data outputs of the latch are enabled, so the vector is put on the bus. Note that the bidirectional buffer must also be enabled at this time: the direction input to this is again determined by CM_0. At the same time, the **clr** input of the second D-type flip-flop is asserted, thus clearing the request. The valid vector fetch detect circuit is, once again, a comparator: it checks that the three-bit address matches the three select switches, that the command signals are correct, and that **ADRSTB*** and **DATSTB*** are both asserted.

It must be possible to load the vector into the latch. This is achieved by a normal peripheral write cycle: another output of the 1 of 8 decoder is used to control the clock signal on the latch for this purpose.

To conform to the STE specification, it must be possible to acquire the vector, etc., by normal read and write cycles. Means must therefore be provided for clearing the second D-type flip-flop (and thus removing the request signal) and for reading the contents of the latch using normal bus cycles. For these actions, further outputs of the 1 of 8 decoder are used.

Note that it is not necessary for a board to be able to respond to vector fetch cycles; thus this board could be simplified, but not by much. If vector fetch cycles are to be ignored, only the latch for the vector and the comparator which detects the vector fetch cycle would not be needed. Also, the decoder with open-collector outputs might be replaced by switches or links for selecting which attention request line is asserted. Circuitry would still be required for generating the request, clearing it and for suitable initialisation.

The address map of the board is shown below:

A_1	A_0	CM_0	action
0	0	0	issue start convert to ADC
0	0	1	read BUSY line and enable/disable
0	1	0	write number to be converted to DAC
0	1	1	read converted value from ADC
1	0	0	write vector
1	0	1	read vector
1	1	0	enable/disable request
1	1	1	clear attention request

Note that some reduction in circuitry could be achieved using PLAs. It should be possible to replace the two comparators which have **DATSTB***, etc., as inputs, the 1 of 8 decoder and the AND and NAND gates by a PLA. The inputs to the PLA would be the address lines $A_3..A_0$, the two address switches and the three vector switches (that is, the switches which are inputs to these two comparators), the $\overline{EQ}$ output of the other comparator, the **CM** command lines, **DATSTB***, **ADRSTB***, **SYSRST*** and the output of the shift register. The outputs of the PLA would be the $\overline{OE}$ and **Sconv** signals on the ADC, the enable of the buffer for BUSY, the $\overline{CP}$ signal on the DAC, the $\overline{CP}$ and $\overline{OE}$ signals on the latch, the **DIR** and $\overline{OE}$ inputs to the bidirectional buffer, the clock input on the first D-type flip-flop, the clear inputs to both flip-flops, the **clr** input to the shift register and **DATACK***. This requires 17 inputs and 13 outputs, which can be achieved by either one large PLA or two smaller devices. Probably, it is not worth using PLAs in this case: very few chips can be replaced.

3.14   Multiple attention requests

Some devices are capable of issuing many interrupts; an example of this is a particular counter timer chip which has five independant counters each of which has an output that can cause an interrupt. As there are only eight attention request lines on STE and no daisy-chain priority system, one board should assert one request line only: if any interrupt is to be issued, this one line is asserted and the processor then determines the particular interrupt source by processing the interrupt vector returned by the device issuing the interrupt.

An interface of this timer chip will now be considered: this is designed to illustrate the use of multiple attention requests as well as to indicate the potentially complex software required when programming some modern microprocesssor support devices, and also to show that the hardware is not always that easy either.

The timer chip

The timer chip has five independent counters each of which can be programmed to count up or down, in binary or binary-coded-decimal (BCD), on rising or falling edges of a clock (selected from a choice of sixteen) until the counter reaches zero, when the associated output bit can be made to give a short pulse up, or down, to invert its current state, or to do nothing. The counter can be programmed to stop then, or to restart counting from an initial value: the same initial value can be used, or one of two values can be selected alternately. The action of one counter reaching zero can be the clock of another counter. Counting can be enabled permanently, or be under software command, or occur only when an external (hardware) level is high, or low, or on a low to high, or a high to low, transition of that signal. The current value of a counter can be read at any time: when it is read the counting action can be stopped if required. Also, two counters can be programmed to give an 'alarm' when a particular count is reached, and two counters can be programmed to provide the current 'time of day'. An internal clock is provided, which can be divided by 2^4, 2^8, 2^{12} or 2^{16} (i.e. in binary) or, of course, by 10, 100, 1000 or 10000 (i.e. in decimal), and these can be used as one of the sources of clock.

These features make the counter a very flexible device, capable of producing most of the conceivable timing requirements: the only problem is to work out how to make it do any particular task! Incidentally, the chip can be connected to either an 8-bit or 16-bit bus.

Each counter has three associated registers: mode, hold and load. The mode register specifies the method of count (binary/BCD, up/down, etc.), the enabling of counts, the source clock and the form of output. The load register contains the initial value. The hold register can contain the alternative initial value or, if the current value of the counter is required, that value is copied into the hold register. In addition there is a master-mode register, which specifies the source of the master clock, the dividing of this clock, whether time-of-day facilities are enabled, etc.

To program a counter, its mode, load, and possibly hold registers need to be set. To use it, a counter must be loaded and armed (which can be done together). The save command is issued to read the value of the counter: the disarm command is used to stop the counter; a counter can be saved and disarmed together. In fact these commands can be applied to any number of the counters at once. The master mode register must also be programmed.

Information is sent to the chip either as command or data. Commands include load, arm, etc., but they can also specify which register is to be loaded or read next. Having accessed one register, the device can be set to point automatically to the next register: for example, having written to the mode register of a counter, the next data access will write to the associated load register. An address line is used to distinguish between a command and a data access.

The outputs from the timer chip are the five counter outputs and the divided master clock. All of these can be used to issue an interrupt request. As mentioned earlier, one only of the STE attention request lines should be used, so that line should be asserted if any of the six sources request an interrupt. When the master responds to such a request, by issuing a *vector fetch* cycle, for example, the appropriate device must put its identification vector on the bus. If more than one request is required, a priority system is needed to decide which interrupt should be serviced. It should be possible to enable or disable each request. These requirements could be met by a number of circuits like that shown in figure 3.19 with suitable priority to determine the order in which the vectors are returned, but a better method is to use an interrupt controller chip, for example, the device in the same family as the timer chip. Such a chip does all the awkward processing, but it also needs programming: no easy task!

The interrupt controller chip

The interrupt controller chip can process eight sources of interrupt; it can decide which of many interruptors is serviced (either a fixed priority is used or the source which was serviced last is given the lowest priority); in response to an interrupt acknowledge, up to 4 bytes of interrupt vector can be returned for each interrupting device; each interrupt source can be enabled separately; a rising or a falling edge signal can trigger an interrupt; and more than 8 sources can be handled by concatenating such chips.

The controller chip also has a data and a command port, distinguished by writing to separate addresses. Commands include enabling, clearing, or reading requests, specifying priority and the active 'edge', and setting the *response memory* so that the vector(s) can be written.

The digital interface

The techniques already described are still applicable for interfacing these chips, although there are a few problems to be overcome, the solution to which may well be applicable to the interface of other devices.

The timings for a data transfer between the master and the timer chip are shown in figure 3.20. The interface must provide the chip select signal $\overline{\text{CS}}$, the command or data input C/$\overline{\text{D}}$, read $\overline{\text{RD}}$ and write $\overline{\text{WR}}$.

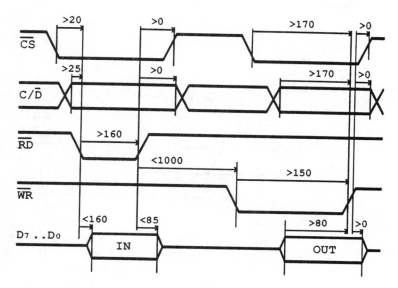

Figure 3.20 Timings for the timer

The timings for data transfer and interrupt acknowledge cycles for the controller chip are given in figure 3.21. Here the interface must provide similar signals: $\overline{\text{CS}}$, C/$\overline{\text{D}}$, $\overline{\text{RD}}$, $\overline{\text{WR}}$ and $\overline{\text{IACK}}$ (interrupt acknowledge) and take account of the signal $\overline{\text{Pause}}$, which is like a $\overline{\text{WAIT}}$ signal in semi-synchronous buses. It must also be possible to read the outputs from the counter without going through the interrupt controller, therefore a normal tristate buffer is required to connect these outputs to the bus: an enable for this buffer must be generated. Close study of these two figures shows that the design is not just a straightforward extension of the techniques described already. The main problems are as follows:

1) The interrupt vector(s) can be read only by issuing $\overline{\text{IACK}}$. Given that it should be possible to read vectors by vector fetch cycles or by 'normal' read cycles, it must be possible to assert $\overline{\text{IACK}}$ during a peripheral read cycle from the correct address, as well as by using a vector fetch cycle.

2) The C/$\overline{\text{D}}$ line on the timer chip (which is implemented essentially by an address line) must be stable before $\overline{\text{RD}}$ or $\overline{\text{WR}}$ is asserted and must remain stable until *after* they are released. For $\overline{\text{WR}}$ there is no problem as the $\overline{\text{WR}}$ signal will be turned off when DATACK* is asserted. But for a read cycle, $\overline{\text{RD}}$ must remain asserted until the end of the cycle (i.e. when the processor removes DATSTB*). Unfortunately, the address hold time after DATSTB* is released is at

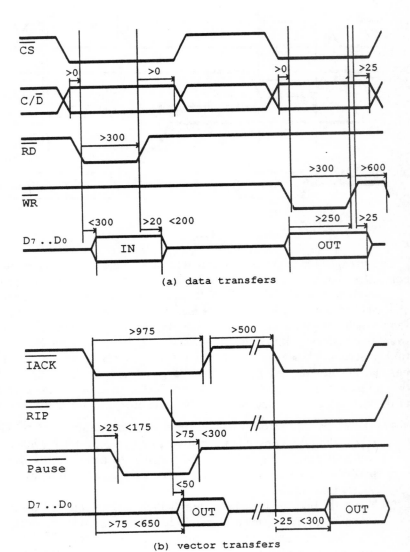

Figure 3.21 Timings for the interrupt controller

minimum 0 ns; thus, given the likely delay between **DATSTB*** and $\overline{\text{RD}}$, it is probable that the address line controlling C/$\overline{\text{D}}$ will change *before* $\overline{\text{RD}}$ is released. There are three solutions to this problem:

i) To latch the address line when **DATACK*** is active using a transparent latch (see section 3.4). Care is required to ensure that the address line passes through the latch sufficiently quickly for the set-up time on C/$\overline{\text{D}}$ to be met.

ii) To latch the data lines: this must be done say one clock cycle before the acknowledge signal is generated (to meet the 35 ns set-up time on data during read cycles). Thus the $\overline{\text{RD}}$ signal will be turned off when **DATACK*** is asserted.

iii) To assume that there is no actual problem. If C/$\overline{\text{D}}$ changes, presumably this means that the data from the chip will be corrupt. However, C/$\overline{\text{D}}$ will change only when the processor releases **DATSTB***, that is, after it has stored the data. Thus the corrupt data may be no problem at all. The design here assumes this to be the case.

3) Successive accesses to the two chips cannot occur too close together. The *recovery* times (time between accesses) are as follows:

```
Timer RD and WR      1 μs    <= 16 clock cycles (at 16MHz)
Int Controller WR    600 ns  <= 10 clock cycles
Int Controller IACK  500 ns  <=  8 clock cycles
```

The solution to these problems is to have a circuit which gives a level active for the prescribed time starting when the appropriate access ends, and this prevents the start of another such access until the recovery time has elapsed. A flat 1 μs delay for all accesses could be used, but with a little imagination, the appropriate delays could be achieved. Again monostables could be used but, for more accurate timings, a shift register is better. A 1 μs delay requires a 16-bit shift register and this needs two chips; if the clock is divided by two, an 8-bit shift register only is needed.

4) The acknowledge times vary depending on the device being accessed. They are as follows (assuming the 8 MHz clock used above):

```
Timer RD               210 ns        <= 2 clock cycles (at 8 MHz)
Timer WR               150 ns        <= 2 clock cycles
Int Cont. RD           350 ns        <= 3 clock cycles
Int Cont. WR           300 ns        <= 3 clock cycles
IACK (first vector)    975 ns + Pause <= 8 clock cycles +Pause
IACK (other vectors)   300 ns        <= 3 clock cycles
Buffer OE               80 ns        <= 1 clock cycle
```

The above times include propagation through a bidirectional buffer and the required data set-up times during read cycles. The divided by two clock (mentioned above) is assumed. The first vector can be detected by testing the *response in progress* line $\overline{\text{RIP}}$ from the interrupt controller when $\overline{\text{IACK}}$ is asserted: this can be achieved by one of the two edge-triggered D-type flip-flops found on a chip, the other flip-flop can be used conveniently to divide **SYSCLK** by two. If one interrupt controller only is used, it is unlikely that $\overline{\text{Pause}}$ will be activated to prolong the cycle, but it should be taken into account.

A block diagram for the proposed circuit is shown in figure 3.22. The basic circuit is similar to those described earlier: bidirectional buffer for data, comparators for checking correct peripheral address or vector fetch cycles, decoder for determining the one attention request line used, etc. The complicated blocks are the decode for generating $\overline{\text{RD}}$, etc., and for acknowledge; PLAs are used in their implementation.

The address lines A_2, A_1 and command line CM_0 determine the device being accessed during a peripheral data transfer according to the following table (A_0 is used to determine the $C/\overline{D}$ lines and so it is not included in the table):

A_2	A_1	CM_0	action
0	0	0	write to timer device
0	0	1	read from timer device
0	1	0	write to interrupt controller
0	1	1	read from interrupt controller
1	0	1	read outputs of timer
1	1	1	read vector

This table is implemented in a PLA which has the following inputs as well: $\overline{\text{Va}}$ which is low during a valid peripheral cycle, $\overline{\text{Vv}}$ which is low during a valid vector fetch cycle, $\overline{\text{Tr}}$ which is low if the recovery time on the timer chip has elapsed, $\overline{\text{Ti}}$ which is low if the recovery time on the interrupt controller has elapsed, and **ACK** which is high if the acknowledge signal has been asserted (so write cycles should terminate). The outputs of the PLA control the signals on the timer and interrupt controller, and the enable inputs on the timer outputs buffer ($\overline{\text{TB}}$) and the bidirectional buffer ($\overline{\text{BB}}$). The following truth table determines the requirements of the PLA:

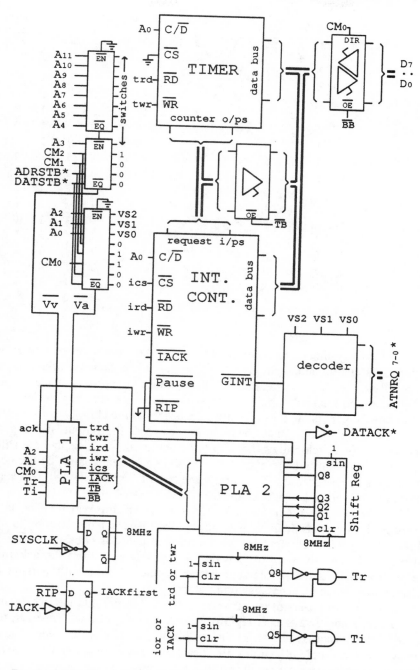

Figure 3.22 Circuit to interface the timer and interrupt controller

								Timer		Int.Controller				Buffers	
$\overline{Va}$	$\overline{Vv}$	A_2	A_1	CM_0	$\overline{Tr}$	$\overline{Ti}$	$\overline{ACK}$	$\overline{RD}$	$\overline{WR}$	$\overline{RD}$	$\overline{WR}$	$\overline{CS}$	$\overline{IACK}$	$\overline{TB}$	$\overline{BB}$
1	0	x	x	x	x	0	x	1	1	1	1	1	0	1	0
1	0	x	x	x	x	1	x	1	1	1	1	1	1	1	0
0	1	0	0	0	0	1	0	1	0	1	1	1	1	1	0
0	1	0	0	0	0	1	1	1	1	1	1	1	1	1	0
0	1	0	0	0	1	x	x	1	1	1	1	1	1	1	0
0	1	0	0	1	0	0	x	0	1	1	1	1	1	1	0
0	1	0	0	1	1	0	x	1	1	1	1	1	1	1	0
0	1	0	1	0	x	0	0	1	1	1	0	0	1	1	0
0	1	0	1	0	x	0	1	1	1	1	1	1	1	1	0
0	1	0	1	0	1	1	x	1	1	1	1	1	1	1	0
0	1	0	1	1	x	0	x	1	1	0	1	0	1	1	0
0	1	0	1	1	x	1	x	1	1	1	1	1	1	1	0
0	1	1	0	0	x	x	x	1	1	1	1	1	1	1	1
0	1	1	0	1	x	x	x	1	1	1	1	1	1	0	0
0	1	1	1	0	x	x	x	1	1	1	1	1	1	1	1
0	1	1	1	1	x	0	x	1	1	1	1	1	0	1	0
0	1	1	1	1	x	1	x	1	1	1	1	1	1	1	0
1	1	x	x	x	x	0	x	1	1	1	1	1	1	1	1

The recovery times are accomplished using the shift registers shown in figure 3.22 and the attendant gates. Essentially, when the appropriate signal is released, the shift registers start shifting and a '1' appears at the output only when the recovery time has elapsed. During the recovery period, the output of the gate is '1' thus disabling the access to the chip (because of the function in the PLA). Once the time has elapsed, the output of the gate becomes a '0' which allows the chip to be accessed. At this stage the shift register is cleared, but the output of the AND gate remains at '0' because the chip is being accessed. To simplify the circuit slightly, the two recovery times for the controller (500 ns and 600 ns) are treated alike.

The acknowledge circuit uses a PLA as well and a shift register. The shift register gives various delay values; one of these is selected according to the device being accessed (that is, the appropriate delay is chosen). $\overline{\text{Pause}}$ is also brought into the chip to provide any extra delay before the acknowledge for when the first interrupt vector is fetched. The shift register is cleared only when no access is taking place.

The above circuit is not trivial and so shows (I hope) that the interfacing to the bus is not always as straightforward as one would like. However, the complicated circuit is just an extension of the simple circuits. Once again, though, the example illustrates the necessity of reading the data sheets clearly and following the requirements given there.

Examples of use

As explained earlier, the timer chip can provide many functions. The following illustrates one example: generating a 50 Hz clock with mark-space ratio 2:1. This is accomplished by having a counter which counts down from two different values alternately, and every time the counter reaches zero, its output bit should invert. Given that the master clock for the counter has a frequency of 6 MHz, by setting the master-mode register to divide in BCD, the master clock divided by 1000 gives a 600 Hz clock frequency. If a counter is loaded alternately with 8 and 4, this 600 Hz clock will be divided by 12, giving a 50 Hz clock, but with the required mark-space ratio.

Thus the following are required. The master mode register needs to be set to divide in BCD. The mode register of one counter must be set to count without enabling, in binary, with clock source being the master clock divided by 1000, loading repeatedly from the two alternative registers, and its output should invert when the counter reaches zero. The load and hold registers of this counter must be set to 8 and 4. Once these data have been sent, the *load and arm* command for this counter should be issued.

Another example is to use the time of day facility and to arrange that the microprocessor is interrupted every one second so that it can display the current time at the top of the screen.

Here the master mode register should be set to count in BCD and to enable the *time of day* facility. The time is kept in counters 1 and 2, and counter 1 should be fed with a 100 Hz clock. This clock is achieved by using counter 5 to divide the 600 Hz clock (obtained in the manner as described in the previous example) by 6, and setting the source clock of counter 1 to be the output of the previous counter. When the program is first run, the current value of the time should be stored in counters 1 and 2.

The program should therefore do the following:

Ask the user for the current time, and load counters 1, 2 and 5 with these values and 6 respectively, and load their mode registers and the master mode register.

The interrupt controller should be set to accept an interrupt from counter 1, and to generate an attention request when such a signal occurs. The response memory should be loaded with a suitable vector (what this should be will depend on the microprocessor used and the operating system software that it runs).

The microprocessor should do anything necessary to set-up the service routine needed to process the interrupt (such as storing the address of the routine in a jump table) and then enable the interrupt.

Then the *load and arm* command for counters 1, 2 and 5 should be issued to the timer chip.

The service routine should first issue the save command to counters 1 and 2 (to save the current value of time), then it should save the current position of the cursor on the VDU screen and put the cursor at the top of the screen, then the saved values of counters 1 and 2 should be read and written to the VDU, the cursor should be restored, and finally interrupts should be reenabled on the interrupt controller chip.

Again the software to control these devices is not easy either, but it can be produced after suitable examination of data sheets.

3.15   Read-modify-write cycles

When a system is configured in which there are many microprocessors (which can happen in STE systems), a suitable protocol is required to allow them to intercommunicate. This is best achieved with some form of shared resource, that is, a device which can be read from and written to by the various processors. Potentially a memory could be used as the medium for communicating data. The system might work as follows. If processor A wants to talk to processor B, it examines the memory to see if no other processor is using it, and if not A marks the memory to indicate that A has control of it. Then the appropriate data are written which can be read subsequently by B. The potential problem with this is that B might also want to communicate and it might read the memory between A finding the memory unused and writing back to indicate that it has control, so that both processors think that they can control the memory. The solution to this is to read and write data in the *same* cycle. This can be achieved by a *read-modify-write* cycle on STE.

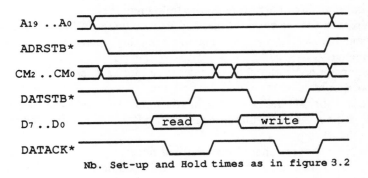

Nb. Set-up and Hold times as in figure 3.2

Figure 3.23 Read-modify-write cycles on STE

The timing diagram for such a cycle is shown in figure 3.23. Essentially the master device specifies the address and (after the set-up time) it asserts **ADRSTB***. Then the command lines are specified (this would have CM_0 in the '1' state to indicate a read operation) and after the set-up time, **DATSTB*** is asserted. The slave then responds to this by putting the data at the specified address on to the bus, and then asserting **DATACK***. The processor then releases **DATSTB*** and the slave **DATACK***. This completes the read operation. Then, the command lines are changed (to specify write) and the data to be written are output on to the bus, followed after a suitable delay by **DATSTB***. The slave then stores the data and issues **DATACK*** and the cycle ends as normal, after which the address lines can change. Essentially, therefore, a read-modify-write cycle is a read cycle followed by a write cycle except that the address is not changed between cycles and that **ADRSTB*** remains active throughout both cycles.

How does this affect the design of a slave circuit? In the simplest case: *not at all!* In all the circuits described above, the circuit operates only when both **ADRSTB*** and **DATSTB*** are active, thus the fact that **ADRSTB*** remains active through both parts of the cycle is irrelevant: **DATSTB*** is released, therefore (to the slave) the cycle has ended. Clearly it is important that the specification for the recovery time (the required delay between successive operations) is met, but otherwise the circuits described above will still work.

Having said this, it sometimes possible to design the slave circuit to optimise for such an occurrence. The access time for a slave is determined in part by the time taken to decode the correct location: in a read-modify-write cycle, the address for the write operation is already set, so, potentially, the access time should be shorter than for the normal access, hence the **DATACK*** signal could be generated earlier. Many dynamic RAMs can handle read-modify-write cycles and so it is possible to account for this. However, it is necessary to check that **ADRSTB*** has remained stable throughout the two parts of the cycle: a nice piece of sequential logic design.

The reader might think that, because there need not be any change in the design to accommodate such cycles, that there is no point to them. The reader would be wrong: the important point, which will become more apparent in chapter 5 when multiple bus masters are described, is that a read-modify-write cycle is a complete cycle which cannot be interrupted, hence the unwanted situation regarding shared resources, described in the first paragraph of this section, cannot occur.

3.16 Burst transfer sequences

Another special form of read, write or vector-fetch sequence which may be used on STE is the burst transfer sequence. During a normal transfer cycle,

DATSTB* and **DATACK*** are asserted once only (by, respectively, the master and the slave). In a burst transfer sequence, there can be many **DATSTB***s and their corresponding **DATACK***s, but the addresses, **ADRSTB*** and the command lines remain stable throughout. In figure 3.24, burst transfer sequences are shown for three successive read operations.

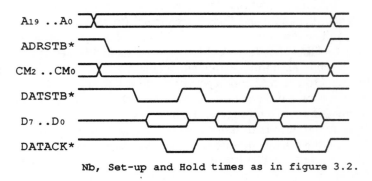

Nb, Set-up and Hold times as in figure 3.2.

Figure 3.24 Burst mode read cycle on STE

The potential uses for this include the transfer of blocks of data to a peripheral: for example, the string of data needed to set-up the mode, load and hold registers of the counters in the timer chip, or the reading of multiple bytes of interrupt vector. When successive addresses of a slave are to be accessed by a master, burst transfer mode can be used if extra logic is included in the slave circuit to increment (or decrement) the on-board address on, say, the trailing edge of **DATSTB***.

Again, the circuits described above could handle such transfers, but they could be optimised to account for burst mode, particularly using page mode on dynamic RAM, and extra logic could be added for automatic address increment, etc.

3.17   Conclusion

The techniques described in this chapter show how slave devices can be interfaced to the STE bus and, with slight modification, to other buses. The basic principles are those required to enable the master device to write to a latch or to read from a buffer. By using these principles and carefully reading the data sheets, suitable interfaces can be designed easily.

4 Other Slave Devices in STE Systems

In chapter 3, some detailed interface circuits are described for various memory and peripheral devices. These circuits show the principles of interfacing: writing to latches and reading tristate buffers. The interfaces of other slave devices use these same principles. In this chapter, therefore, these other devices will be discussed, although their detailed interface to the bus is not given.

4.1 Serial communication

Inside a microprocessor system many bits of data are transferred at one time (in parallel): the data bus is 8 bits wide on STE, but on other systems it can be 16 or even 32 bits wide. However, when information is transferred between different computers, or between computers and related devices such as printers, plotters, terminals, etc., often one bit only of data is transferred at once. This is termed *serial communication*. Clearly, serial data transfers will be slower than parallel transfers. However, fewer wires are needed for serial communication, and this is especially significant when data are transferred over long distances, including transfers over the telephone network.

In principle all that is required is two wires: one for the data, the other for the earth return. This *simplex* system is appropriate for sending data in one direction only, to printers for example. The same system can be use for two-way communication (*half duplex*), provided that it is ensured that data are not sent in both directions at once. A more practical system, *full duplex*, uses three wires: data in, data out and a common earth return.

Thus, for a computer to transmit information to another device, some means is required whereby the parallel data in the computer are transformed into serial data for transmission, and serial input data must be converted into parallel data for reading by the computer. In principle this is relatively simple and all that is required is a shift register; to output data, the values are loaded in parallel into the register, and on every subsequent clock cycle the next bit of data appears on the output; for input, the serial data stream is clocked into the shift register, and after 8 clock cycles the 8-bit parallel data can be read from the device. The problem for this is how to synchronise the transmitting and receiving devices. This is achieved by either synchronous or asynchronous means.

Asynchronous communication

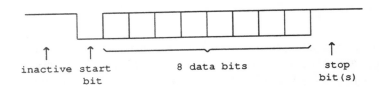

Figure 4.1 Asynchronous data stream

In figure 4.1 is shown the data format used in asynchronous communication. Normally no data are being sent, so the data wire is in the inactive state. When a data stream is about to be sent, the transmitter sends a signal to inform the receiver that communication is about to start; it does this by turning the data line on: this is termed the *start bit*. After this has been sent, the data are transmitted one bit at a time (the data line being set to '0' or '1' as appropriate for each bit). Then the line is turned off for a period (the *stop bit*). The receiver must know how long one bit lasts so that it can tell when one bit has been sent and the next bit is being sent (it cannot test for changes in the data line as two successive '1's may be sent, for example). Thus, for any link, the length of time that one bit is transferred is set: the length of the bit time determines the number of data bits that can be sent in one second (the *baud rate*). Most computers are able to transmit at 9600 baud, which is approximately 1000 bytes per second; some can go higher, others are capable only of lower speeds. Practical speeds are $300 * 2^n$ baud (n is an integer).

The receiver knows therefore the length of each bit, and it must sample the data line during each bit and feed the sampled value into a shift register. Ideally, it should sample the line in the middle of the 'bit period' when the data line is most likely to be in a stable state. This is achieved by having a clock signal whose frequency is 16 times the baud rate. Eight clock cycles after the receiver detects the beginning of the start bit is approximately the middle of the start bit; sixteen clock cycles later is about the middle of the first bit, etc. Thus the receiver is able to detect the approximate middle of each bit and so sample the serial data line at that time.

Traditionally, serial communication was used for connecting terminals to computers, so the data traffic consisted of characters which are represented by the 7-bit ASCII code. Thus the data transmitted are sometimes 7-bits only, though a parity bit is often sent as well: this produces some checking against errors, the parity bit being set or cleared such that an even number of '1's is transmitted. More recently, when data are being sent between computers, other binary data are sent. This can cause problems as computers interpret certain codes sometimes (e.g. control characters), so it is often better to transmit 'printable' characters. Some systems require 1, 1.5 or 2 stop bits: during the stop bit the received data can be transferred to some suitable location and the receiver can get ready for the next transmission.

Circuitry to perform this operation does not sound trivial. However, suitable chips are available: they are termed *UARTs* (Universal Asynchronous Receiver/Transmitters). UARTs are capable of both receiving and transmitting serial data, and they provide a parallel interface to the computer.

Early UARTs are simple devices to use: their interface to processors is easy, the options for length of stop bits, 7 or 8 data bits, parity, etc., being set by hardware connections: a set of wires being connected to '0' or '1' as appropriate. More modern devices can perform other functions as well and so this information has to be programmed into the UART.

A potential problem when transmitting data is that the receiving device may not be ready. For example, when sending data to a computer, the computer may be doing something other than servicing the UART. A system is needed such that the receiver can prevent the transmitter from sending data. This can be achieved by *hardware handshake* or by *software* means.

Hardware handshake requires two more wires, and sometimes four are used. These are effectively status signals: a device outputs one (for receiving data) and monitors another (for transmission). Before sending data, the transmitter should look to see if the receiver is ready and, if it is not, no data are sent. When a receiver has read in a byte, it asserts the 'do not send' wire, only releasing that signal when it is ready to receive again. One problem with this is over long distances when the 'do not send' signal does not arrive until after the transmitter has started to send the next data item.

Software methods are often used where a receiver has an area of memory in which it can store many bytes of data: this is termed a buffer. The receiver can therefore accept many characters before it is full. To prevent extra data being sent, the receiver outputs a command down the serial data line when the buffer is about three quarters full: this command requests that transmission should be turned off (called *XOFF*). It does not matter if the transmitter is already sending the next byte of data, as there is still space in the buffer, so long as transmission stops soon. Transmission is restarted only when the buffer is say one quarter full, when the receiver sends the transmit on character (*XON*). This protocol is termed *XON/XOFF*. It has the advantage that no extra wires are needed. However, there are problems if the XON or XOFF character is corrupted during transmission, so that they are not understood. Also, it becomes awkward if the XON or XOFF character is to be sent as data. However, XON/XOFF is used frequently.

In practical communication links the most reliable data transfer can be achieved by having some extra processing of the data being sent. That is, the transmitter and receiver should 'talk' to each other: the transmitter sends a set of data (including some error detection/protection codes) and then the receiver sends back an acknowledgement of the data, perhaps even a copy. Thus if an error is detected, the transmitter can be asked to send the packet again. This adds an overhead to the system: it takes longer to send data, but it provides security. The public domain program *Kermit* utilises this method. Kermit (some say it is so named from the Celtic word for free, others after the frog) is a useful program for sending data between similar computers or between different type machines (from main frames to PCs, for example). For transmitting large amounts of data, Kermit, or a similar program, is recommended.

RS-232-C

RS-232, or more formally the Electronics Industries Association's EIA RS-232-C, is a standard defined for transmitting serial information. It defines the logic levels and other electrical parameters, and it specifies the mechanical connections: those pins to be used on a 25-way D-type plug or socket. It may seem odd that a system which requires at minimum 2 wires only and normally only 7 or 8 wires maximum, should be defined to use a 25-way connector, but there are uses for most of the connections. Unfortunately, the specification is potentially ambiguous as to which pins on the connector should be used and, true to form, given the opportunity to interpret anything in different ways, computer manufacturers grasp it in both hands. Thus it is a non-trivial task to connect two devices both of which, it is claimed, conform to the RS-232 specification. Hence the well known witticism: 'The only standard thing about RS-232 is that it is not standard'!

To a certain extent the problem is historical. RS-232 was defined when the two devices being connected were typically a terminal and a MODEM (MOdulator DEModulator, a device for processing the signal so that it can be sent over telephone networks, etc.): devices are categorised as being either *DTE* (Data Terminal Equipment) or *DCE* (Data Communication Equipment) respectively. The problem comes when connecting two computers together: which computer is the terminal and which one is the modem?

In general, the pins that are commonly used are as follows:

1) *Protective Ground*
2) *Transmitted Data (from DTE to DCE)*
3) *Received Data (sent from DCE to DTE)*
4) *Request to Send ($\overline{RTS}$): when on it tells a DCE to start to transmit*
5) *Clear to Send ($\overline{CTS}$): when on it tells a DTE that it can transmit*
6) *Data Set Ready ($\overline{DSR}$): its use is similar to that for $\overline{CTS}$*
7) *Signal ground*
8) *Data Carrier Detect ($\overline{DCD}$): often used by DCE to stop transmission*
20) *Data Terminal Ready ($\overline{DTR}$): used by DTE to say transmission can occur*

In practice lines 1, 2, 3, 7 and two or four of 4, 5, 6, 8, 20 are used.

However, RS-232 is used, so its deficiencies should not be expounded too much. It is well defined as to logic levels, line characteristics and other such parameters. In practice all that one needs to know is that a logic '0' is a voltage value between 3 V and 12 V, and a '1' is between -3 V and -12 V, and that these levels and all the other electrical requirements are met by the special driving chips which convert between TTL logic levels and RS-232 levels. Either two chips are used: one containing four transmitters and the other four receivers, or a single chip with two of each is utilised. One advantage of the latter is that it does not require a separate +/-12 V power supply. One word of warning: all unused data inputs to the drivers should be connected to 0 V, otherwise they may output +12 V back down their other inputs and blow up the normal logic chips.

Data can be sent at rates of up to 20,000 bits per second over distances of 20 m or so, or further at slower speeds. To transmit data over greater distances and/or at faster speeds, other similar standards can be used, for example *RS-422*, *RS-423* or *RS-449*. RS-422 allows faster and further transmission by having balanced lines, thus preventing data corruption because of reflections at the end of the transmission line.

Another method used for sending logic levels is the 'current loop': a logic '1' is specified by the presence of a current in a circuit. Old teletype terminals used a 20 mA current. One advantage of this is that an opto-isolated circuit can be used to generate the current and thus the link is isolated electrically from the computer.

More detailed information can be found in the many references on the subject. See for example *Technical Aspects of Data Communication* by McNamara, *Communicating with Microcomputers* by Cullimore, etc.

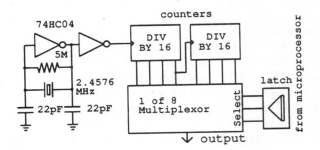

Figure 4.2 Hardware selectable baud rate generator

Thus providing a serial interface to an STE system is achieved by connecting a UART to the bus (in a manner similar to that described in the previous chapter) and connecting the appropriate driver chips between the actual serial link and the UART. Also required is a clock signal at the appropriate frequency; this is best achieved using a clock generator circuit based around a 2.4576 MHz crystal (this being $300 * 2^n$) followed by a series of counters which divide the frequency of the clock. The circuit shown in figure 4.2 provides such a clock. The latch is used to store a three-bit number which selects one of eight possible baud rates: the output of the latch controls a multiplexor. Remember that the UART requires a clock whose speed is 16 times the baud rate. The clock generator circuit is one of many such circuits: nearly everyone has his own favourite. Care is required to ensure that the clock oscillates at the frequency determined by the crystal and not at a harmonic.

Synchronous communication

One disadvantage of asynchronous communication is that 10 or 11 bits have to be sent for every 8 bits of data: this is clearly inefficient, but not a problem if data are sent only occasionally. To improve this a system is needed which does not require a specific beginning and end of each byte. This is achieved by sending many bytes of data, each one following the previous byte directly. Such collections of data are termed *packets*.

Some means is still required for synchronising the transmitter and the receiver, but this is achieved by sending special data at the start of the packet, after which the information is sent at the specific rate. Once the devices are synchronised, it is assumed that they will remain so for the period of the packet. A packet can contain other information as well, the address where the data are to be stored, for example, or error checking. Cyclic Redundancy Checks (CRCs) are often used for error detection. The precise structure of the packet is determined by the *protocol* used in the transmission. Various protocols are used, the more popular ones include *BISYNC* and *HDLC*.

BISYNC (Binary Synchronous Communications) relies on one or two successive synchronising characters to identify the start of the useful information in a packet. The receiver establishes synchronisation by studying each bit read from the serial channel until a special synchronising pattern is established. When the receiver is synchronised it tells the transmitter to stop sending the synchronising pattern and instead send the packet. The packet consists of the start of header character (SOH), a header (which could contain an address), the start of transmission character (STX), the actual data, the end of transmission character (ETX) and then the data necessary for the CRC. To send an ETX character as part of the data, the data link escape character (DLE) is sent before the ETX data.

HDLC (High level Data Link Control) uses a unique character for synchronisation (in binary 01111110). If six '1's are to be sent as data, a dummy '0' is sent after the fifth '1'. A packet in HDLC consists of this synchronising character, a one-byte address, one or two bytes of control information, the data, two bytes of checking and then the synchronising character again.

Handling these protocols is not easy in software, especially at fast speeds, but again chips are available for the purpose. Some such chips provide synchronous communication only, others can handle asynchronous protocols as well. The interfacing of these chips is again straightforward, though their programming can be complicated.

Local Area Networks

In these days where microprocessors have proliferated just about every-where, it is useful to be able to transfer information from one machine to another. Also, when a high quality printer (like a laser printer) costs two or three times the price of a computer, it is necessary to be able to connect many different computers to that one printer. A system is needed therefore which allows many computers and related devices to communicate with each other. This is achieved by a *local area network* or **LAN**. Local area networks have been achieved only because of the advances in micro-processor technology, but then they are required only because of those advances!

A LAN is a collection of devices which are interconnected and positioned close together: in the same building, say, or on the same site. Networks covering larger areas are termed wide area networks. There are various topologies used in LANs, the most common being *star*, *ring* and *bus*; examples of such are shown in figure 4.3. In a star system there is a central

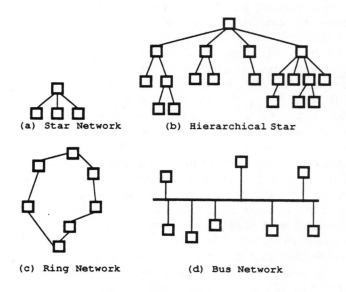

(a) Star Network   (b) Hierarchical Star

(c) Ring Network   (d) Bus Network

Figure 4.3 Various LAN topologies

controller and all data traffic is sent to the controller and then from there to the appropriate device. The disadvantage of this is that the speed of the system is restricted by the response of the controller. In a hierarchical star system, there are a number of 'sub' star networks, each servicing a number of devices and having its own controller. Each controller is itself connected to a 'master' controller, so data traffic may have to be passed through many devices before reaching its destination. In a ring system there is a continuous link which passes through each node in the network; thus the data are passed from one node, to the next, to the next, etc., until they return to the first. In a bus system there is one common medium on to which each node can write data, and which each device can read. Modern LANs usually use a ring system or a bus system: the main types used being Cambridge Ring and the Ethernet bus system.

Ring systems

The exact protocol used in a ring configuration depends on the system, but the basic principle is like the following. One, or sometimes many, packets of information are sent around the ring continuously. A packet is either empty or it contains data. If a device wishes to send data to another device, it waits until an empty packet arrives, then it marks the packet full, puts the data in it and specifies the address of the destination node and its own address. The packet then continues around the ring until it reaches the destination node. This node, if it is able to accept data, marks the packet read, and removes the data. The packet continues on around until it reaches the sender, which then marks the packet empty, and so available for use by another device. If the receiver is unable to read the data, the packet is not marked read, so the transmitter can tell that it must try to send again at some later time; it still marks the packet empty so that another device can use it, thus data can still be transmitted between other devices. The packet also contains error checking data, so corrupt data can be detected and retransmitted. Some ring systems also contain a master controller which organises packets, notes unread packets, handles errors in the system, etc.

Bus systems

In a bus system, when a device wishes to transmit data, it monitors the bus until no device is writing on to it, then it takes control and puts a packet on to the bus: the packet is *broadcast* to all other devices. This packet also contains the address where the data are to be stored. All other devices monitor the bus continuously, and when a device sees a packet addressed to it on the bus, that device reads the packet. After a packet has been sent, the receiving device should transmit an acknowledge packet. If no such packet is sent, the receiver is unable to accept the data, so the transmitter knows that it should try to send again at a later stage. There is the potential problem that two devices may both see that the bus is free, and so both start to transmit. This problem is handled by having the transmitter monitor the bus and compare the values that it is sending with those on the bus. If these differ, a *collision* has occurred, so the two devices stop sending and only restart transmitting at some random time later (random so that both devices do not start to retransmit at the same time). This technique is termed *Carrier Sense Multiple Access with Collision Detect*. A receiver which is unable to accept data could itself generate a collision to prevent the packet being sent, and thus get the data sent at a later stage, although the author knows of no system which uses this method. The advantage of this method is that less time is used for sending ignored data.

Thus these topologies of LAN use synchronous communication techniques. Again, suitable chips are available for handling these protocols; some are designed specifically for controlling LANs. Again their interfacing is quite simple, but the programming requires careful scrutiny of the data sheets.

OSI seven layer model

When designing or analysing any system it is important to have a model of the system. For a communications link, a useful model to adopt is the Open

Systems Interconnect, OSI, seven layer model. The lowest level is the *physical layer*, which is the actual link between two devices; above this is the *data link control layer*, which controls the physical layer and handles errors; the next layer is called the *network layer*, which handles the flow control of packets: it knows when to send or receive them; above this is the *transport layer*, in which the packets of data are formed: the data stream is divided into suitably sized packets; above this is the *session layer*, which sets up access rights between systems on the network; and then the *presentation layer*, in which data are encrypted or compressed, etc.; and at the top is the *application layer*, which is determined by the actual job being done by the network. For more information on the OSI model see for example, *Open Systems Interconnection* by Tolhurst et al.

Transmission media

It is important that the communications link should have a low error rate and be able to transmit information rapidly. The physical connection is therefore important, and various technologies are used.

One method used is *twisted pair*: here two wires are wound around each other to form a helix: one wire contains the data, the other the earth, and this gives fairly constant electrical characteristics. If good conductors are used, transmission rates of a million bits per second (bps) are possible over distances of up to 100 m. For longer distances, repeaters are needed.

Another method is *multiway cable* (also called *ribbon cable*). This is useful as IDC connectors are available allowing connection to the wires without the need for soldering. The performance of links using such cables is improved if every other wire is connected to earth. Data rates of 10 Mbps are possible.

Coaxial cable is also used, being better than ribbon cable but more expensive. 'Middle' quality cable is often used in LANs (the same as used in Cable TV).

Fibre optics are very good, but still expensive. Their advantages include their speed and their light weight; they also have good noise immunity and provide a secure link: it is difficult to tap into an optical link without causing attention.

Having alternate signal and ground wires helps reduce the effects of noise. Another method of improving the performance of the system is to have a balanced link, where at the end of the link there is an impedance load equal to that of the link. These factors are discussed in the literature (see for instance *Microcomputer Interfacing* by H.S. Stone) and in chapter 7 (with regard to their uses in buses).

The MIDI interface

Recently, sophisticated musical instruments, including synthesisers, drum machines, etc., have been produced, and people want to be able to connect them together or to a computer. One reason for doing this is to allow a composer to enter his music into a computer using a piano-type keyboard; this music can then be stored, possibly edited, and subsequently printed. To allow this connection, a suitable interface is required, and this has been provided by the **MIDI** system which has become standard (the music industry realised the problem existed very early, and acted quickly to produce a standard to which most manufacturers conform).

The MIDI system is another serial interface. The data rate is fixed at 31250 baud (faster than RS-232) and a 5 mA current loop and the 5-pin DIN connectors are used. The asynchronous protocol is used: one start bit, eight data bits and then one stop bit. A 5 mA current indicates a logic '0'. The standard is thus much more rigidly defined than say RS-232, and less flexible (fixed baud rate and connections), so connecting two devices together is very straightforward. More detailed information on the system can be found in the literature, for example Cullimore.

4.2 Parallel communication and input/output devices

The main advantage of serial communication is that it is cheap because few wires are required. However, only one bit of information is transferred at any time, so this form of communication is slow. Often this does not matter; mechanical devices such as printers and plotters cannot respond as quickly as computers, so there would be no particular advantage in being able to send information at the fastest possible rate (unless the printer has a large enough buffer). But when transferring between computers, or when sending a graphical image to a fast printer like a laser printer, the slow serial link can be a problem. For example, to send an image filling an A4 size sheet of paper to a printer with a resolution of 300 dots per inch, the amount of data to be sent is about 300 * 7 * 300 * 11 bits (plus any protocol for setting graphics mode, etc.). If the speed of the link is 9600 baud (a typical speed from a microcomputer), that is, about 1000 bytes are sent per second, it will take about 14 minutes to send the data. This assumes that the whole picture is sent, but if the image is made up of lines and the printer is capable of accepting such commands, it will probably be faster to send just the coordinates of the ends of each line. Alternatively, some form of data compression can be used to reduce the amount of data being sent. One such technique, called *run length coding*, divides the data into *runs* of data of the same colour and sends the colour and the number of consecutive dots of that colour. This method reduces the time taken for transmission of an image, but it can still take much time to send an image over a serial link.

Thus there is also a need for parallel communication, and many micro-computers have a parallel 'printer' port for this purpose. This is normally a uni-directional link only: data can be sent from the computer to the printer. It should be possible to send at least 10^5 bytes of data per second over such a link, so the transfer described above would take about 8 seconds: this is much better than using a serial link.

Centronics standard

Many microcomputers are provided with a parallel printer port, and the standard for such ports is the *Centronics interface*. This interface is relatively standard: most computers and cheap printers conform to it (though do not take it for granted). The interface uses 36 lines and, like RS-232, it does not need them all. In principle all that is required are eight data lines, an earth and two control signals: a *strobe* to indicate that a byte of data has been output, and a *busy* signal which is issued to the transmitter to show when data may be sent. In operation, the transmitter waits until the *busy* signal is inactive, then the eight data bits are output, and when these are stable, the *strobe* signal is turned on (to low). The receiver uses the strobe to latch the data, and immediately asserts the *busy* line, which it releases only when it has processed the incoming data.

IEEE-488 instrument bus

The instrument bus can also be considered as a parallel interface for transmitting information between computers and other devices. As explained in chapter 2, it is used for connecting instrumentation devices like signal generators, oscilloscopes, voltmeters, etc., to computers. For more informa-tion on the bus, see chapter 2 and also such references as Cullimore. Various commercial boards are available for STE which allow the STE master to be the controller of a system using the instrument bus.

Parallel input/output chips

Most microprocessor manufacturers produce devices which provide parallel input/output ports: such chips are called *PIO*s (parallel input output), or *PIA*s (programmable interface adaptors), etc. Essentially, these provide a means whereby a number of different logic signals can be connected to the main processor. Each device has a number of input/output lines, each of which can be configured as being an input or an output, and a suitable interface to the microprocessor. Some devices can also be programmed to issue interrupts when data are input, and some have timers built in.

A typical device will have two 8-bit ports associated with which are registers and control lines. The registers determine whether each bit is an input or an output, the current values on the port, and control information (such as whether interrupts are enabled). The control lines provide the *busy* and *strobe* lines described above for the centronics interface.

The interface to the microprocessor will include the data bus, control signals specifying read and write, and register select lines (similar to the command/data input on the timer chip described in chapter 3). Often there is also a reset input, which is used to define the state of the ports when the system is first turned on: in general the ports are configured as inputs initially, as this is the 'safe' state. Often, therefore, it is a good idea to have a suitable 'pull-up' resistor on a line used only as an output, which is temporarily set as an input when the system is reset.

Again, as the various manufacturers provide different facilities on their own devices, it is essential to read the data sheet before selecting and then interfacing such devices. It is important also to consider the amount of power that these devices can output: the load current must not be too high, nor the length of the output wire too long, or the capacitance on the wire too great. See chapter 7 for more information on the practical aspects of connecting such devices to STE.

Many manufacturers provide parallel input/output boards for STE. One such board has 40 input/output lines and the ability to generate an interrupt when new data are provided. This board is based around two parallel I/O devices. The outputs to the real world are buffered, so as to provide necessary protection for these devices.

4.3 Disks

The principle of operation of a floppy disk, a hard disk, or even magnetic tape, is the same: information is stored in the form of magnetic fields on a magnetic medium, and that medium travels relative to a head which has a coil of wire wound round it. To read data, the changes in field as the medium passes the head induce current in the coil, and this current is detected; to write data, signals are put in the coil to induce fields into the medium. In the case of a tape, the medium passes the head serially, so the data can be accessed in a sequential mode: the first bit, then the second, etc. In the case of disks, the data are stored in concentric tracks; to access any data, the head must be moved radially until it is over the particular track and then it waits until the disk has revolved around so that the appropriate part of the track is under the head. The disk spins continually, but at a speed much slower than microprocessors can process data, so data are not accessed in single bytes, rather they are grouped together and read in a block. These groups are called *sectors*. Thus the data in a sector are accessed sequentially, but the access to sectors is more random. In a floppy disk, one head is used to read from one surface; in a hard disk, there are many heads, one for each surface, so many bits can be accessed at one time; thus access to hard disks is much faster than for floppies, especially as hard disks revolve more quickly than floppy disks.

Data encoding

Data are recorded as transitions of magnetic fields and this information must contain a clock signal so that the read back circuitry can be synchronised with the data and so compensate for any differences between the timings for read and for write. These differences can occur because tape stretches or because of tolerances on resistors, etc., used in timing. This is achieved in various ways including **FM** (frequency modulation), **MFM** (modified frequency modulation) and **NRZ** (non return to zero). These methods are illustrated in figure 4.4.

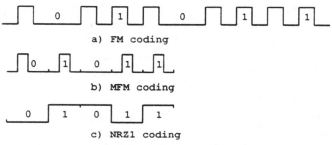

a) FM coding

b) MFM coding

c) NRZ1 coding

Figure 4.4 Disk data encoding

In FM, the data are stored in regular periods; a '1' is stored for the first quarter of the period: this is the clock signal; the data bit for the period is put in the third quarter: a '1' is stored there if the bit is a '1', otherwise no signal is stored.

In MFM, the length of the period is half that for FM, so twice as much data can be stored (hence FM is single density, MFM is double density). In general, a '0' is indicated by a pulse stored for the first third of the period, and a '1' by storing a pulse in the second third of the period. This means that a '0' following a '1' results in two pulses too close together, so such a '0' is indicated by there being no pulse during the period.

There are various forms of NRZ. In one, sometimes called NRZ1, a '1' is recorded by changing the current value output to the medium, whereas no change is made when writing a '0'.

More data can be stored on disk by methods of data compaction. Here, instead of writing data for each bit, some grouping is used which can result in fewer bits of data being stored. For example, rather than writing five consecutive '0's, the number five is written to indicate that there are five such '0's. One such system, *run length limited* or RLL, is used in some modern systems.

In each case there is an effective (with FM explicit) clock signal, and this can be recovered together with the data by using a phase locked loop. Thus for reading data, the signal from the disk is obtained and then passed through suitable circuitry which extracts the clock and thus the data. When writing data, the values must be encoded and then written. There is an extra problem: *bit shifting*, which occurs when domains of magnetic data are too close together and so affect each other. This is more significant on MFM encoded data, especially on inner tracks of the disk where the data are much closer together. If a sequence of magnetic data is 0 1 1, the first 1 is influenced on one side by the second 1, but not on the other, so that the 1 will appear earlier than expected. Similarly, the last 1 in a sequence 1 1 0 will appear late. Three techniques are used to compensate for this problem (these are possible because the problem can be predicted):

1) reducing the flux density on the read/write head on inner tracks
2) adjusting the window during which the data bits are read
3) writing earlier so the bits are read in the 'right' place.

The first two methods are used in both FM and MFM, the third is also used on MFM recording. Thus the reading and writing of data is non trivial.

As mentioned earlier, the data are stored in sectors containing groups of data bits. Just as with packets in serial communication, so in sectors on disks, the data are stored with other information. This information must first indicate the start of a sector. On *hard-sectored disks*, a series of holes are put on the disk to mark the start of the sector, whereas on *soft-sectored* disks, a unique pattern (the *leader*) is stored to show the start of the sector (compare the opening flag in the HDLC protocol). The advantage of soft-sectored disks is that they are more flexible: different sized sectors can be used. After the leader, some identification mark is stored followed by a *CRC* block (for error checking). Often this is followed by a gap which is used to ensure synchronisation (this is necessary so that disks can be used on various machines with slightly different timing parameters: perhaps due to tolerances on capacitor values) and thus to allow for different-sized data, and then the data are stored followed by a code for error checking.

The extra data in the sector are specified when the disk is *formatted*. Thus a disk on which 1.6 M bytes can be stored say, can have only 1.2 M bytes of actual data when it has been formatted, the rest specifies the start of the sector, etc.

The blocks of data read from the disk must be stored somewhere: normally they are put in memory. Each byte could be read separately by the processor and then stored. Alternatively, the data can be written directly to (or read from) memory without going through the processor. Such action is termed *direct memory access*. DMA is described in more detail in chapter 5.

Clearly, the control of disks is not trivial, but again there are special chips for the job, some for floppies, others for hard (Winchester) disks. Such *disk controller* chips interface easily to microprocessors, although they also need to be programmed. They perform all the functions described above, that is, moving to the correct track, encoding data and then writing them, decoding data using phase-locked-loops, etc., error handling, direct-memory access (if required), decoding of RLL, etc. Normally the controllers can handle many physical disks.

The organisation of a disk is determined by the operating system which is controlling the computer. Certain tracks are often used for storing the operating system itself (the *system* tracks). Other tracks are used for specifying whereabouts on the disk the data are stored (the *directory* tracks). Normally the information on the disk is stored in a number of different files, each with its own name. These names, together with the actual location of the file on the disk, are stored in the directory tracks. Thus to find a file, the directory tracks are searched until the file is found, and using this information the position of the file can be determined and data read from or written to the file.

Optical disks

A more recent development are optical disks, including CD-ROMs, where the data are stored using laser light. There are various advantages to this, including the absence of physical contact, hence less wear on the disk and the drive, greater reliability and greater packing density. Originally such disks were **WORM** (write once, read many times), but disks which can be both read and written many times are now available. These are of more general use in computing as it is necessary to read and write files. However, for storing vast quantities of data which need to be written once only, WORM devices are very suitable. Again, suitable controllers will be produced to allow a simple interface to computers.

4.4 Graphics

'A picture is worth a thousand words', according to the Chinese proverb; thus it provides a good method of communicating information. It is certainly true that it is often easier to determine pertinent facts from a graph rather than from a table of figures.

Requirements for graphics

There are two parts to a graphics system: the generation of the image and its display. In most modern graphics systems the information which makes up the image is stored in a memory, and these data are read from the memory into a suitable display device. Often that display device is a cathode ray tube (CRT); basically this is a television, the principle of which is that a dot can be shown at a particular position on the screen by firing an electron beam on to a phosphor at that position. The effect of this is to put energy into the phosphor atom, which pushes its electron up to a higher energy level: when the beam is removed, the electron comes down from that level and, in accordance with physical law, it must lose energy. This it does by emitting light: the time it takes to lose the energy is determined by the *persistence* of the phosphor. The greater the intensity of the electron beam, the more energy is put into the atom, so the brighter the light emitted. To show a complete picture, all the pertinent dots on the screen must be energised. If these dots are reenergised sufficiently often, the picture appears to be stable. The human eye can be fooled into thinking that this has happened if the picture is redrawn about 30 times a second, though it need not be refreshed that often if a *long persistence phosphor* is used. For colour graphics, each position on the screen has three dots (one for red, one for green and one for blue), and there are three electron beams, each directed at their respective dots. To ensure that the green beam only excites a green dot, etc., a *shadow mask* is used. Essentially this is a screen with carefully positioned holes in it which allow each beam to see only its respective dots.

In early graphics systems, the image was stored as a series of end coordinates of lines. The picture was drawn by turning the beam off, then adjusting the electrostatic plates so the beam would appear at the start of a line, then the beam was turned on, and then moved to the end coordinate of the line. This type of system is termed *vector graphics*.

More modern systems are termed *raster scan* systems which operate in a manner similar to televisions. The picture is drawn line by line, starting at the top of the screen and working down. As the beam progresses along a line, the intensity of the beam (or beams in colour systems) is adjusted according to the brightness of the dot (or dots) at that position. Thus the data which make up the image are stored serially in memory as a series of intensity values. On a television in the UK there are 625 lines, 313 lines of which are drawn in one 20 ms period or frame time (50 times a second) when every other line is drawn. In the USA the picture is redrawn 60 times a second (which reflects the different power frequencies in the UK and USA) and there are only 525 lines. In the next frame the intermediate lines are drawn. This method is termed *interlace*, and has the problem that any line is redrawn only 25 times a second (30 times in the USA), and so each line will appear to 'flicker'. If no interlace is used, that is, the same lines are drawn every frame, there is no problem. This is why the graphics provided on many cheap computers have a vertical resolution of around 300 lines, or less. More advanced high definition TVs get around this problem by redrawing the screen more often.

A line of video signal is shown in figure 4.5. First there is a blank period (the front porch), then a dip which is used for synchronisation, then another blank period (the back porch); after this the actual data are sent with colour information included if necessary. The peak-to-peak voltage of the signal is 1 V, with the synchronisation signal being 0.3 V below the porch levels. The porch levels indicate no signal, that is, the colour black. The actual d.c.

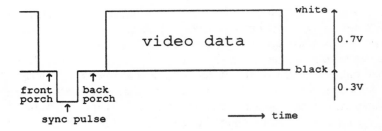

Figure 4.5 Timings of one line of video

level of this signal is not specified, so its decoder should be a.c. coupled, and the porch times can be used to set the 0 V level. The length of the line period is about 60 µs; this includes a period of about 10 µs when the electron beam is moved back to the start of the next line: the memory is not being accessed during this time. There is a similar (longer) period at the end of a frame when the beam is moved from the bottom right corner of the screen to the top left corner.

Circuitry required

Thus for most of the time the image is being read from memory and the data used to control the intensity of the electron beam(s). The circuitry needed to achieve this action is not trivial. First it must generate the appropriate addresses and the other signals necessary to read the data from the memory. Then it must convert the data into the correct voltage range and add the synchronisation signals. This action must be fast: for a horizontal resolution of 256 dots (a low resolution system), the data for each dot must be read every 50/256 µs, that is, about every 200 ns. The circuit can be made easier if many bits are read at once and converted into serial form using a shift register.

Colour graphics systems have separate memory for the different colours: these are accessed in parallel. Multiple shades of colour (or grey levels) also require multiple planes of memory and the n-bits of data must be converted to the appropriate voltage using a digital-to-analog converter. A nice facility on colour systems is to be able to select different colours depending on the application. This can be achieved by having a number of notional or 'logical' colours which are converted to actual or 'physical' colours at the last stage where the appropriate amounts of red, green and blue components are generated. This conversion is achieved by a look-up table which is a memory whose addresses are the logical colour and whose data are the colour components. The contents of the memory can be changed depending on the application to give the correct colours.

The circuit to implement a graphics system is not too difficult, but it is complicated because it should also be possible to change the image being displayed. To write new data, the controller must either interrupt the almost continuous accessing of memory for display purposes, or wait for one of the 'flyback' times. In the former case, the display is interrupted: this can disturb the viewer. In the latter case, the accessing of the display memory can be slow.

The design of suitable controlling circuitry now looks increasingly difficult. However, once again, special purpose chips have been designed for the purpose, and these are becoming increasingly powerful.

Early video controllers provided the necessary timing signals only: suitable counters for addresses, shift registers, multiplexors for allowing access by either the display or the microprocessor, had to be provided externally. The next generation had these external chips built in. Thus the display was generated, and the user could specify where a new dot was to be drawn. The next stage was to provide higher level commands: drawing a line, circles, plotting characters, filling areas. More powerful still are chips with commands for windowing and clipping, icon handling, etc. The latest chips are themselves microprocessors with built-in graphics instructions, handling three-dimensional images and even shading, for example.

But even with these sophisticated chips there is still the problem of fast access to the image whilst the display is being produced. There is a special solution to this as well: video dynamic RAMs (also called dual-port RAMs, although there are also 'proper' dual-port RAMs with different features, which should not be confused with video RAMs). These RAMs have the normal random-access mode: specification of row-address, then column address, etc., but they also have a serial access mode. To use this serial mode, a row of data is loaded from the main matrix into a buffer configured as a shift register. The data in the shift register can be read out serially, exactly as is required for graphics display. The important point is that the serial access to the shift register can occur at the same time as any normal (parallel) access, so that a conflict can occur only when the next row is being loaded into the shift register. The most modern graphics controller chips can be configured so that they can use these memories.

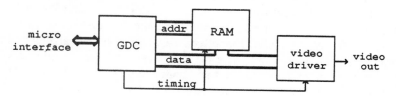

Figure 4.6 Block diagram of a graphics system

A block diagram of a graphics system based around a graphics controller chip (GDC) is shown in figure 4.6. This describes a typical configuration, though the exact system will depend on the characteristics of the GDC. Here the image is stored in the RAM and data are extracted from here for display at the times determined by the GDC. The output from the RAM is fed into the video driver circuitry which combines the video data with blanking and synchronisation signals so as to generate the information needed by the display device. The microprocessor in the system controls the image contents by issuing commands to the GDC. These commands would include line and circle drawing, etc., and the GDC would modify the data in the RAM accordingly. The GDC would also allow the processor to read back the contents of the RAM to allow some image processing, for example. There are various commercial graphics boards available on STE.

VDUs

The above systems are used for displaying pictures, and they can be used to show characters if the appropriate patterns for characters are stored in the image memory. However, to use a graphics system for showing characters only is often wasteful: more memory is required than is necessary, and manipulation of the image can be slow. For example, most PCs can show 25 lines of 80 characters: this requires 2000 bytes of information. The resolution of the equivalent graphics system is 640 * 200 dots, that is 16000 bytes. Also, if the screen is to be scrolled up a line, the data on (character) lines 2 to 25 must be moved: that is, either 1920 or 15360 bytes of data must be transferred. (Note that there are techniques which allow the scrolling operation to be performed without moving the data, but the main point is: character-only displays are best implemented with special hardware and not as purely graphics systems.) However, many modern word processors require that characters in different fonts should be shown on the screen, so that italic, bold, underlined or mathematical symbols can be seen. These are implemented easily in a graphics system, but the system can be slow.

The memory for a character VDU contains the binary codes for the characters which are to be shown at each position on the screen. To display those characters, their codes must be converted into the appropriate patterns for controlling the electron beam of the monitor. These patterns are a series of dots arranged in a matrix: on many PCs the size of the matrix is 8 by 8 dots, which gives readable characters. However, better characters could be generated by having more rows of dots, but this often requires a vertical resolution of more than 320 lines and hence interlacing flicker occurs which makes the display worse, or more expensive wide band monitors need to be used.

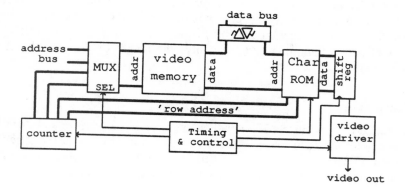

Figure 4.7 Block diagram of a character VDU

The requirements for the control of the electron beam are the same for the VDU as for graphics: the first line of dots must be drawn, then the second, etc. Thus the first line of each character in the first row must be drawn, then the second line of these characters, etc. Generating the appropriate pattern is usually done using a look-up table implemented in a ROM: the character to be read and which row of the character are connected to the address lines of the ROM and the appropriate binary pattern comes out of the data lines. This pattern is then fed into a shift register whose output is the serial binary data which is passed through special driver circuitry to generate the necessary video waveform. A block diagram of such a circuit is given in figure 4.7. Counters provide the necessary addressing: the least significant three bits of these specify the row *in* the character, the other bits specify the address of the character and are connected to the address lines of the RAM. The data lines from the RAM and the bottom three bits from the counters are passed to the character ROM to generate the appropriate pattern. These counters are controlled by a timing circuit which also ensures that the video data are output at the correct times with the necessary synchronisation added. Incidentally, scrolling without moving the data can be achieved by adding an offset of one row to the address of the image memory. With no offset, the first byte read is the first character of the first row. After scrolling, the first byte to be read should be the first character of what was the second row; if an offset of one row is added to the address, the first byte read is indeed that character.

This arrangement allows the image to be displayed, but it is also necessary to be able to update the image. Hence the controlling processor must also have access to the memory. This is achieved by passing the address to the memory via a multiplexor: either the VDU circuitry specifies the address of the memory, or the controlling microprocessor does.

Much of the circuitry required for VDUs is provided by the standard CRT controller chips. Again the sophistication of these chips has increased and the amount of external circuitry required has diminished, but (often) the amount of programming and (certainly) the length of the data sheets has increased!

Frame stores

A related type of system is one which can take a video image and store it in memory for later processing. This requires circuitry to decode the synchronisation signals, to process the video data, and to then store these in the appropriate memory locations. This can be achieved in various ways.

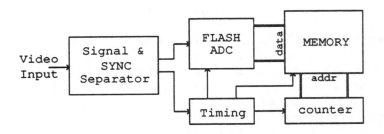

Figure 4.8 Block diagram of a frame store

The fastest systems can store a whole picture in one frame period: they wait for the start of the frame, and then for each row in the frame they convert the video signal into a stream of digital numbers and store each byte in successive memory locations. For a low performance system with a horizontal resolution of 256 pixels, the video data must be converted and then stored about every 200 ns; for a higher resolution system the data must be obtained more quickly. The type of converter used must also be very fast: the appropriate devices are called *flash* converters. A block diagram of a frame store is shown in figure 4.8. In the first block the synchonisation signals are extracted from the video signal, and these are used to provide the necessary timing. The signal is a.c. coupled (because the d.c. level is not specified), and the black level is set (or *clamped*) during the porch time, and the video signal is passed to the flash converter. The digital outputs from this are passed as data to memory, the address where they are stored being determined by counters controlled by the timing circuit. As the 'Sync Separator' is quite complicated the frame store could generate the synchronisation signals for the video source, although this is not possible if the source is a television.

Flash converters can be expensive: an 8-bit converter can cost about £80, whereas an 8-bit succesive approximation converter costs only about £4. The cheaper converter can be used if a slower video digitiser is employed: consider the following. Rather than digitising the whole image in one frame, that is, acquiring many values for each line, get one value only per line. This will require converting the analog signal and storing the digital value in the line time (60 μs): that is trivially easy. The signal should be digitised a certain period after the start of *each* line. If this is done for each line in one frame, a column of data will be stored. If on the next frame, the delay before digitising on each line is slightly longer, the next column of the image will be digitised. Thus by increasing the delay by a small amount each frame, the complete image can be collected. For a horizontal resolution of 256 dots, this process will take 256 frame periods, that is about 5 s. This may be reasonable for certain applications (though from experience of such a system, it is not easy sitting still in front of a video camera for this period!) If the video source sends interlaced data, it might be necessary to read every other frame to stop vertical 'jitter', so the process will take about 10 s.

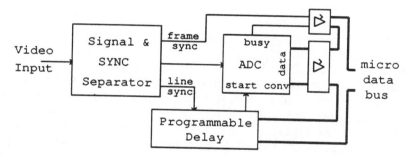

Figure 4.9 Block diagram of 'slow' video digitiser

A block diagram of such a system is shown in figure 4.9. Again there is a circuit for extracting the synchronisation pulses and deducing the start of a frame and each line. The video signal is again a.c. coupled, processed using the 'black level clamp' and passed to the converter via a sample-and-hold circuit. When the requisite time has passed since the start of the line, the video signal is latched and the start convert signal asserted. When the conversion is complete, the digital value is read and stored in memory. This action can be done by the microprocessor itself (if interrupts are disabled) so there is no need for any DMA circuitry or any memory in the digitiser circuit. The delay after the start of the line is achieved by a counter: this is loaded with an initial value before the start of the line and when the counter is zero, the data are processed. The initial value of the counter is changed (to give a longer delay) at the end of each frame.

5   Bus Masters on STE

5.1   Bus masters on STE

In this chapter the design of master devices will be considered, that is, interfaces will be described for connecting different microprocessors and similar devices to the STE bus. A bus master is a device which issues addresses, data, command signals, etc., that is, it is a device which instigates data transfer cycles. At any one time there is only one master device, but there can be many potential masters. The allocation of different masters will be described first, followed by their design.

The STE specification defines that an STE system should have a *system controller*, an *arbiter*, *master devices* and *slave devices*. The system controller provides the clock signal, **SYSCLK**, the reset signal, **SYSRST***, and handles the transfer error signal, **TFRERR*** (which is asserted when an erroneous bus cycle occurs). The arbiter determines the one master which at any time is in control of the bus. A master is usually a microprocessor or a logic circuit which issues similar signals, such as a DMA (direct-memory-access) controller. One such master is the *default* master: this is the device allocated control of the bus when the system is first switched on or reset. Other master devices can request control of the bus, though they may take control only if and when the arbiter allows it. In many systems the system controller, the arbiter and the default master are provided on the same board. Many commercially available processor boards can be configured as either a default master or a sub-master: they provide the signals for **SYSRST*** and **SYSCLK**, etc., but switches are used to prevent these signals reaching the bus if the board is being used as a sub-master.

5.2 Transferring control between master devices

If a sub-master wishes to take control of the bus, it must issue a request signal to the arbiter. Only when the arbiter acknowledges this, by issuing a grant signal, should the sub-master take control of the bus. Essentially there are two ways of requesting the bus: asserting one of the bus request signals, or asserting an attention request line.

The two bus request signals are called $BUSRQ_1*$ and $BUSRQ_0*$; both are open-collector lines. Associated with them are two acknowledge signals, $BUSAK_1*$ and $BUSAK_0*$. Either BUSRQ* line may be asserted by any potential master in the system, but $BUSRQ_0*$ has the higher priority. A request line should remain asserted until after the device has finished with the bus, thus bus requests are *level-triggered* rather than *edge-triggered*. Note that multiple masters may be connected to a single bus request line only if it can be ensured that at most one device can assert that line at any time.

In response to a request on one of the lines, the arbiter should, when control of the bus can be transferred, assert the *corresponding* BUSAK* line. The qualification is to allow the current transfer cycle to be concluded. In a read-modify-write cycle (section 3.15), the acknowledge will not be sent until after the whole cycle is complete, thus avoiding the shared-resource problem. While the acknowledge line is asserted, the master which requested it can take control of the bus. Note that at most one only of the two BUSAK* lines can be asserted, and it should be turned on only if the corresponding BUSRQ* line has been asserted: thus when the sub-master has finished with the bus, it should release the BUSRQ* line and then the arbiter will release the BUSAK* line, and then the default master can retake control of the bus.

A device must not assert a BUSRQ* line if the corresponding BUSAK* line is asserted already. This is because there is no means of determining which device should have control of the bus if many devices assert the same line.

For some system configurations, having only two bus request lines may be limiting, particularly if it has many slave devices which wish to transfer data to memory rapidly and so wish to use direct memory access. One solution to this problem is for the slave devices to issue an attention request when they have data to be sent, and have this request processed by a suitable DMA controller. For more detail on this technique, see p. 153.

5.3 The design of microprocessor-based master devices

In this section techniques will be described for interfacing various micro-processors to the STE bus. The resultant circuits convert the signals used by the microprocessor into the signals required for the STE bus so as to allow the transfer of data to and from slave devices and to handle attention requests. Included also in such circuits will be the system controller and arbiter, as most commercially available boards adopt such a strategy. Having a separate board for these functions is quite wasteful, given the overheads in such a board: the board itself, edge-connector, etc.

Philosophy

Most microprocessors communicate with slave devices using either a semi-synchronous bus or an asynchronous bus (some have both). STE is an asynchronous bus, therefore the time taken to complete a data transfer cycle will vary. Thus only a microprocessor whose transfer cycles can be of varied length can be interfaced directly. Thus connecting the Z8 single-chip processor for example, which has a synchronous bus, is more complicated.

Connecting a microprocessor with an asynchronous bus is relatively straightforward: the microprocessor will instigate a cycle and terminate it again only when the slave device has acknowledged the cycle (or a transfer error has occurred). Thus all the interface has to do is to convert the similar signals from the microprocessor into those required on STE. This is not necessarily that easy, in that the timings for STE must be adhered to rigidly, and may not correspond to those for the 'real' microprocessor.

For a semi-synchronous bus, a little more effort is required. Here a bus cycle will end after a fixed period unless the *wait* signal is asserted, in which case the cycle will then continue until after the wait signal is released. To convert to an asynchronous bus, a circuit is required which asserts wait immediately a cycle begins and releases it only when the data acknowledge signal has been asserted. In addition to this, the other STE bus signals must be synthesised from those provided on the microprocessor.

For a processor with a synchronous bus, a data transfer cycle on STE is probably best achieved using several synchronous cycles. First the transfer is instigated and the necessary signals (addresses, data, control) latched. The processor then, during subsequent cycles, tests whether the acknowledge signal has been returned, and when it has the cycle is terminated.

Another factor to be considered is the addressing of the bus. Many 8-bit microprocessors have an address bus only 16 bits wide: how is a 20-bit address provided? Also, some processors do not distinguish between memory and I/O: how is this handled? What about interrupts? In general, the extra lines are provided by a latch, written to during one cycle, the outputs of which provide the top address lines. For I/O, a suitable range of addresses is allocated; thus when such a location is accessed, command line CM_1 is made '0' to indicate a peripheral transfer as opposed to a memory transfer (when CM_1 is '1'). With interrupts, some microprocessors, like the Z80 and 68000, can handle interrupt vectors directly: whenever an interrupt is acknowledged, the address of the appropriate service routine is determined in part by the vector returned during the acknowledge cycle. For other microprocessors, like the 6809, no such facility is provided; in which case the facility can be synthesised: a vector fetch cycle initiated and the vector returned stored in a suitable latch and then processed subsequently. Alternatively, the interrupt can be handled by normal data transfer cycles:

the vector read by reading from one address and the attention request line cleared, etc. A further complication is that a device which can issue attention requests does not have to respond to a vector fetch cycle; so how should a processor, which generates such a cycle automatically, be connected to the bus? Specific methods of handling these problems are given below.

Also to be considered are any on-board memory or I/O. As the STE data bus is only 8-bits wide, the full potential of a microprocessor with a 16 or even 32-bit wide data bus cannot be achieved unless 16 or 32-bit wide memory is provided on the *same* board as the microprocessor. If the board is configured as a sub-master, it can continue to run its own program independently of the master device, provided that it has the necessary facilities on board. If it is to communicate with the master, it must either request control of the bus or allow access to its own memory. Some processors have other facilities (for example a UART) which cannot be exploited on the bus, but which can be used on board and brought out on to the front of the board. Most commercially available processor boards have their own memory and also some I/O including, usually, serial communication.

Also required in the circuit are the system controller and bus arbiter circuitry. The system controller must provide the clock, reset and transfer error signals, and the arbiter must handle bus request circuitry. Suitable circuits for these, described below, are given in figure 5.1.

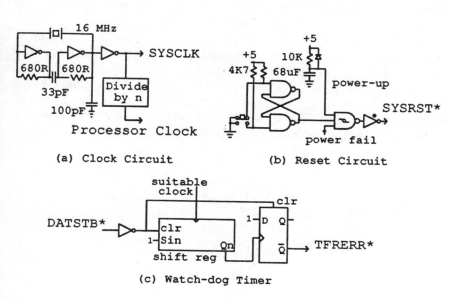

Figure 5.1 System controller circuitry

The bus clock signal, **SYSCLK**, must be a 16 MHz signal, which is faster than many microprocessors require. For STE the period of the clock signal should be 62.5 ns +/-1 ns, and the period when the clock is 'high', and when it is 'low', should be 31.25 ns +/-10 ns. Such a signal can be provided by one of the many standard circuits, like that shown in figure 5.1a, and then divided down (where necessary) for direct use by the microprocessor.

The reset signal, **SYSRST***, is an open-collector signal which may be asserted by any board in the system. When the system is first powered-up, any device performing on-board self-diagnostics (such as a micro-processor), should assert **SYSRST*** until the completion of such tests. On the *system controller* board, **SYSRST*** should be asserted for between 200 ms and 500 ms after the +5 V power supply has reached its designated minimum specification (see chapter 7). It should also be asserted if the power supply falls below its specified lower tolerance (again see chapter 7). The microprocessor should also respond to the reset signal if it is asserted elesewhere in the system. The board should also have its own debounced reset switch, so that the user can abort an erroneous program. These are shown in figure 5.1b.

When the processor attempts to access a non-existent slave device, no acknowledge signal will be returned, and the system will stop. To obviate this a watch-dog circuit is required. If it notices that a cycle has been in operation for, say, 20 times the length of a normal cycle, the circuit should deduce that a faulty transfer cycle is in operation and thus issue the **TFRERR*** signal. On detecting this the master should terminate the current cycle and, possibly, go to a suitable service routine to handle such an error. Such an occurrence is often an indication that the program being obeyed is in error and has 'got lost', so the program is best aborted and an appropriate error message printed. Generating **TFRERR*** is quite simple: again either a monostable can be used, or a shift register as in figure 5.1c. In the figure, the shift register operates when **DATSTB*** is asserted, and the flip-flop is triggered after the requisite delay and **TFRERR*** is generated.

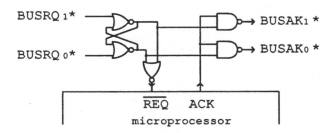

Figure 5.2 Circuit for the arbiter

Most of the circuit for the *arbiter* is usually provided in the micro-processor itself. Most microprocessors have a bus-request input and a bus-acknowledge output (though they call these signals by different names), thus the arbiter can use these signals. Care is required for handling the two BUSRQ* signals for when both are asserted at the same time and to ensure that the correct BUSAK* signal only is returned, but this is relatively simple. A suitable circuit is given in figure 5.2. Essentially this uses an inverse S-R latch for handling priority. In the inactive state, both BUSRQ* lines are '1', so the outputs of both the NOR gates (in the latch) are '0'. When one BUSRQ* line is asserted, the output of the corresponding NOR gate goes to '1' and this is used to assert the bus request signal on the microprocessor. If the other BUSRQ* signal is asserted while the first is active, it has no effect until the first BUSRQ* signal is released. The outputs of the NOR gate are gated with the bus acknowledge signal from the processor to ensure that the appropriate BUSAK* line only is asserted.

Circuits for connecting some real microprocessors

In the following sections circuits will be presented for connecting some microprocessors as bus masters on the STE bus. In so doing, the principles of interfacing bus masters will be shown, and also, the techniques for inter-facing to real microprocessors will be described. Each circuit will include the STE interface, but some will also provide on-board memory and peri-pherals as most commercially available boards do this.

The 6809
The following specification will be adopted for the 6809 circuit:

1) The board will have on-board 16K EPROM, 8K RAM and 4K internal I/O. A further 4K of the address space will provide the STE peri-pheral addresses and the other 32K will provide STE memory addresses. A latch (accessed as part of the internal I/O) will be used to provide the upper 5 address lines for such memory accesses. The address map for the board (using the 16 address lines from the 6809) will be as follows (all addresses in hexadecimal):

address range	device
0000 - 7FFF	STE memory
8000 - 8FFF	STE peripheral
9000 - 9FFF	on board I/O
A000 - BFFF	on board RAM
C000 - FFFF	on board EPROM

The EPROM is mapped into the top of memory as the address of the first program to be run is stored in addresses $FFFE and $FFFF.

2) As the 6809 has no vectored interrupt facilities, no vector fetch cycle will be generated: vectors will be read by normal peripheral accesses. The three most significant attention request lines, $ATNRQ_0*$.. $ATNRQ_2*$, will be connected to the three interrupt lines on the 6809, **NMI, FIRQ** and **IRQ**.

3) Also included in the circuit will be the circuitry for providing the *system controller* and *arbiter*.

4) A 68B09 microprocessor will be assumed. This is one of the fastest 6809 processors: it can operate with a 8 MHz clock. The B in the number indicates the speed of the device.

A block diagram of the circuit is shown in figure 5.3. At the top of the figure are the on-board extra facilities: EPROM, RAM and I/O. The I/O is drawn as a block in which various devices could be connected, one of which is a latch to provide the upper five address lines. The EPROM, RAM and I/O require address and data lines, the read/write signal and some enable lines: each enable line is active only when the appropriate device is accessed.

Down the right hand side of figure 5.3 are shown some tristate buffers. These provide the necessary buffering for signals and also allow for other master devices: the outputs of these buffers are put in the high impedance state when another master has control of the bus. At the bottom of the figure are two blocks providing the clock signals (16 MHz for **SYSCLK** and 8 MHz for the 6809 microprocessor) and the reset signals (**SYSRST*** on the bus and **RES** for the 6809).

The final block in the circuit, marked control, covers a multitude of sins! First it generates the enable signals for the on-board facilities. Also, it takes the control signals from the 6809 and converts them into those required for the STE bus: **DATSTB***, CM_2, etc. Finally it handles the bus request/grant signals. This block will now be considered in more detail.

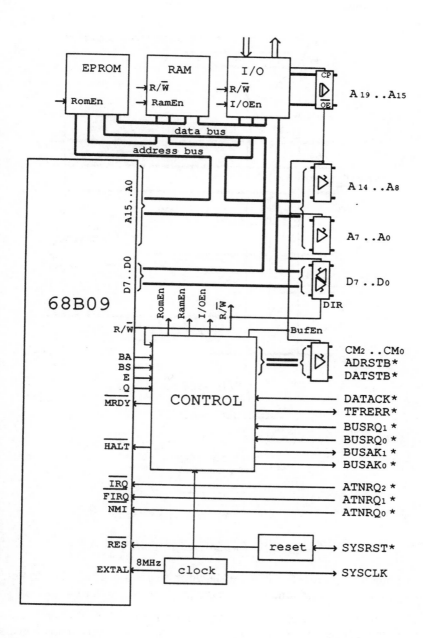

Figure 5.3 6809 board system diagram

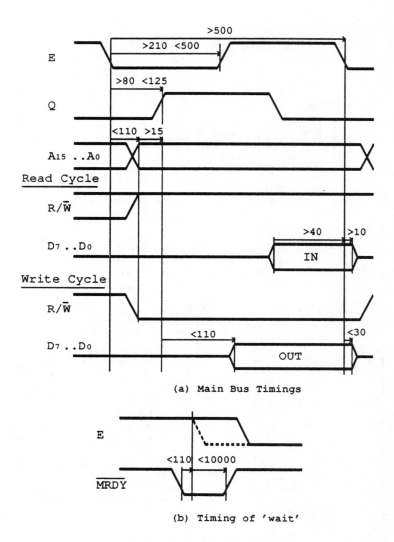

(a) Main Bus Timings

(b) Timing of 'wait'

Figure 5.4 Bus timings for 68B09

The bus timings for the 6809 are shown in figure 5.4. The points to note from this, and other information from the data books, are as follows:

1) A data transfer cycle starts when **Q** goes high and ends when **E** goes low. The address lines, read/write strobe (**R/$\overline{W}$**) and bus status signals (**BA** and **BS**) are valid when **Q** is asserted. The cycle can be extended by asserting the $\overline{\text{MRDY}}$ line on the 6809, the effect of which is to delay the

falling edge of **E**. Note that the maximum time that $\overline{\text{MRDY}}$ can be asserted is 10 μs (if this is exceded the 6809 may lose the contents of its registers), thus the **TRFERR*** signal should be asserted, say, 8μs after the start of the cycle.

2) **ADRSTB*** and **DATSTB*** cannot be asserted immediately after **Q** goes high because the 35 ns set-up times on addresses and command lines cannot be guaranteed. Also, for write cycles, the data do not appear on the data lines until at maximum 110 ns after the rising edge of **Q**. Thus, given the required 35 ns set-up time for data, **DATSTB*** cannot be asserted until at least 145 ns after the cycle starts. These delays will be achieved using a synchronous sequential logic circuit; thus, on read cycles **ADRSTB*** and **DATSTB*** will be asserted one complete clock cycle after the rising edge of **Q**, and for write cycles the delay should be two complete clock cycles.

3) The signals **BS** and **BA** from the 6809 determine the type of cycle, as shown in the following table:

BA	BS	cycle
0	0	normal data transfer cycle
0	1	reset or interrupt acknowledge
1	0	SYNC acknowledge
1	1	HALT or Bus Grant

During a reset or interrupt acknowledge, the 6809 is reading the address of the appropriate service routine from memory. Thus **BA** = 0 means that some form of data transfer cycle is occurring. Thus a data transfer cycle starts when **Q** goes high and **BA** is '0'.

The main part of the interface circuit uses the signals **E**, **Q**, **BA**, **R/$\overline{\text{W}}$** and the address lines $A_{15}..A_0$ to generate either suitable signals for the on-board memory or I/O, or the signals for the STE bus. For the on-board devices, a synchronous interface is required (it will be assumed that these devices are sufficiently fast for no wait state to be necessary). On the STE bus, however, an asynchronous bus is required. For the on-board devices: during a write cycle the data will be written when the cycle ends, and for a read cycle the processor will read in the data and then terminate the cycle. Thus any on-board cycle can begin as soon as **Q** is asserted, **BA** is low and the address is correct. As regards the STE signals, the timing is more complicated (as explained above) and the strobe signals must be delayed. The state diagram shown in figure 5.5 describes the required signals. Note that this diagram describes a synchronous sequential machine: the system remains in each state for at least one complete clock period.

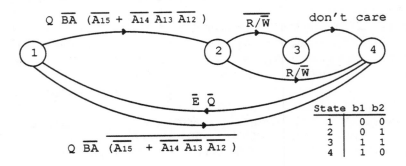

Figure 5.5 State diagram for 6809 interface

In state 1), no cycle is in operation. In state 4), the cycle is occurring, and remains so until the end of the cycle (which can be detected when both E and Q are low). If in state 1), Q is high, BA is low, and an on board device is accessed (the address is above 9FFF), a cycle can begin immediately: thus state 4) is entered. If, however, in state 1), Q is high, BA is low, and the STE bus is addressed, state 2) is entered. From state 2), if a read operation is to begin, the STE bus cycle can start on the next clock cycle (when there will have been the required one clock period delay after Q has been asserted). If, however, a write cycle is about to start, the STE cycle cannot begin until two further periods have elapsed (until after the data have been put on the bus), hence state 3) is entered and, on the following clock period, state 4).

Following the design procedure given in appendix 2 and more fully in Lewin, the four states can be represented by two signals, b_1 and b_2, encoded as shown in figure 5.5. Thus b_1 should be set if the next state is state 3 or state 4, and b_2 set if the next state is state 2 or state 3. Thus, as shown in appendix 2, the following logic expressions can be determined for b_1 and b_2:

$$b_2 = \overline{b_1}\,\overline{b_2}\,Q\,\overline{BA}\,(\overline{A}_{15} + \overline{A}_{14}\,\overline{A}_{13}\,\overline{A}_{12}) + \overline{b_1}\,b_2\,R/\overline{W}$$

$$b_1 = b_2 + b_1\,E + b_1\,Q + \overline{b_1}\,Q\,\overline{BA}\,A_{15}\,(A_{14}\,R/\overline{W} + \overline{A}_{14}\,A_{13} + \overline{A}_{14}\,A_{12})$$

The other signals are then as follows:

$$CM_2 = \overline{A}_{15} + \overline{A}_{14}\,\overline{A}_{13}\,\overline{A}_{12}$$

$$CM_1 = \overline{A}_{15}$$

$$CM_0 = R/\overline{W}$$

$$\overline{ADRSTB*} = \overline{DATSTB*} = b_1\,b_2 + b_2\,\overline{R/\overline{W}} + b_1\,(E+Q)\,\overline{DATSTB*}$$

$$\overline{EPROM} = \overline{b}_1\,\overline{b}_2\,Q\,\overline{BA}\,R/\overline{W}\,A_{15}\,A_{14} + b_1\,\overline{b}_2\,(E + Q)\,\overline{EPROM}$$

$$\overline{RAM} = \overline{b}_1\,\overline{b}_2\,Q\,\overline{BA}\,A_{15}\,\overline{A}_{14}\,A_{13} + b_1\,\overline{b}_2\,(E + Q)\,\overline{RAM}$$

$$\overline{I/O} = \overline{b}_1\,\overline{b}_2\,Q\,\overline{BA}\,A_{15}\,\overline{A}_{14}\,\overline{A}_{13}\,A_{12} + b_1\,\overline{b}_2\,(E + Q)\,\overline{I/O}$$

The above expressions can be included in a registered PLA with the 16 MHz clock providing the sequential timing.

Also required is the wait signal on the 6809 ($\overline{MRDY}$): this should be asserted when **DATSTB*** comes on and released when either **DATACK*** or **TFRERR*** is asserted. Thus MRDY can be generated by a circuit implementing the following expression:

$$\overline{MRDY} = \overline{DATSTB*}\ DATACK*\ TFRERR*$$

The **TFRERR*** signal can be generated using the circuit shown in figure 5.1.

Next the bus request lines must be considered. When either of the two request lines is asserted, the 6809 should relinquish control of the bus. To request the bus from the 6809, its $\overline{HALT}$ line should be asserted. The acknowledge can be detected by testing **BA** and **BS** on the rising edge of **Q**: when they are both high the processor no longer controls the bus. Whilst the 6809 is halted, it continues to assert the signals **E** and **Q**, thus the acknowledge line will be turned off when it is determined that either **BA** or **BS** is low. The complete bus arbitration circuit (extending figure 5.2) is shown in figure 5.6. The flip-flop in the figure is used to sample **BS** and **BA** on the rising edge of **Q**: this provides the acknowledge signal which is used to generate the appropriate **BUSAK*** signal. The output of the flip-flop is also used to turn off the buffers which drive the STE bus. Note that the flip-flop is cleared when the system is reset to ensure that this board is the master device. Extra switches and hardware could be added to allow the board to be configured as a sub-master and to control the bus only when it has requested and been granted it by the default master.

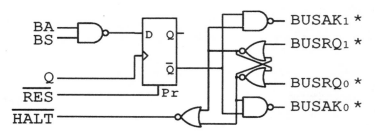

Figure 5.6 6809 bus arbitration circuit

As regards reset, the 6809 will sample the $\overline{\text{RES}}$ line when Q goes low and the set-up time for this is at least 110 ns. There is no other timing constraint on $\overline{\text{RES}}$. It is best therefore to latch the SYSRST* line on the rising edge of Q, and pass this latched signal to $\overline{\text{RES}}$. Also required are circuits to provide a reset signal when the system is first switched on, to handle the 'panic' button so the user can manually reset the computer, and a power supply fail circuit. A suitable reset circuit is shown in figure 5.7. The reset switch is debounced using an I-S-R latch, the output of which is gated with the power-up reset circuit; these are 'wired-ored' with the open-collector SYSRST* line so that any of these sources generates the system reset condition. The result is then sampled on the edge of Q, using another flip-flop whose clear input is controlled by the power-up reset signal, so that the processor is reset when the system is first switched on.

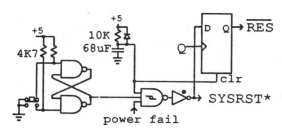

Figure 5.7 6809 reset circuit

These various circuits can then be put together to form the complete 68B09 processor board for STE. In addition, certain other I/O devices could be connected, such as UARTs and timers. As an exercise, the reader could draw the complete circuit diagram and then add in the necessary circuitry for a UART. This circuitry would need some form of circuit (probably using a decoder chip) to differentiate between the UART, any associated circuitry, other peripherals and the latch providing the extra memory addresses.

The Z80

The Z80 is another 8-bit microprocessor with a semi-synchronous bus and only 16 address lines, so that extra address lines must be provided to conform to the STE specification. In many respects, therefore, the design of the processor board for the Z80 is very similar to that for the 6809. There are major differences, however, and these differences and the methods to solve them will be described here, rather than a complete circuit.

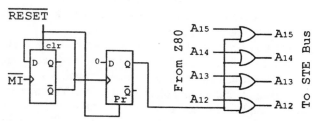

Figure 5.8 Z80 start address circuit

The first program run by the Z80 after it is reset begins at address 0, thus any EPROM should be put at the bottom of the memory map rather than the top (as was done in the 6809). This can be a problem if, say, the CP/M operating system is to be implemented as this requires RAM at the bottom of memory, but there are various methods for circumventing this problem: for example, consider the circuit shown in figure 5.8 which forces the upper 4 address lines to be all '1' until after two instructions have been obeyed. $\overline{MI}$ is a signal from the Z80 which is asserted when an instruction is being fetched. Thus, the first flip-flop is cleared when the Z80 is reset, so its $\overline{Q}$ is about '1'. After $\overline{MI}$ is released a second time, this $\overline{Q}$ signal goes high and this clears the second flip-flop, thus subsequently the upper address lines are passed through the OR gates directly.

The Z80 distinguishes between memory and I/O whereas the peripherals used with the 6809 are memory mapped. However, only 8 address lines are output for peripheral accesses: the required extra lines must be provided in a similar manner to that used for generating the extra lines for accessing memory.

The Z80 does have vectored interrupt facilities; thus vector fetch cycles can be generated, although extra circuitry is required to handle the eight potential interrupt sources and to cope with circuits which generate interrupts but do not respond to vector fetch cycles.

The reset on the Z80 must be asserted for at least three clock cycles.

The Z80 has a bus request line and a bus acknowledge line, so no extra decode is required for determining when the Z80 has responded to the request for the bus: thus the circuit shown in figure 5.2 can be used directly.

Given these points, a suitable system diagram for the Z80 board can be derived similar to that given in figure 5.3 for the 6809. Then it is necessary to design circuitry to convert the signals from the Z80 into those required for STE. As the system diagram is sufficiently similar to that for the 6809, in this section the signal conversion circuitry only will be described. This circuitry is worth considering as the signals from the Z80 are very different from those of the 6809, and so a different strategy is employed for generating the STE signals.

In figure 5.9 the bus timings for the Z80 are shown (an 8 MHz Z80H is assumed). Six types of bus cycle are shown: memory read (instruction fetch, with the extra refresh cycle, and normal), memory write, peripheral input, peripheral output and interrupt acknowledge. The bus timings for the Z80 are more complicated than those for the 6809. They are somewhat confusing, with oddities like the 'late' write strobe ($\overline{\text{WR}}$) during memory write, though not for peripheral write, and the extra clock period for peripheral accesses and the extra two for interrupt acknowledge. Although these signals are not as elegant as those for the 6809, suprisingly, it is more straightforward to generate the STE signals from the Z80 signals. Essentially, this is because all signals are stable on the rising edge of the processor clock signal, and this edge can be used for sampling the various signals.

For example, if on the rising edge of clock, $\overline{\text{MREQ}}$ is low and $\overline{\text{RFSH}}$ is high (a non-refresh memory cycle), the data transfer cycle can start, in which case $\overline{\text{WAIT}}$ on the Z80 should be asserted immediately and then the STE signals should be generated (although it is necessary to wait for $\overline{\text{WR}}$ to be asserted if it is a write cycle). The refresh cycle occurs after an instruction has been fetched, while the Z80 is decoding the instruction and so deciding what to do next. However, as there is no line on the STE bus for refresh, this cycle is wasted completely although it could be used for refreshing any dynamic-RAM on the Z80 board itself.

Adopting this approach, a simplified diagram can be drawn showing when $\overline{\text{WAIT}}$ should be asserted and when the cycle should start: see figure 5.10. The address, data and command lines can be asserted as soon as the cycle starts, but the address and, particularly, the data strobes (**ADRSTB*** and **DATSTB***) must be delayed to account for the required 35 ns set-up time: this delay can be achieved by passing the 'strobe' signal through a flip-flop whose clock is the 16 MHz system clock signal, as shown in figure 5.11, although it is necessary to verify that the required delay is achieved (by checking the slew between the STE clock and the 8 MHz processor clock, and the propagation delay in the circuit generating the command lines, etc).

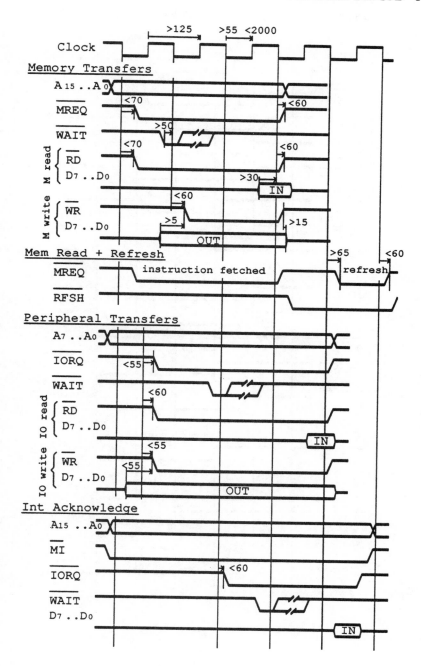

Figure 5.9 Bus timings for the Z80

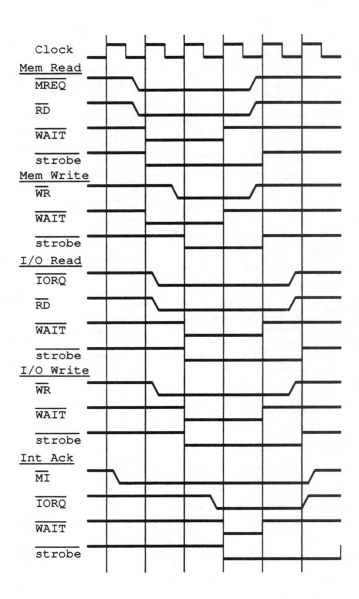

Figure 5.10 Wait and strobe timings for Z80

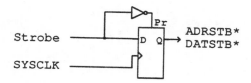

Figure 5.11 Strobe delay circuit

The following expressions describe the logic required to generate the STE signals:

$$WAIT = (\overline{MREQ} \ RFSH + \overline{IORQ} \ ) \ DATACK* \ TFRERR*$$

$$CM_2 = \overline{MREQ} + \overline{IORQ} \ MI$$

$$CM_1 = \overline{MREQ} + \overline{IORQ} \ \overline{MI}$$

$$CM_0 = \overline{RD} + \overline{MI}$$

$$strobe = \overline{MREQ} \ (\ \overline{RD} + \overline{WR} \ ) + \overline{IORQ} \ (\ \overline{RD} + \overline{WR} + \overline{MI} \ )$$

The outputs from circuits implementing these expresssions should be connected as D-inputs to a latch whose clock is the processor clock edge. The only potential problem with this is to ensure that $\overline{WAIT}$ is asserted sufficiently before the next falling edge of the clock as that is when the signal is sampled by the Z80. Thus the circuit is probably best implemented using a fast registered PLA. Note that the above expressions do not take account of any on-board memory or peripherals: address lines would have to be considered to decode access to such devices, as was done for the 6809.

As regards interrupts, the Z80 can generate a vector fetch cycle in response to an attention request, although extra circuitry is required to handle the 8 request lines (the Z80 has one vectored-interrupt line) and to generate the correct 3-bit address. This circuitry must take the 8 lines and assert the **INT** line on the Z80 if any line is '0', and then generate the appropriate 3-bit address. This seems to require a relatively complicated logic circuit, but it can be achieved very easily using standard chips. Most of the work is done by a *priority encoder* chip: this has 8 data inputs, $I_0..I_7$, 3 address outputs $A_2..A_0$ and a control output, C, whose actions can best be described by the following table:

I_7	I_6	I_5	I_4	I_3	I_2	I_1	I_0	A_2	A_1	A_0	C
x	x	x	x	x	x	x	0	0	0	0	0
x	x	x	x	x	x	0	1	0	0	1	0
x	x	x	x	x	0	1	1	0	1	0	0
x	x	x	x	0	1	1	1	0	1	1	0
x	x	x	0	1	1	1	1	1	0	0	0
x	x	0	1	1	1	1	1	1	0	1	0
x	0	1	1	1	1	1	1	1	1	0	0
0	1	1	1	1	1	1	1	1	1	1	0
1	1	1	1	1	1	1	1	1	1	1	1

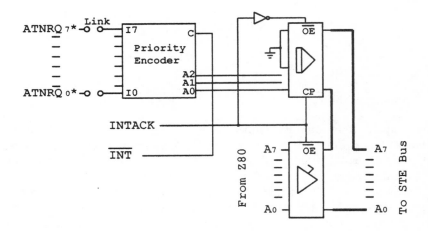

Figure 5.12 Vector address generation

Such a chip is exactly what is required: the attention request lines can be connected directly to the I lines, the A lines form the required 3-bit address, and the C output can be fed directly into the interrupt line on the processor. The only extra requirement is to prevent the address lines changing during an interrupt acknowledge cycle (which would happen if an attention request line with a higher priority than that being serviced was asserted during the cycle). The simple solution to this is to latch the A outputs at the start of the vector fetch cycle. The circuit to handle interrupts in this way is shown in figure 5.12. Links are used so that only those attention request lines which should generate interrupts actually cause an interrupt. The interrupt acknowledge line is generated in the same PLA as the command lines, etc., the required boolean expression being:

```
INTACK  =  IORQ MI
```

This signal latches the address from the encoder and enables the outputs of the latch, and its inverse disables the buffer which normally connects the lower address lines from the processor to the bus. If the slave cannot respond to vector fetch cycles, these A lines could be returned as the vector. Note that the vector returned must be an even number.

The Z80 also has a non-maskable interrupt (NMI) which could, in principle, be connected to the highest priority request line. The only problem with this is that there is no vector fetch cycle associated with an NMI, although a vector could be read using a 'normal' peripheral read cycle generated by an instruction in the NMI service routine.

The 64180   The 64180 is a Z80 microprocessor with some extra facilities. These extra facilities include more address lines, a memory management unit, a two channel DMA controller, two UARTs and a two channel 16-bit timer. The 64180 can also enter a mode termed *SLEEP* where it consumes little power. Although software compatible with the Z80 (that is, any program written for the Z80 will run on the 64180), the 64180 also has some extra instructions including multiply.

The basic interface to STE is therefore similar to the Z80 interface and so will not be described here. As regards use of DMA controllers, see section 5.4. A commercial 64180 board for STE is available.

The 68000

The 68000 is a 16-bit microprocessor with effectively 24 address lines and an asynchronous bus. Thus it appears that the 68000 connects to the STE bus almost directly (not quite: nothing in life is that simple!). The processor can also access devices using the semi-synchronous protocol (this ability was provided to allow the direct interface of some 8-bit peripheral chips used with the earlier 8-bit microprocessor, the 6800), but this mode can be ignored and all peripherals mapped into the asynchronous memory. Given the (relatively) large number of address lines, the STE addresses can be configured as just part of the 68000 address map, and the rest of the address range used for on-board facilities.

The bus timings for the 68000 are shown in figure 5.13. At first sight most of the signals can be connected directly to the STE bus: $\overline{\text{AS}}$ (address strobe) is ADRSTB*, R/$\overline{\text{W}}$ (read/write) is CM_0, $\overline{\text{DTACK}}$ (data transfer acknowledge) is DATACK*, $\overline{\text{BERR}}$ (bus error) is TFRERR*, either $\overline{\text{UDS}}$ or $\overline{\text{LDS}}$ (upper or lower data strobe) is DATSTB*, etc. However, there are problems which make the design tricky.

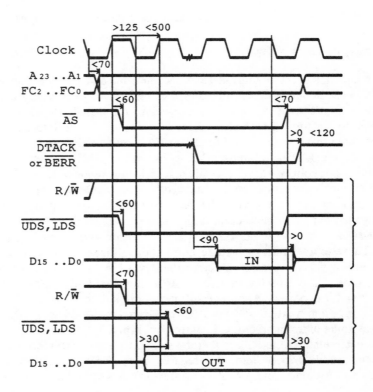

Figure 5.13 Bus timings for 68000

The 68000 does not have address line A_0, instead it has two strobes, $\overline{UDS}$ and $\overline{LDS}$, which indicate, respectively, whether the data being accessed are a byte from an odd address, a byte from an even address or a word (two bytes from both addresses). This strategy is very reasonable for designing 68000-based systems: the memory is divided into two 8-bit wide banks, one is connected to data lines $D_{15}..D_8$ and the other to lines $D_7..D_0$. Thus if $\overline{UDS}$ is asserted, the first bank is enabled and if $\overline{LDS}$ is asserted the second bank is enabled; thus both banks are enabled if both strobes are asserted. However, this nice elegant scheme really upsets the interface to STE because STE is an 8-bit bus. Contiguous addresses from the 68000 must be contiguous addresses on STE (the 68000 must be able to read from successive addresses), hence address line A_0 must be generated, and this can be done quite easily by processing the two strobes. However, this address line can be determined only after the data strobes are generated, and hence *after* the address strobe, $\overline{AS}$, is asserted.

Thus **ADRSTB*** cannot be generated directly from $\overline{\text{AS}}$, instead it must appear at least 35 ns *after* A_0 is produced. This problem can be surmounted relatively easily. However, an even worse problem exists.

All 68000 instructions are at least two bytes long and the processor reads them as words, that is, both data strobes will be asserted. Thus, if the program being obeyed is stored on another board in the STE system, the processor *must* be able to read 16 bits at a time: this is awkward in that 8-bits only can be transferred along the bus at once. Thus if the 68000 wants to read 16 bits of data, two separate cycles must be generated: the first should read the byte from the low address and this should be stored in a latch (when the acknowledge signal is returned) whose outputs are connected to the lower half of the processor data bus; then the other byte should be read and passed to the upper half of the processor data bus, and only then should the acknowledge input on the 68000 be asserted. A similar (complicated) procedure is required for writing words. All this is possible, but the circuitry is involved. A better solution is to use the 68008.

The 68008

The 68008 is a 68000 with an 8-bit data bus. Instead of having two data strobes, the 68008 has the required extra address line, A_0, and one data strobe, $\overline{\text{DS}}$. Thus no complicated cicruitry is required for generating the STE signals for memory and peripheral transfers. The only disadvantage of using the 68008 is that on-board memory must also be only 8 bits wide and so the system will be correspondingly slower than one using the 68000. The basic interface is easy, but interrupts must also be considered and also bus requests as well as the memory mapping of the on-board facilities.

The 68000 and 68008 have vectored interrupt facilities, so they can generate vector fetch cycles. The following text describes how interrupts work on these chips. There are three interrupt inputs, IPL_2, IPL_1 and IPL_0, the logic signals on which can be considered as a three-bit number in the range 0..7: 0 means no request, 1 is a level 1 request, 2 a level 2 request, etc. If the level on these lines exceeds the current *masking level* (as set in the processor status register), the processor will be interrupted at the end of the current instruction and an interrupt acknowledge cycle initiated; otherwise the interrupt will be ignored. Then (ignoring 6800 semi-synchronous compatibility mode) the processor expects the interrupting device to return a vector which is used to calculate the address of the service routine. While the interrupt is being serviced, the masking level is set to the level of the interrupt request, thus the service routine can be interrupted only by a higher priority interrupt (note level 7 is non-maskable interrupt: if the level on the **IPL** lines is number 7, the interrupt is always serviced).

An interrupt acknowledge cycle is like a normal transfer cycle as regards the address lines, data lines, $R/\overline{W}$, $\overline{AS}$ and $\overline{DS}$, the only difference is in the state of the function code lines from the processor, FC_0, FC_1 and FC_2. The state of these lines determines the type of cycle, as shown in the following table:

FC_2	FC_1	FC_0	
0	0	0	undefined/reserved
0	0	1	User Data
0	1	0	User Program
0	1	1	undefined/reserved
1	0	0	undefined/reserved
1	0	1	Supervisor Data
1	1	0	Supervisor Program
1	1	1	Interrupt Acknowledge

The processor can distinguish between supervisor mode (when the operating system is running) and user mode (when the user program is in operation), and it is useful to be able to assign different areas of memory depending on the current mode: the function code lines can thus be used to generate an extra address line (as well as indicating an interrupt acknowledge cycle). Note that their timings are the same as for the address lines.

The 68000 has a special instruction for handling shared resources: **TAS** or test-and-set. In this instruction a memory location is read, so its contents can be tested, and then data are written to that location. The signals generated on the bus when this instruction is obeyed form a read-modify-write cycle in exactly the form required for STE: a read cycle followed by a write cycle with the address (and function codes) and address strobe ($\overline{AS}$) stable throughout. This cycle cannot be interrupted by an interrupt request or a bus request. Thus read-modify-write cycles can be implemented without any extra thought or circuitry.

With this information it is now possible to design the logic required to generate the command signals on STE. In addition, it will be assumed that the memory addresses on STE will be those for which the upper four address lines are all '1', and peripheral accesses occur when the top three lines are '1' and A_{20} is a '0'. The following boolean expressions describe the required logical functions:

$$\text{ADRSTB*} = (\ \overline{A_{23} \ A_{22} \ A_{21} \ + \ FC_2 \ FC_1 \ FC_0 } \ ) \ \overline{\overline{AS}}$$

$$CM_2 = \overline{\overline{FC_2 \ FC_1 \ FC_0}}$$

$$CM_1 = A_{20} \ + \ FC_2 \ FC_1 \ FC_0$$

$$CM_0 = R/\overline{W}$$

$$\text{DATSTB*} = \overline{DS} \ + \ \text{ADRSTB*}$$

The **IPL** signals could be coded directly from the attention request lines using a priority encoder (as long as at maximum only 7 of these lines are configured as interrupts). The disadvantage of this is that it does not allow any on-board devices to generate interrupts. Alternatively, the C output of the priority encoder could be used to control one of the **IPL** lines. There is still the problem (as there was for the Z80) of handling boards which do not respond to the vector fetch cycle, but returning a suitable vector which includes which attention request line was asserted (as was suggested for the Z80) can be done.

One other requirement is that the transfer error and bus acknowledge signals on the processor should be stable at least 20 ns before the falling edge of the processor clock signal (which is when they are sampled). This can be achieved easily by connecting the STE signals **DATACK*** and **TFRERR*** to the D-inputs of two positive, edge-triggered flip-flops with the processor clock signal connected to the clock inputs of the flip-flops, and their outputs are connected directly to $\overline{\text{DTACK}}$ and $\overline{\text{BERR}}$ on the processor.

The 68008 (or 68000) can be made to do one of two things when an erroneous bus cycle occurs: it can either obey an 'exception trap', which is like an interrupt service routine, or it can be made to retry the cycle. This latter 'rerun' mode, which is invoked by asserting both the $\overline{\text{BERR}}$ and $\overline{\text{HALT}}$ lines on the processor, can be used when the bus error is caused by an error in the data being transferred (perhaps a parity error), rather than because a non-existent slave is accessed and so no acknowledgement has been received. As there is no extra line on the bus to provide a parity bit on the data bus, the rerun mode cannot be utilised. Thus the exception trap should be used.

As regards bus requests, the requirements of the 68000/68008 are slightly different from the other processors. When a device wishes to take control of the bus from the processor, it must assert the bus request line, **BR**. In response to this, the processor asserts its bus grant line, $\overline{\text{BG}}$, which indicates that the processor will be willing to allow the requesting device to have control of the bus at the end of the current cycle. The requesting device should then release the $\overline{\text{BR}}$ line and, when the current cycle ends ($\overline{\text{AS}}$ is '1' and $\overline{\text{DTACK}}$ is '1'), it should assert the bus grant acknowledge line, $\overline{\text{BGACK}}$, to tell the processor that it has actually taken control of the bus. If the $\overline{\text{BR}}$ is not released before $\overline{\text{BGACK}}$ is asserted, the processor assumes that a second bus request has occurred.

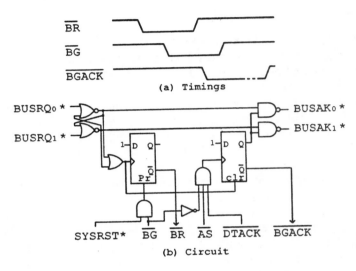

Figure 5.14 Bus arbitration on 68000/68008

A circuit to achieve this is shown in figure 5.14: it is an extension of figure 5.2. When either **BUSAK*** line is asserted the $\overline{\text{Q}}$ output of the first flip-flop goes low, and this generates $\overline{\text{BR}}$. When the processor responds by asserting $\overline{\text{BG}}$, the request is cleared and then when both $\overline{\text{AS}}$ and $\overline{\text{DTACK}}$ are high, the $\overline{\text{Q}}$ output of second flip-flop is low, and this generates $\overline{\text{BGACK}}$ and also enables the appropriate **BUSAK*** line on the STE bus. Note the use of the reset signal to remove the bus request signals. Also, if the other **BUSRQ*** signal is active (low) when the first is released, the $\overline{\text{BGACK}}$ will remain active, and the second **BUSAK*** line will be asserted and control of the bus passed directly to the second requesting device. Only when neither **BUSRQ*** line is active will $\overline{\text{BGACK}}$ be released.

As regards reset: the $\overline{\text{RESET}}$ signal is bidirectional (the processor or an external device can assert the line). To reset the processor, external signals should assert both the $\overline{\text{RESET}}$ and $\overline{\text{HALT}}$ lines. After the system is first switched on, the processor should be reset for at least 100 ms, so the STE requirement of 200 ms is compatible with the requirements of the 68000 or 68008. After $\overline{\text{RESET}}$ is released, the processor finds the initial value for the stack pointer and program counter from the first 8 locations in memory. These locations are the start of the *exception* page where the addresses of interrupt service routines, divide-by-zero handler, etc., are also kept. These are best kept in RAM so they can be changed, but the first 8 locations must be in ROM. This can be handled quite neatly as the first locations are considered to be part of supervisor program memory (see the definitions of the function codes) whereas the rest are part of supervisor data memory.

The 68020

The 68020 is a 32-bit processor in the same family as the 68000. Thus it might be expected that the same problems exist (or worse) in trying to put the 68020 on to STE as for the 68000 with regard to the STE bus being only 8-bits wide. Wrong! The 68020 can be connected easily.

The bus timings for the 68020 are much the same as for the 68008 as regards addresses ($A_{31}..A_0$), data, the address and data strobes, the $R/\overline{W}$ signal, the function codes and acknowledge and bus error signals. In addition, there are two signals, SIZ_1 and SIZ_0, which appear at the same time as the address lines and function codes, and these specify whether the processor wishes to transfer 8, 16, 24 or 32 bits of data during the cycle. Also, there are two acknowledge lines, $\overline{DSACK_1}$ and $\overline{DSACK_0}$, and these can be used to allow the easy interface to the STE bus: they not only tell the processor that the data transfer has occurred, they also specify the width of the data bus when it reaches the adddressed slave. See the table below:

$\overline{DSACK_1}$	$\overline{DSACK_0}$	Meaning
0	0	Cycle complete, bus size is 32 bits
0	1	Cycle complete, bus size is 16 bits
1	0	Cycle complete, bus size is 8 bits
1	1	Cycle not finished

Thus if the processor requests 32 bits of data, but the interface can give 8-bits only, $\overline{DSACK_0}$ only will be asserted when the cycle is complete, and thus the processor will deduce that the remaining data must be fetched in separate cycles; these cycles will then be instigated. Thus the STE DTACK* line can be connected directly to $\overline{DSACK_0}$ and $\overline{DSACK_1}$ held high.

Another difference between the 68020 and the 68008 is with regard to interrupt acknowledge. If the three function code outputs are all '1', this indicates *CPU space* which can mean interrupt acknowledge, but it can also show, for example, that the processor is communicating with a *coprocessor*.

A coprocessor is a support chip in the same family as the 68020 like the 68881 arithmetic processor which performs floating-point calculations. When the processor wishes to communicate with a coprocessor, or acknowledge an interrupt, a 'CPU space' transfer occurs; address lines $A_{19}..A_{16}$ determine the type of CPU space transfer. For example, if all these address lines are '1', then an interrupt acknowledge cycle is occurring. If only A_{17} is a '1', then a coprocessor communication cycle is in operation: which (of 8) coprocessors is determined by the number on address lines $A_{15}..A_{13}$.

As the 68020 can transfer 32 bits of data at one time it is obviously advantageous if the on-board memory is 32 bits wide. How this is achieved needs to be explained. Even with such memory the processor must also be able to access 8 bits only, or 16 or even 24. This is where the two size lines, SIZ_1 and SIZ_0, come in; their function is best described by the following:

SIZ_1	SIZ_0	Meaning
0	0	32 bits of data to be transferred
0	1	8 bits of data to be transferred
1	0	16 bits of data to be transferred
1	1	24 bits of data to be transferred

Note that these two lines specify the amount of data which the processor would like to be transferred, the **DSACK** lines are used to tell it the actual width of the data bus during that transfer, and if the width is less than the amount being transferred, the processor knows that further cycles are required in order to complete the transfer which it then instigates.

This is not the complete story: addresses must also be considered. The 68020 outputs 32 address lines and these specify the unique address of each byte of data. When the memory is 32 bits wide, it is divided into four 8-bit banks, so A_1 and A_0 identify one of those four banks, just as in 16-bit wide memory A_0 identifies one of the two banks of memory. The remaining address lines are common to all the banks. When the 68020 accesses memory, the two **SIZ** lines specify the number of bytes to be transferred, and the address lines specify the address of the first byte to be read: the table below describes, for 32-bit wide memory, which banks are accessed depending on SIZ_1, SIZ_0, A_1 and A_0: a '1' in a bank column specifies that bank is being accessed. Note that bank 3 is connected to the highest data byte $(D_{31}..D_{24})$, bank 2 to $D_{23}..D_{16}$, etc.

SIZ$_1$	SIZ$_0$	A$_1$	A$_0$	bank3	bank2	bank1	bank0
0	0	0	0	1	1	1	1
0	0	0	1	0	1	1	1
0	0	1	0	0	0	1	1
0	0	1	1	0	0	0	1
0	1	0	0	1	0	0	0
0	1	0	1	0	1	0	0
0	1	1	0	0	0	1	0
0	1	1	1	0	0	0	1
1	0	0	0	1	1	0	0
1	0	0	1	0	1	1	0
1	0	1	0	0	0	1	1
1	0	1	1	0	0	0	1
1	1	0	0	1	1	1	0
1	1	0	1	0	1	1	1
1	1	1	0	0	0	1	1
1	1	1	1	0	0	0	1

For STE, where the data bus is 8 bits wide, all the addresses are used to specify the one element in the memory to be accessed. The data bus should be connected to the highest data byte ($D_{31}..D_{24}$). Incidentally, when memory is only 16 bits wide, the upper 16 data lines are used, and A_0 indicates which bank of memory is accessed.

Note that the next chips in the 68000 family, the 68030 and the 68040, are more advanced versions of the 68020 with extra inbuilt facilities. Their interface to STE, however, is very similar to that for the 68020 and so will not be described here.

The 8088

The 8088 is the 8-bit bus version of the 16-bit processor the 8086, and it is better to describe the interface of the 8088 to STE, rather than the 8086, for reasons similar to those given in the description of the 68000. The 8088 and 8086 evolved from the 8-bit 8080 processor and many features were copied from the earlier 8-bit processor and so are not very applicable to 16-bit or, as regards the more modern members of the 8086 family (the 80286 and 80386), to 32-bit processors.

As regards interfacing to these chips, there are various factors to be considered. First the function of certain pins can change depending on whether *minimum* or *maximum* mode is used. The former mode is for relatively simple systems, the latter is used in systems where there can be many micro-processors and coprocessors. A system must be configured in one of the two modes. Also, some signals are multiplexed, for example, during one part of a transfer cycle the **AD** lines contain addresses, for the rest of the time they are data lines. Various other signals are designed so that certain support chips (bus controllers, etc.) should be used in the system, rather than having the proper set of signals on the chip itself. For example, it is important that the set-up and hold times for the **READY** (or wait) line are adhered to (otherwise unpredictable results may occur), and this is best achieved by using the clock generator chip which synchronises a ready request. Synchronisation is also required for the bus request signal.

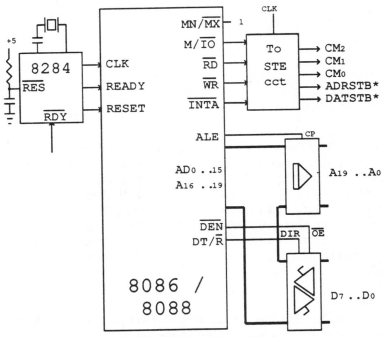

Figure 5.15 8086/8088 based system

In minimum mode a suitable system diagram for an 8088 configuration on STE is shown in figure 5.15. The mode select line, **MN/$\overline{\text{MX}}$**, is set to '1'. The 8284 clock generator chip provides the clock, reset and synchronised ready signals. The latches take the multiplexed address/data lines and store the address when it appears (on the falling edge of **ALE**). The bidirectional data buffer must be enabled only when the processor expects data on the multiplexed lines: **$\overline{\text{DEN}}$** indicates when this can occur, and **DT/$\overline{\text{R}}$** specifies the direction of data transfer through the buffer. Finally, there is the circuitry required for conversion from 8088 signals to STE signals.

As regards the timings of signals, they are similar to those of the Z80 (which is not suprising as both the Z80 and 8086/8088 evolved from the 8080). The control signals to be used are $\overline{RD}$, $\overline{WR}$ and $\overline{INTA}$ which indicate respectively that a read, write or interrupt cycle is occurring; memory and I/O are distinguished by the $M/\overline{IO}$ line. The timings of these signals (in relation to the data and the clock) are sufficiently similar to that for $\overline{RD}$ on the Z80 for the same design strategy to be used. Hence the design of circuits to process such signals will not be considered here. Before designing a circuit the reader should consult the data sheets carefully (as always), but the above comments should help.

Interface to the PC IO channel

A related interface is one which allows a standard IBM PC (or clone) to be a master on an STE bus. The author has found an interface similar to the following quite useful. An alternative method of achieving a similar result is to buy the 'PC compatible STE system'. One advantage of the interface described here is that it provides an extension bus to a standard unit, and these days many people already have such a PC.

The circuit described below is designed to act in two capacities: either as the default bus master or as sub-master. In the first mode, the interface provides an expansion box outside the PC allowing various devices to be connected to the system without having to take the PC apart to install the new interface. This is also useful in that a separate (clean) power supply can be provided for these interfaces. The second mode provides a fast communication link between the PC and the master in the STE bus. When data are to be transferred to the bus, the PC requests control of the bus and then writes suitable data into memory in the STE system.

The first stage in the design is to consider how to synthesise the STE signals from those provided in the PC. Interfacing to the PC consists of designing circuits to plug into the PC expansion bus (or I/O channel). To do this, in particular when one is trying to conform to the STE specification, it is necessary to know precise timings of signals on the channel. These are hard to find. In the technical reference manuals one can find the circuit diagram for the system which shows the various chips which are connected between the processor and the channel. In data books one can find the timings of these chips. Thus to deduce the timings of the channel, one has to start with signals at the processor and then calculate the propagation delays through the chips until the signals reach the channel. It would be nice if the required information were available in the manual. For most design purposes, there are not too many problems because data are stored at the end of a transfer cycle and the timings at the end of the cycle are straightforward. But as regards interfacing to STE, it is important to know when, at the start of the cycle, the data to be written are actually on the bus in relation to the control signals (because of the required set-up time before asserting **DATSTB***, etc). Thus the circuit below may not be the most efficient possible because signals are delayed until it can be guaranteed that they meet the STE specification.

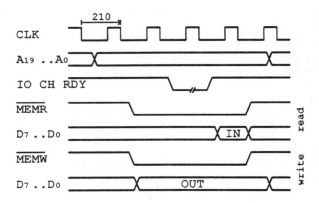

Figure 5.16 Timings on PC I/O channel

Simplified timings for memory cycles on the I/O channel are shown in figure 5.16 and the PC to STE interface is shown in figure 5.17 (this is not complete as the system controller circuitry is not included). The **CLK** signal, which has a period of 210 ns and a 2:1 mark space ratio, can be used as the basis of timings. The two main strobe signals are $\overline{\text{MEMR}}$, $\overline{\text{MEMW}}$, which indicate respectively that a memory read or a memory write is in operation. Peripheral cycles are very similar: different strobes are used, $\overline{\text{IOR}}$ and $\overline{\text{IOW}}$, and there is an automatic wait state (as with the Z80). In read cycles the data are expected near the end of the cycle; in write cycles the data appear on the bus a short time after the appropriate strobe. Thus **DATSTB*** must be delayed until 35 ns after the data appear: a suitable time to generate **DATSTB*** is on the *falling* edge of the clock signal. The wait signal is called **I/O CH RDY**: to synthesise an asynchronous bus, this signal should be asserted as soon as one of the strobes is active and the address is valid, and then released when the slave device has issued an acknowledgement. Note that valid addresses occur only when the **AEN** signal is low (if it is high, a DMA cycle is in operation).

As regards addresses: a 20-bit address is output on the channel, but some of those addresses have already been used in the system. Depending on the graphics cards, etc., already installed in the PC, there is normally a 64K page of memory which is not used at (hex) address Dxxxx or Axxxx. Thus the interface should be able to generate a 16-bit memory address, the extra address lines required on STE must (again) come from a latch.

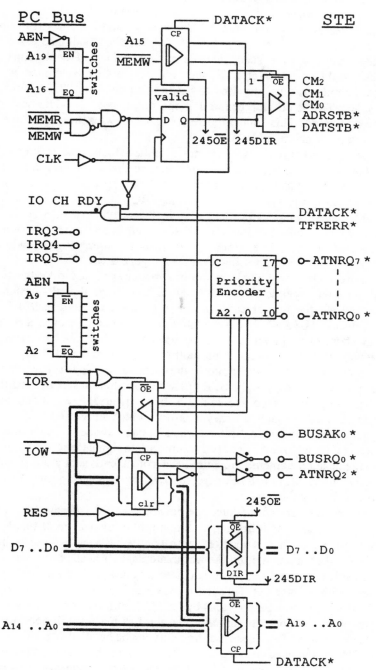

Figure 5.17 PC to STE interface

As regards peripherals, the PC decodes 10 address lines (the upper lines are ignored) and A_9 must be '1' for valid channel addresses. Most of these addresses are used; there is no large block of contiguous addresses that could be used for STE, thus the best policy is to memory map the peripherals: A_{15} can be used to distinguish between STE memory and I/O cycles. The latch (for generating the extra, now 5, addresses) must also be addressed. This (and a buffer, which allows some input lines) is best put at a peripheral address.

As regards interrupts, there are 6 request lines. The technical reference manual specifies uses for each of them, so that it appears that none can be used by the interface. However, each line is used only if the appropriate device is in the system; for example, **IRQ5**, is used in the interface for a hard disk: if there is no hard disk in the machine, **IRQ5** can be used for interrupts. Thus the interface has an adjustable link to connect to an available request line. Note that there is no interrupt acknowledge signal on the bus, so no vector fetch cycles are generated.

Also to be considered are the bus request and acknowledge lines. Their generation depends on whether the circuit is the default master or a sub-master. In the former case, the circuit should respond to a **BUSRQ*** and produce a **BUSAK***, but in the latter case, it should generate a **BUSRQ*** and take control of the bus when it receives a **BUSAK***. In each case the signal generated by the circuit will be another output from the latch, and the received signal will be one of the inputs to the extra buffer. Thus software will be used to prevent accesses to the STE bus when another master is in control, rather than stopping the processor in the PC by hardware. Note that one output of the latch is used to enable the tristate buffers which allow the PC to drive the STE bus. These outputs are disabled when another device is the bus master. Links are again used to connect only the appropriate signals to the bus. It is important that the latch contents are initialised consistently: they are cleared by the active high reset line, **RES**. After reset, the tristate buffers are disabled: the PC is not driving the bus.

As regards the communication between the PC 'sub-master' and the STE default master, the following system might be envisaged. If the PC wishes to send data to the bus, it must get control of the bus so as to write to the memory. Then, when it has written the whole message, it needs to let the STE master control the bus and also tell it that there is a message in the memory: this is best done with an interrupt. Thus it is a good idea if the interface circuit also allows for the generation of interrupts by the PC. Similarly, messages will need to be passed in the opposite direction, so the bus master will need to attract the attention of the PC. These requirements can be handled either using the buffer and latch signals exclusively where the testing of message transmission can be done entirely in software, or by using an interrupt request line as well. In the circuit given in figure 5.17, the attention request lines are connected to a priority encoder whose control output initiates an interrupt request, and whose A outputs, which indicate the particular ATNRQ* line, are connected to the buffer. Links are used to connect the appropriate attention request signals to the encoder.

At the top of figure 5.17, the $\overline{\text{valid}}$ signal is asserted when the address is correct, $\overline{\text{AEN}}$ is asserted, and either $\overline{\text{MEMR}}$ or $\overline{\text{MEMW}}$ is active. This indicates that an STE cycle should begin. The top half of the 64K page so addressed is allocated to memory, so 5 extra address lines are needed, the other half is for peripherals: thus CM_1 is generated from A_{15}. No vector fetch cycles can occur, so CM_2 is always '1'. CM_0 is effectively generated from $\overline{\text{MEMW}}$. However, a little extra processing is required.

As mentioned earlier, ADRSTB* and DATSTB* are generated by delaying the $\overline{\text{valid}}$ signal until the next clock edge. Hence there will be sufficient set-up time for address, command and data lines before the strobes are asserted. However, as the strobes are also released later, care is required to ensure that addresses, etc., do not change until after the strobes are released. Hence the control signals on the data buffer, the command lines and the address lines must be maintained until after the strobes are released. The easiest method of doing this is the technique described for slave interfaces in chapter 3, that is, to use a transparent latch controlled by DATACK*: when DATACK* is not asserted, the inputs to the latch are passed to the outputs, but the outputs do not change when DATACK* is asserted. As the strobes are released *after* DATACK* is asserted, the required signals will be latched when the strobes are released, and hence the hold time requirements will be met. The outputs of these latches are enabled only when the PC is the STE bus master. The wait signal, I/O CH RDY, is asserted as soon as $\overline{\text{valid}}$ is active, and turned off when the cycle ends (DATACK* or TFRERR* asserted).

The peripheral latch is written to or the buffer enabled when there is a valid peripheral address and $\overline{\text{IOW}}$ or $\overline{\text{IOR}}$ is asserted. The latch is cleared when the system is reset (using RES). Five outputs from the latch provide (via a tristate buffer) the extra address lines, the others can be used to generate the $BUSRQ_0$* or $BUSAK_0$* signal (which ever is appropriate) or some attention request signals. The other bus request/ acknowledge signal is one input to the buffer, other inputs to which could be some attention request signals or, as shown in the figure, the A outputs from a priority encoder.

The Z8

The Z8 is a single-chip microcomputer, that is, it is a device which contains not only the central processing unit itself but also some memory and I/O. It is intended that minimal systems be designed around such processors. The justification for including a description of it in a book about non-minimal systems like STE is that a Z8 on STE could be used in the development of Z8 systems, and it allows a description of how to interface a processor with a synchronous bus to an asynchronous system like STE.

The Z8 comes in various forms, some with built-in ROM (including one version with a mini BASIC interpreter). The version being considered here is one with no such ROM, 124 bytes of general purpose RAM, and some I/O.

Most of the external connections of the Z8 form four 8-bit programmable ports. These can function in various ways depending on the application for the system. However, having chosen the ROM-less version of the Z8, it is necessary to have some external memory, so ports 0 and 1 must be configured to provide the address and data bus for the memory and some I/O. Two bits on port 3 can be used for serial communication as one on-board facility in the chip is a UART. The other ports can be used to provide some I/O lines. The Z8 STE board described here will contain 16K of EPROM, 16K of RAM, have some on-board I/O (including a latch for the extra STE memory addresses, etc., and serial I/O) and provide the necessary STE bus signals.

As regards the address and data buses: port 0 can provide the upper half of the 16-bit address bus and port 1 provides the lower half of the address bus and the data bus: these functions are multiplexed (the address strobe signal $\overline{AS}$ is low when port 1 contains the address bus, and this signal can be used to latch the lower half of the address, and when the data strobe signal $\overline{DS}$ is low, the port is the data bus). The slight problem with this is that the lines on port 0 are configured as inputs when the processor is reset, so it does not provide the upper address initially: external resistors must be used to pull these lines to a '1' when the Z8 is not driving them. Thus the upper half of the address of the first instruction must be (in hex) FF, so ROM should be placed at the top of memory. However, for handling interrupts, there must be memory in the bottom page as well.

A suitable memory map for the system being considered is shown below:

```
0000 to 3FFF : on-board RAM, including routines to handle interrupts
4000 to 5FFF : on-board I/O devices, including extra STE address lines
6000 to 7FFF : STE I/O devices
8000 to BFFF : STE memory
C000 to FFFF : on-board ROM
```

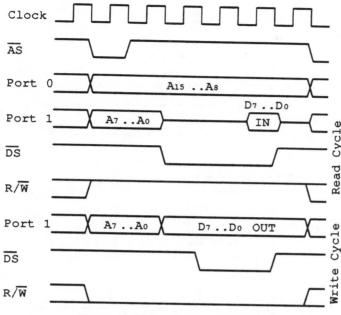

Figure 5.18 Bus timings for the Z8

The external bus timings for the Z8 are shown in figure 5.18. The addresses are output on to ports 0 and 1, the read/write signal is asserted as appropriate, and these signals are valid when $\overline{AS}$ is released. After this, port 1 becomes the data bus (and in a write cycle the data are output immediately), and then the data strobe ($\overline{DS}$) is asserted. After a fixed period $\overline{DS}$ is released. Note that the cycle can be extended (by software) for a further two clock periods, but this is of no use in the STE interface where greater variation of the cycle period is required, though it does allow the connection of relatively slow devices. Interfacing to the Z8 is very simple (assuming that the devices are not too slow) as addresses, data, etc., are set-up and then the data strobe is asserted. Thus a device should be enabled if the address is correct and $\overline{DS}$ is active, and R/$\overline{W}$ is used to determine direction of data transfer.

A block diagram for the board is shown in figure 5.19. Note that the system controller and arbiter are not included. The latch connected to port 1 is used to store the lower address lines. The decode circuit uses the upper three address lines and $\overline{DS}$ to generate the control signals for the on board memory and I/O and the enable for STE accesses. Two lines from port 3 provide the serial interface. But the main block, marked STE

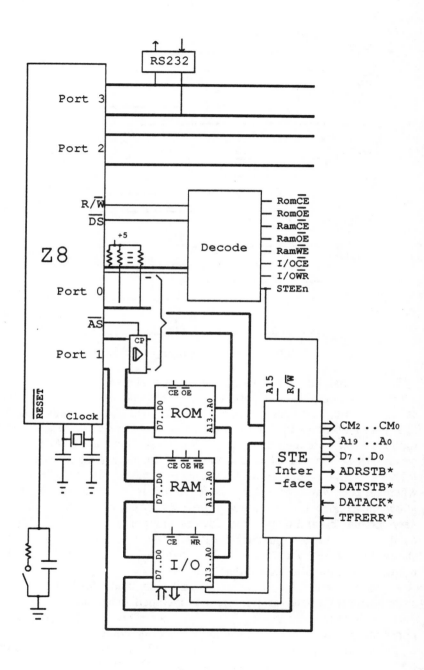

Figure 5.19 Block diagram of Z8 board

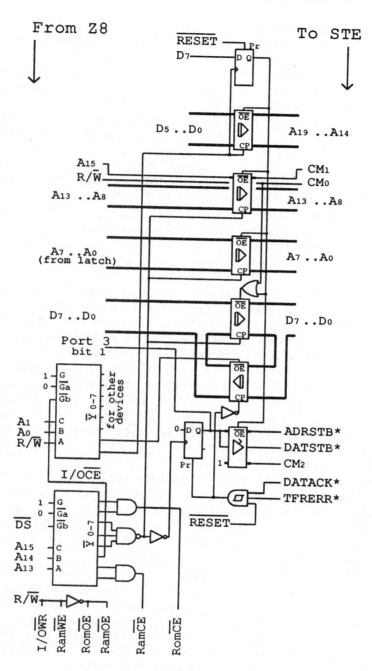

Figure 5.20 Z8 to STE conversion circuit

interface, is the interesting part as here the synchronous bus from the Z8 is converted to the asynchronous STE bus. The stategy adopted for this is as follows:

Whenever an STE access occurs, that is, whenever one of the addresses between 6000 and BFFF is read or written to by the Z8, an STE cycle is started, though it cannot be assumed that it will end before the Z8 cycle finishes. Thus addresses, command lines, data (if a write cycle) and the address and data strobes should be latched and output to the STE bus. The Z8 will then, under program control, and in separate cycles accessing on board I/O lines, keep testing until it sees that the cycle is complete. Then, if a read operation was instigated, the Z8 can read the returned data; otherwise no further action is required. Thus, during a write cycle, the data from the Z8 must be latched and output to the STE data bus, but for a read cycle, the data from the STE bus must be latched when the acknowledge signal is returned by the slave device. When **DATACK*** is asserted, **ADRSTB*** and **DATSTB*** should be released automatically. Thus, the Z8 can determine when the cycle is complete by reading the state of **DATSTB***.

A circuit to achieve the decode and STE interface blocks is shown in figure 5.20. At the top of this is shown a flip-flop whose output controls the output enables of the tristate devices: if these are disabled another board can drive the bus. Below this is a latch which contains the upper 6 address lines and these are loaded during an on-board access. In the two latches under this are stored the 14 significant address lines output by the Z8 during an access to the STE bus, as well as the **R/W̄** line and A_{15} as these provide the STE command lines CM_0 and CM_1 (for an STE I/O access, the address is between 6000 and 7FFF, so A_{15} is '0', but for a memory access, A_{15} is '1', thus the address line determines CM_1). These signals should be stored when the cycle begins, that is, on the falling edge of **D̄S̄** during an STE cycle.

The two latches beneath these are used for storing data: in a write cycle, the data from the Z8 are stored in the top latch at the start of the cycle and its outputs are enabled, but in a read cycle, the data from the bus are stored in the lower latch when the slave issues the acknowledge or the cycle is terminated by **TFRERR*** and its outputs are enabled only when the Z8 reads the latch during an on-board I/O cycle.

Under these is the circuit which generates **ADRSTB*** and **DATSTB***. To maintain the set-up times required for STE, these signals are output on the rising edge of **D̄S̄**, whereas the address and command lines were output on the earlier falling edge of **D̄S̄**. Then the output of the flip-flop is driven low, and passed through the tristate buffer to the STE bus. When the slave acknowledges (with **DATACK***) or **TFRERR*** is asserted, this output is released and the cycle is complete. This signal is connected to an input bit on port 3 so it can be tested, thus the Z8 can determine by software if the cycle is complete. Note that no vector fetch cycles are generated, so CM_2 is always '1'.

The 1 of 8 decoder at the bottom of the figure (with the extra gates) generates the signals for enabling memory, I/O and STE interfaces. Each output of the decoder is active when the appropriate 8K block of memory is accessed and $\overline{DS}$ is active; for example, $\overline{Y}_5$ is '0' if the address is between A000 and BFFF, that is, it is an STE memory access: an STE access occurs if $\overline{Y}_3$, $\overline{Y}_4$ or $\overline{Y}_5$ is asserted. Then, the addresses and data from the Z8 are stored in the appropriate latches.

The other decoder chip in the circuit is used to enable on-board devices; two of these are the latch for the extra address lines, and the latch for the data from the STE bus. The other decoder outputs could be used for any other devices required on the board.

As regards the software for accessing a device on the STE device, the routine for writing a data byte is as follows:

```
If necessary, output upper 6 bits of address to latch
Output byte to correct address
REPEAT UNTIL bit 1 of port 3 is '1'
```

To read a byte, the algorithm is:

```
If required, output upper 6 bits of address
Read from correct address
REPEAT UNTIL bit 1 of port 3 is '1'
Read byte from 'data' latch
```

Thus connecting a processor with a synchronous bus to STE is not straightforward. The alternative to the above convoluted system is to assume that the STE access is sufficiently fast and so is always completed before the Z8 cycles ends. This is like setting the time out for **TFRERR*** to a value of around 1 µs, but it is rather unsatisfactory.

Note that the Z8 does have a handshake mode: an output bit on port 3 provides the strobe and the acknowledge is returned on an input bit on the port. When the acknowledge is returned an interrupt is generated and, for a read operation, the returned data are stored in port 2. This method could have been used to connect to STE, but extra hardware would still have been required for holding addresses, etc., more software would be needed to load the hardware, configure the ports and the interrupt service routine. Another way of connecting a Z8 to STE is as an intelligent slave. This is described in more detail in section 5.5.

Note also that in figure 5.19, if the STE interface circuit is excluded, there is a general block diagram which could be used as the basis for the design of a stand-alone board based around the Z8 microcomputer.

5.4   Design of direct memory access interfaces

In the ordinary way, if a peripheral device wishes to transfer data to memory, it can signal the processor of its desire (perhaps by issuing an interrupt), the processor will then read the data into one of its registers and then output the data to memory. This action takes many operations: the servicing of the interrupt is needed, as well as the two data transfers. A faster method is to by-pass the processor completely. In this *direct memory access* mode, DMA, the control of the bus is requested from the processor, and when this is acknowledged, data transfer cycles are instigated, that is, addresses, data and command lines are issued, so that data are transferred between the memory and the peripheral. This can be achieved by the peripheral issuing the signals on to the bus, or by having a separate DMA controller to do it. DMA is used in many situations where such data transfers must be handled quickly, or where it is required that the processor be interrupted for the shortest possible time. Examples of use include a disk interface where successive bytes of data are read from (or written to) the disk quite rapidly. Also, a fast data communications link, like the Ethernet system, can transmit over a million bytes of data per second which is faster than most processors can handle.

To accomplish such DMA, special chips have been designed. These *direct memory access controllers*, DMACs, are themselves microprocessors which have been preprogrammed to transfer data between peripherals and memory.

Another use of DMA is for copying data from one part of memory to another. Again this can be done by a processsor, but it can be slow as the processor has to read the instructions as well as obeying them, rather than just transferring the data. The required algorithm is of the form:

```
      initialise source and destination index registers, and block size register
loop: load data register from location addressed by source index register
      store data register at location addressed by destination register
      increment both index registers
      decrement block size register
      branch to loop if not zero
```

Admittedly , some processors have block copy instructions, the Z80 and Z8000 for example, but the procedure can be slow. A faster method is to have special hardware to do it. This again can be accomplished by a DMAC, though not all controllers are capable of this mode.

Direct memory access controllers

In general, DMACs have two modes of operation: cycle stealing and burst mode. In cycle stealing, the processor is held up for one cycle only, just enough time for one byte of data to be transferred, and this occurs whenever the peripheral requests the transfer. In burst mode, control of the bus is requested from the processor for much longer, during which period data are transferred at the fastest possible rate. This is used, for example, when a complete packet of data has been received already and stored in some local memory, and this is then transferred to the memory of the main processor. In this latter mode, data can be transferred more quickly than in the former as there is not the overhead in requesting the bus and waiting for the acknowledge. However, extra hardware is required for storing the data.

Thus DMACs must be programmed as to what mode is required. Additional information required for the transfer includes the start address of the memory where the data are stored, the amount of data to be transferred, the direction of the transfer (to or from memory), whether an interrupt is to be issued when all the data have been transferred, etc.

A block diagram of a DMA interface is shown in figure 5.21a. There are six parts to this: the DMAC itself; the interface to the processor, which allows the DMAC to be programmed; the bus control circuit, which handles the request for the bus and the acknowledgement; the bus interface, which converts the signals from the DMAC to those required for controlling the bus when the main processor has relinquished control; the interrupt control circuit, which allows the DMAC to assert the attention request lines; and the peripheral request interface, where the peripheral (or peripherals) indicate a desire for data to be transferred. Most DMACs can process several requests (as the interrupt controller of chapter 3 can handle several interrupts), thus some form of priority handling is in-built.

In figure 5.21b typical timings are shown for the operation of the circuit. When a peripheral needs servicing it issues a request (Peri.1 REQ) in response to which the DMAC issues a bus request on STE ($BUSRQ_0$*). At the end of the current STE cycle (or later), the arbiter acknowledges this request by asserting $BUSAK_0$*. The DMAC is now the bus master, so it issues the address, commands and strobes, and data are transferred to or from the peripheral (which is triggered by the signal Peri.1 ACK from the DAC). At the end of the cycle, the DMAC releases the bus request line and control of the bus is returned to another master.

Most DMACs are designed to work with one particular processor or family of processors (the Z80 DMA chip with the Z80, the 6844 with the 6800 or 6809, the 68450 with the 68000 family, the 8089 with the 8086

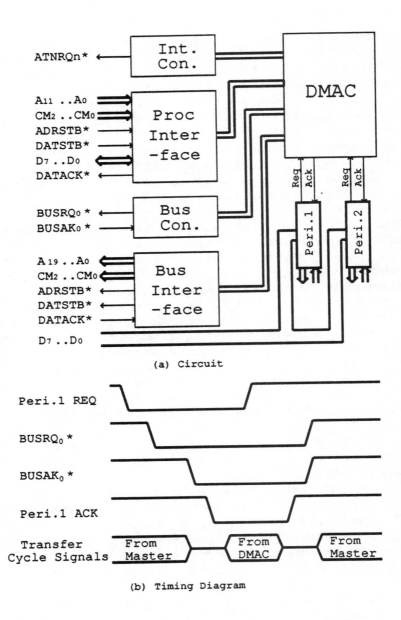

(a) Circuit

(b) Timing Diagram

Figure 5.21 DMA interface circuit and timings

family, etc.), thus the bus interface from a controller to the STE bus is very similar to that between the corresponding microprocessor and the STE bus. Hence such circuitry will not be repeated in detail here.

As regards the processor interface, this is just like the circuitry described in chapter 3: here the main processor is reading from or writing to a slave device (the DMAC). The interrupt circuitry converts interrupt requests from the DMAC into attention request signals, and handles vector fetch cycles. Again, the circuitry described in chapter 3 is appropriate.

The bus control circuit for STE converts the request signal(s) from the DMAC into **BUSRQ$_1$*** or **BUSRQ$_0$***, and **BUSAK$_1$*** or **BUSAK$_0$*** into the appropriate acknowledge signal(s) for the DMAC. When the acknowledge occurs, the DMAC controls the bus, so it outputs the necessary address and control lines, and the peripheral either outputs the data to be written to the STE bus, or prepares to accept data from another device on the bus.

A practical example: a serial communications interface

The system described here is a node on a local area network. This node can both transmit and receive serial data: it could, therefore, be part of a ring system where the data come from one node and are passed on to another, or a star network where data are sent to and received from a central controller. Thus there are two devices in the node: the transmitter and the receiver, both devices are UARTs. Whenever a byte of data is to be sent, the transmitter will request the next byte of data from memory. But if a byte has been received, the receiver will want to store that byte into memory. In each case, therefore, the device will request control of the bus so that the appropriate single byte transfer can occur. The data sent will be in fixed length packets.

The block and timing diagrams shown in figure 5.21 are applicable to this problem. Here the two peripherals are the transmitting and the receiving UARTs. When a data byte has been sent to the receiving UART, a status output from the UART is asserted and this is used as a request signal to the DMAC. The DMAC then asserts **BUSRQ$_0$***, say. When the bus arbiter acknowledges this, by asserting **BUSAK$_0$***, the DMAC outputs the address where the data are to be stored and relevant control signals (which are converted in the bus interface block into the command lines and strobes required for STE), and the data from the UART are output on to the data bus. The DMAC then increments an internal register so that when the next byte of data is received, it is written into the subsequent address. When a complete packet has been sent, that is, when the requisite number of bytes have been received, the

DMAC issues an interrupt. The processor can then examine the packet, which is now in its memory, check for errors, etc.

A similar procedure is used for the transmitter. When it is ready for the next byte of data, the appropriate signal from the UART asserts another request input to the DMAC. The DMAC then issues a bus request and, when the acknowledge is received, it outputs the address and command signals. The addressed memory then puts the data on to the data bus and these are then written into the transmitting UART, thus allowing the byte to be sent. Again, the DMAC then increments the address. When the whole packet has been sent, an interrupt is generated by the DMAC to inform the processor so that it can ready itself to send the next packet.

This system must be programmed for it to operate. Both the receiver and transmitter are serviced by separate registers within the DMAC, so each set of registers must be programmed appropriately. To both sets must be given the start address of the memory to be accessed, the length of the packet, the direction of data transfer and whether an interrupt should be generated at the end of a packet. The actual mechanism for programming will depend on the DMAC; it could be like the timer chip of chapter 3 where the registers are programmed in sequence, or the particular register to be accessed is addressed explicitly (that is a number of address lines are input to the DMAC). The transmitter facilities will be programmed when the processor has formed a complete packet of data to be sent, as only then can the packet be output. The receiver will be programmed when the processor is ready to accept a packet, and reprogrammed after processing each received packet.

DMA using attention request lines

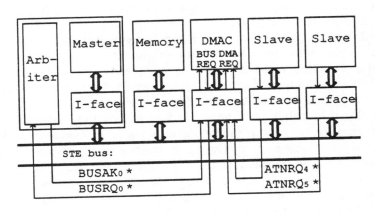

Figure 5.22 STE system with one DMA controller

The STE specification states that the attention request lines could be used for DMA accesses. This could be achieved in various ways: consider the following, as illustrated in figure 5.22. Given that DMACs require a certain amount of extra hardware and that typically one DMAC can handle several DMA requests, and that there can be only 3 bus masters on STE, it might be appropriate to have one DMAC on one board and this be accessed by various slaves wishing for DMA transfers. This is shown in the figure where there are two slaves which issue DMA requests and these are passed to a board on which there is a DMAC using $ATNRQ_4$* and $ATNRQ_5$*. When either request line is asserted, the DMAC requests control of the bus from the current arbiter, and the DMAC instigates the necessary data transfer when this is acknowledged.

How this is achieved needs some consideration. Usually two transfers will be needed, one between the slave and the DMAC and the other between the DMAC and the memory. The transfer between the slave and the DMAC may be used to clear the request. Thus a DMAC which is capable of these double transfers is required. The circuit for the slave would be no different from those described in chapter 3, as it need only respond to 'normal' data transfer cycles, except that an attention request line would be asserted to request a DMA transfer and released when the data are transferred.

Alternatively, it might be possible to arrange the transfer in one cycle, so that when the DMAC instigates the transfer, by setting the address and command lines and the strobe signals, the slave outputs the data. This requires careful thought to handle the situation when two DMA requests occur at about the same time: the slave needs to know which DMA request is being serviced by the DMAC. This could be achieved by the DMAC using other attention request lines as acknowledgements. Consider the circuit shown in figure 5.23. When the slave requires data to be transferred, it asserts $ATNRQ_4$*. In response to this the DMAC requests and is granted control of the bus and then instigates a DMA data transfer cycle in which $ATNRQ_6$* is asserted. The slave detects this request line and so knows that it should provide (or receive) the data transferred during the current cycle. One disadvantage of this method is that extra attention request lines must be used, and that extra hardware is needed to handle the data. The advantage, of course, is that the data transfer is quicker, as one cycle only is needed, but this may not be significant because of the overhead in requesting the bus, etc.

5.5 'Intelligent' slaves

Another method of connecting a microprocessor to STE is to have a self-contained system on a board: here the processor has its own memory and

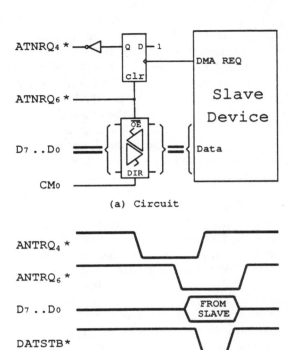

(a) Circuit

(b) Timing Diagram

Figure 5.23 One cycle DMA circuit and timings

peripherals, but it cannot drive the STE bus itself. Hence the board is a slave device. To communicate with the STE bus master, the slave must pass messages to the current bus master, and this is best accomplished using a shared resource, say a memory. To send a message, one device (the processor or the bus master) takes control of the memory, and then writes the data. Subsequently the other device reads the message. If the other device is writing to the memory, the potential sender should not do so. This leads to the problem described in section 3.15 of both devices testing the memory and finding that it is free, and both taking control. This problem can be solved using read-modify-write cycles. Alternatively, extra lines could be provided for this purpose. Both methods will be described here.

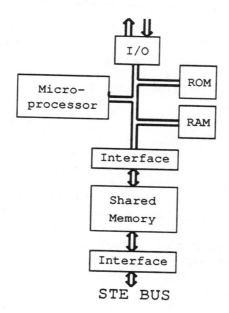

STE BUS

Figure 5.24 Block diagram of a microprocessor slave

A block diagram of such a system is shown in figure 5.24. At the top of the figure is the microprocessor with its own memory and I/O devices. At the bottom is the shared memory which can be accessed by either the processor or the STE bus master. In the following it will be assumed that the capacity of the shared memory is 32K bytes, that the microprocessor can support read-modify-write (RMW) cycles and it has a semi-synchronous bus. If it had an asynchronous bus, its interface would be very similar to the STE interface, so this circuit is more informative. The control signals from the processor are assumed to be:

$\overline{VALID\_ADDR}$: indicates that the processor is addressing the shared memory. This signal will stay valid throughout both parts of a RMW cycle. The timings of **VALID_ADDR** are like those of **ADRSTB*** on STE.
$\overline{STROBE}$: this is equivalent to **DATSTB*** on STE.
$\overline{WRITE}$: this is like CM_0 on STE: it indicates if data are being read or written by the processor.
$\overline{WAIT}$: this is the ready line, it is asserted by the memory interface to prolong the cycle from the processor.

In addition, address lines are stable while $\overline{VALID\_ADDR}$ is active, and the data lines are stable on the rising edge of $\overline{STROBE}$.

Shared memory interface with read-modify-write cycles

The basic requirement of the interface is to allow both devices to access the memory, but not at the same time. Thus, if one device instigates a data transfer cycle while a transfer from the other device is occurring, the earlier cycle should continue as normal and the 'interrupting' cycle be delayed until after the other has finished. Thus, for an STE cycle, the acknowledge signal, **DATACK***, will not be asserted until the data from the STE bus has been transferred successfully, but for the processor (with its semi-synchronous bus), the ready signal, $\overline{\text{WAIT}}$, should be asserted as soon as the cycle is instigated and released only when the data have been transferred between the processor and the memory.

In addition, the circuit should process RMW cycles correctly, that is, an *interrupting* cycle should not be allowed to access the memory until both halves of the RMW cycle have been completed. In an STE RMW cycle, as shown in figure 3.23, the address lines and **ADRSTB*** remain stable throughout both the read and the write operations. Thus the RMW cycle begins when **ADRSTB*** is asserted (and the address is correct), and ends only when **ADRSTB*** is released. Thus the processor will not be allowed to access memory during this time.

The circuit to achieve the memory interface is shown in figure 5.25a. The basic arbitration is achieved by the I-S-R latch at the top of the figure (the same arrangement as was used for handling the two bus request lines, as shown in figure 5.2). Normally both inputs to the latch are in the inactive '1' state, so neither device has control of the memory. If, however, one device instigates a cycle, the appropriate input to the latch goes to the '0' state, the corresponding output goes to the '1' state and this is fed back to the other gate, thus preventing the second input from having any effect until after the first input is released. For STE the input to the latch is the output of the comparator circuit (note that this is just like the circuits described in chapter 3 except that **DATSTB*** is not included: as **DATSTB*** goes inactive during a RMW cycle the output of the comparator would be turned off, so the RMW cycle could be interrupted). The input to the latch from the processor is the signal $\overline{\text{VALID\_ADDR}}$.

The outputs from the latch are gated with the two data strobes (**DATSTB*** on STE and $\overline{\text{STROBE}}$ from the processor) to generate signals indicating when a transfer is occurring. These are gated together to provide the chip enable signal on the RAM: this is active if either device is accessing the memory. This signal is also used to provide the delay to overcome the access time of the memory: the signal is fed to a shift register, the output of which is used to produce either **DATACK*** or $\overline{\text{WAIT}}$. During a write cycle the enable is released, so the data are written, and then **DATACK*** generated. Note that **DATACK*** is asserted after the

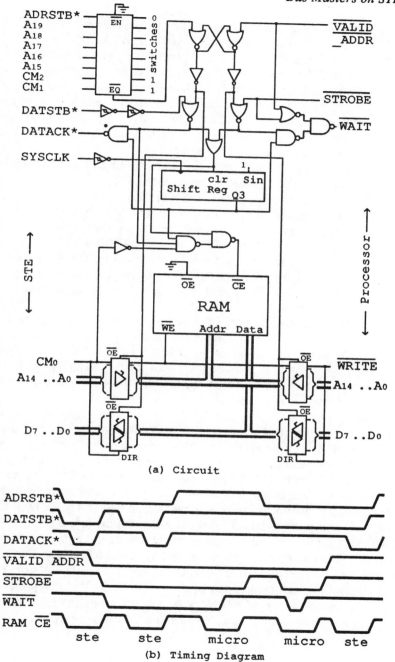

(a) Circuit

(b) Timing Diagram

Figure 5.25 Shared memory interface

necessary delay (using the shift register output) if an STE cycle is occurring, and $\overline{\text{WAIT}}$ is asserted when both $\overline{\text{VALID\_ADDR}}$ and $\overline{\text{STROBE}}$ are on and released when the delay after the start of a processor cycle has elapsed.

The other signals required for the memory are the output enable, the write enable, the address lines and the data lines. Output enable can be connected to ground permanently. The other lines are generated from the respective sources via tristate buffers. The buffers are enabled by the outputs from the latch, and the direction control of the data buffers is determined by the write signals (CM_0 and $\overline{\text{WRITE}}$).

The operation of the circuit is described in the timing diagram in figure 5.21b. This shows the STE master issuing a read-modify-write cycle during which the other processor attempts to access the RAM. Immediately this is detected, $\overline{\text{WAIT}}$ is asserted to delay the processor. Only when both parts of the STE cycle are complete can the other processor access the memory: $\overline{\text{WAIT}}$ is released a short time after the processor has access to the memory. During the processor read-modify-write cycle, the STE master also attempts to access the memory, but it has to wait until the other cycle is complete, thus **DATACK*** is not asserted until sometime after the processor cycle has finished.

In use, if the STE bus master, say, wishes to send a message to the processor, it tests and sets the first byte in the memory. If that byte contained 0, the processor was not using the memory, so the bus master can write its message. Otherwise it must wait until the processor has finished with the memory, when it should read any message from the processor, and then it can send its own message.

If the processor cannot instigate RMW cycles, and many processors cannot, the circuit described above is still applicable, but the way it is used must be changed. Instead of using the whole memory for each message, one half of the memory should be used for sending from the processor to the STE master, and the other half for sending from the master to the processor. Thus one device writes in one half of the memory only and reads from the other half, and the other device writes in the second half and reads from the first. The only exception to this is for verification that the message has been read. When the sender has put a message in the memory, it must inform the receiver: this it can do by storing 0 in the first byte, and this can be detected by the receiver. When the receiver has read the message, it should write FF in that byte, and this can be detected by the sender. Note that this protocol does not require uninterrupted RMW cycles, it just needs the interface to handle transfers from both devices (which the interface described above does).

Shared memory interface with interrupts

The following is another protocol for passing messages via a shared memory which uses software instead of hardware to prevent both devices accessing the memory at the same time. In this it is assumed that one device 'has' the memory, the other does not. When the system is reset it will be assumed that the processor 'has' the memory.

If the device which 'has' the memory wishes to send a message, it loads the message into memory and then 'grants' the memory to the other device. This other device then 'has' the memory and is able to read the message.

If the 'not has' device wishes to send a message, it must 'request' the memory. In response to this request, the 'has' device loads the memory with data if it has a message to send, and then 'grants' the memory to the other. On being granted the memory, the first device reads any message in the memory, loads its own message and then 'grants' the memory back.

Thus a device needs two variables: 'ihave' and 'iwant'; the former is true if the device 'has' the memory, the latter if it does not have it, but wants it so that it can load a message.

The 'request' and 'grant' operations are best sent as interrupts from one device to the other. So interrupt service routines are needed to handle the communications between the two devices. The software for handling each device in the system is as follows:

```
Initialisation:
      initialise ihave (true for processor, false for bus master)
      iwant := FALSE
      set-up interrupts (service routine, enable interrupts, etc.)
Routine for sending message:
      iwant := TRUE
      IF ihave THEN 'load and grant'
                  ELSE issue 'request' interrupt to other device
load and grant routine:
      load message into memory
      ihave := FALSE
      iwant := FALSE
      issue 'grant' interrupt to other device
grant from other device interrupt service routine:
      IF message in memory THEN unload message
      IF iwant THEN 'load and grant'
request from other device interrupt service routine:
      IF NOT (iwant) AND ihave THEN
            ihave := FALSE
            issue 'grant' interrupt
```

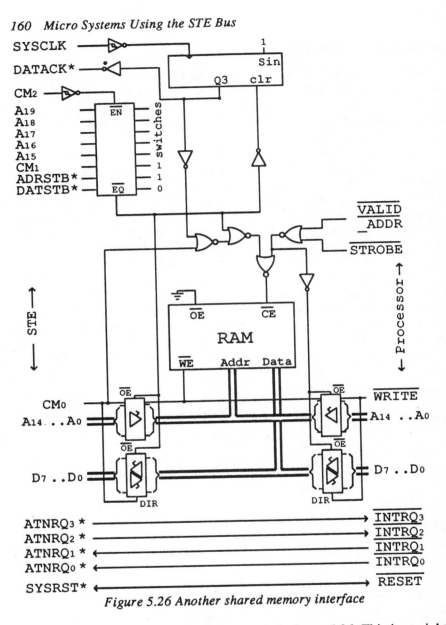

Figure 5.26 Another shared memory interface

The hardware to accomplish this is shown in figure 5.26. This is straight-forward as the memory interface does not need to handle two cycles at the same time. Thus the interface between the STE bus and the memory is just like that given in chapter 3, and between the processor and the memory a simple semi-synchronous interface is needed. As regards interrupts, these could be generated by special purpose peripherals lines implemented using latches or, if there is little else in the system, the attention request lines could be used directly. This latter method is adopted here. Thus two lines from the processor are connected directly to two **ATNRQ*** lines, and two other such lines are input from STE to the processor: no vector-fetch cycles are used.

Initialisation is important: if one device is reset problems can occur. For example, if the device which initially does not 'have' the memory resets when the other device does not 'have' it, neither device believes that it has the memory and so communication will stop. Worse still is when the 'have' initially device is reset when the other 'has' the memory, then both devices will access the memory and conflicts occur. The simple solution to this is that when one device is reset, the other should also be reset. Hence both devices are able to assert **SYSRST***.

Thus a simple method is provided for connecting an independent microprocessor system on STE, with communication to STE via a shared memory. This is probably the best method of connecting a Z8 to STE. In a standalone application only the shared memory interface would not be needed. Hence the STE system could be used for initial development and debugging of a stand-alone Z8 system. Alternatively, an STE system could be developed in which there are many Z8 (or other processor) boards.

Commercial boards are available which contain a microprocessor, its own memory and some I/O, interface to STE and an area where the user can develop his own application hardware. In one such system, the user can send his completed design to the manufacturer who will incorporate the user circuit into the existing processor hardware and produce a complete PCB.

5.6   Conclusion

The designs in this chapter show how a variety of different microprocessors can be connected to the STE bus system. STE is a truly processor-independent bus, so the appropriate chip for the particular application can be chosen. Also shown are methods of connecting other bus masters to the system and hence how a multi-processor system can be generated. Thus the STE bus, although considered to be a relatively low performance system, can be configured as a relatively high performance multi-microprocessor system.

6   *Software and Testing*

6.1   System development

For a computer system to work correctly, both the hardware and the software must be right. Unfortunately, it is impossible to guarantee that both parts will be correct: the hardware may be at fault, or the software. Certainly the software can be in error: a computer does exactly what it is told and not necessarily what you *thought* you told it to do. The hardware may have been designed incorrectly, an error may have occurred during construction, or one of the components may be damaged. Thus when a system is first configured and it does not work (which happens all too often), is it the software that is wrong, or is the hardware faulty?

Building a complete system (including the software) and expecting it to work first time is a mistake. It is far better to develop and test the system in stages. This is certainly true of software: in the recommended top-down method of programming, the program is divided into suitable parts and each part is written and tested separately; then the parts are brought together and tested gradually. The same applies to hardware: it should be divided into many modules and each module tested separately. A bus system inherently contains modules, so it is relatively easy to adopt this philosophy. Unfortunately, there is the problem that the complete testing of a module requires that the bus master device is working and running suitable test software to exercise the module. Thus the master must work as well as the memory which contains the program in order that the other modules can be tested. One potential solution to this is to buy a master board (and many are available for STE) and use that to test the other modules. Testing master devices is more complicated than testing slave devices, so the testing of the latter will be described first.

Computer-aided design (CAD) systems allow the user to enter a circuit diagram from which a printed circuit board (PCB) layout can be produced. In such an integrated system checks can be made that the PCB connections match those of the original circuit. More advanced CAD systems also allow the user to run a simulation of the circuit to verify that it will work correctly (at least in those instances that are tested by the simulation). For those who cannot afford such systems, or who are producing one-off boards for a particular application, or who are developing a prototype, it is perhaps easier just to build the circuit. In this section, therefore, the strategies for testing such a board will be described, though many of the techniques are equally applicable to any other circuit boards.

Testing is not easy, whether on hardware or software. There are certain rules which should be followed, and these help to sort out most of the problems. If the system is still at fault, testing can be tricky. Then it involves the acquisition of information about the system by injecting suitable stimuli and then processing that information, removing those parts which are irrelevant and using the rest to deduce the problem or to suggest further tests. The following anecdotes illustrate how trivial mistakes can cause baffling problems, thus making testing difficult.

The first system tested consisted of a 6809-based board connected to a PC via a serial link. The PC was running a program such that it appeared to be a terminal, thereby providing a keyboard and a VDU for the 6809 board. When the board was turned on a suitable 20-character message should have appeared on the VDU: it did not. However, the complete message did appear if the 6809 was reset; the system worked, but then it stopped again. The program on the board was known to work as it had been tested on another copy of the board, so that was not the problem. Eventually it was discovered that the reset button was wired upside down: the system worked only when the button was pressed!

The second system was a 68000 board which again used a PC as a terminal. Here the software for the board was tested in an EPROM simulator (see section 6.2), that is, the program was in the memory of another computer connected to the board under test by a cable which plugged into the socket for the EPROM. The software worked, so it was decided to replace the simulator with a real EPROM. Then the system stopped working. Checks were made regarding the speed of the memory (if anything the simulator was slower!), etc., but to no avail. Then it was discovered that the system worked when an oscilloscope (CRO) was connected to the reset line. This suggested that the capacitance of the CRO was having a significant effect (this has been observed in the past, the CRO acts as an expensive capacitor! The problem is that the CRO cannot then be used to help find the fault). However, the 'capacitor theory' seemed dubious as there was no reason why the system should have worked when the EPROM simulator was used. Then it was discovered that the CRO could be connected anywhere on the board to make it work! Then it was noticed that the important point was that the earth of the CRO had to be connected to make the board work: without it there was no earth link between the board and the PC. Such a link was provided by the simulator, hence the board worked then, but there was no earth link when the EPROM was installed. In this case the CRO was an expensive piece of wire!

Testing software can also have problems. Recently, the author was working on a problem which involved considerable amounts of arithmetic including some matrix routines. Approximate values for the final results were known, but not the intermediate values, so it was hoped that the program would be correct, as debugging would be a problem. Unfortunately the program went wrong: incorrect answers were produced. As usual, by default, the compiler does not put any checks on (to ensure data are in range, indexes are not outside arrays, etc.): this ensures that the program runs slightly faster and is shorter, which gives good performance in the standard tests (benchmarks). So, in response to the error, checks were put on, and then the program worked, but no report of any error was made. The program also worked when debugging statements were added to the program. Eventually the problem was diagnosed: an uninitialised variable. In the original program the contents of memory where the variable was stored contained a value which caused the program to be in error. When the checks were on or the debugging code added, the address of the data variable changed, to where the memory contained zeros, and the program worked.

6.2   Testing a slave module

Testing a peripheral slave

To illustrate the strategies the testing of the analog-digital conversion board of chapter 3 (figure 3.19) will be described. It will be assumed that a working microprocessor board is available and that suitable test software can be written. It is a good idea to have an 'extender board' which allows the board under test to protrude out of the bus so that CROs and other test equipment can be connected. A potential problem with this is that the signals will take longer to reach the board, but this should not be significant because of the asynchronous bus protocol.

The board should be tested in stages. The first test should be made before plugging the board in: a check that the system still works. Then there should be a check that there is no short circuit between the power rails on the board. Then, with no chips connected, the board should be plugged in and a check made that the system still works: if it does not then there is probably a short circuit between some lines on the bus. If the board now works it is time to start inserting chips.

The first part of the circuit to be tested is that which verifies that the address is correct and which generates DATACK*. Thus the two comparators at the top of the circuit (see figure 3.19), the shift register and the NAND gate chip should be inserted and the board plugged in. Static tests could be employed by driving the appropriate lines from switches and measuring other points using a test probe, but these tests do not show any hazards or glitches, so it is better to exercise the board repetitively and watch the signals on a CRO. This requires a simple program of the form:

```
loop:      read from an address allocated to board
           jump back to loop
```

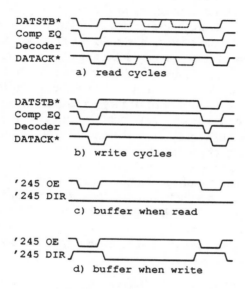

a) read cycles

b) write cycles

c) buffer when read

d) buffer when write

Figure 6.1 Expected signals on CRO

On a CRO the signals that should be seen are like the somewhat idealised signals shown in figure 6.1a: first the comparator output should be go low, and then a little time later **DATACK*** should be generated, then all signals should be turned off for a period longer than they were on (enough time for the jump instruction to be fetched and obeyed and the read instruction to be fetched) before the process is repeated. This assumes that the program is read from memory on the same board as the processor, and so the accesses to the memory do not appear on the STE bus: hence the dotted lines shown in figure 6.1a will not be there. If, however, the program instructions are transferred along the STE bus, it will be possible to see those extra **DATSTB*** and **DATACK*** strobes.

The **DATSTB*** signal could be used as the trigger for the CRO as it provides regular timings: alternatively **SYSCLK** could be used. If the **DATACK*** circuit is not working, the cycle should be ended by the watch-dog timer circuit; so there will be a longer delay before the pattern repeats, or the program might abort because of the error, so the regular pattern will not be visible on the CRO. If the comparator circuit does not work, the switch settings may be incorrect.

When this part of the circuit works, connect the 1 of 8 decoder. Now check that the same program still works. If it does then one output of the decoder should go low just after the comparator output (this is also shown in figure 6.1a). If this does not happen then the decoder chip is probably wired incorrectly: check connections to it. Next modify the program so that it writes continually to one address. Now a different decoder output should go low, but for a shorter time: it should go high before **DATACK*** is generated (see figure 6.1b). Then try accessing different addresses.

Now check the output enable and direction pins on the bidirectional data buffer: for a read cycle they should be like those in figure 6.1c and for a write cycle like that in figure 6.1d. If they are correct then insert the buffer. Note that the whole system may stop working if the buffer is wired incorrectly, as the buffer may drive the data lines at wrong times and thus corrupt all data transfers on the bus.

The next stage is to test the DAC: write a suitable value to the DAC and check that the analog voltage output is about right (the potentiometer settings will probably need adjusting for the correct voltage to be output). If this is correct, insert and test the buffer providing the busy line and then the ADC itself. The output from the DAC provides a useful input signal to the ADC. Note that to test the ADC it is necessary to write a program of the form:

```
        write to appropriate address to start conversion
loop:   read byte at address to provide busy line
        check bit 7 of this byte
        jump to loop if not ready
        read the ADC
```

Once these parts of the board work, the interrupt circuitry can be tested. This is left to last as interrupts are not easily tested, since they do not occur at regular intervals and so do not provide regular triggering for the CRO. Also, much programming is required to handle interrupts. The first stage of testing is to insert the D-type flip-flops and verify that, when they are enabled, the end of conversion causes the $\overline{Q}$ output of the second flip-flop to go low. After that the rest of the circuit must be connected and suitable software written.

Testing a memory slave

The testing of a memory module follows much the same strategy as that described above: the circuit is tested gradually. However, there are a few extra problems associated with memories because one memory chip contains a number of different locations: a circuit which appears to work, in that data are transferred to or from some locations, can be found to be in error when other addresses are accessed.

The first problem is that the address lines to the memory may be in the wrong order. This is significant for EPROMs, because instructions will be read in the wrong sequence, or for battery-backed RAM modules which may be transferred to other systems. For RAMs there is no problem: although the wrong location will be read, data will have been written to that same wrong location.

One problem with using EPROM is that every time the contents of the chip have to be changed, for a new program or test pattern, the EPROM has to be removed from the socket, put in a u.v eraser for about 20 minutes, then reprogrammed and then reinserted into the socket. This takes a long time and can reduce the reliability of the chip and the socket. A better method is to use an *EPROM simulator*.

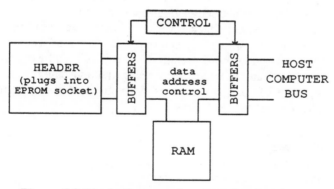

Figure 6.2 Block diagram of an EPROM simulator

A block diagram of an EPROM simulator (also called a pseudo-EPROM) is shown in figure 6.2. Essentially the simulator is a piece of RAM in a computer which is connected by a suitable cable to a header which plugs into the socket of the EPROM in the system being tested. To the circuit under test it appears that there is an EPROM in the socket, but in fact the memory is RAM whose contents can be set by the other computer. Thus changes to the contents of the 'EPROM' require only that the contents of the RAM be changed, and this can be done very quickly. Such a device is very useful when developing the initial software for a system: it allows the user to try out a series of simple test programs very rapidly.

Referring to figure 6.2, the central part of the circuit is the RAM which can either be accessed as RAM by the computer or as EPROM by the board under test. Therefore (like the dual-port memory of chapter 5) the address, data and control lines to the memory must be buffered so that only one set of signals controls the memory at any time; which one is normally controlled by a switch. Care is required with the simulator that the characteristics of the RAM (access time, etc) are sufficiently similar to that of the EPROM, that the wires from the EPROM header are not so long that they affect significantly the circuit under test, and that the address lines of the RAM are in the correct order. For the second point, it is a good idea if there are buffers sufficiently close to the header.

Another problem with memory devices occurs when there is a short circuit between two address lines, or an address line is not connected. The effect of either of these is that two different addresses are decoded as the *same* memory location. Testing for this requires some thought.

A simple program of writing a value to a location and then reading back immediately to verify that data were written correctly is not a good test, because capacitance in the wires may help preserve the data for a short time. A longer delay between the write and read operations may help to reduce this problem, or (better) an intermediate access to another location. However, this test does not check for short-circuited address lines. A better test is to write to the whole of memory and then read back from each location. There should be no correlation between the address and the data written there. This can be achieved by using random data, generated such that the sequence of random numbers does not restart until after many locations. The algorithm is as follows:

```
initialise random number generator
for each memory location
        write next random number to memory
reinitialise random number generator
for each memory location
        if value at location <> next random number then
            report error
```

6.3   Testing a master module

The testing of a master module is more difficult because for the device to operate correctly both the microprocessor and the memory circuits should be working. If there is another master device, the system can be configured with the other master as the default master, the master under test as a potential master, and any necessary slaves. The system is then switched on and the default master used to set up all necessary devices (including loading a suitable program into memory). Then the test master requests and is given control of the bus, it then runs the test program in the memory. If, on the other hand, the memory is on the same board as the master, as in the circuit described in figure 5.3, much more of the circuit must be tested in one go. An EPROM simulator is very useful in such circuits.

The first tests on a master module are to check the power supply, then the clock circuit, as this provides a good signal for triggering the CRO. After checking that the signals are correct around the socket for the micro-processor, the chip itself can be inserted. Without other circuits in place the processor will try to instigate data cycles, and these can be observed. For a processor with an asynchronous bus, a suitable acknowledge signal should be generated. If the processor seems to be working correctly, the memory circuit should be connected with a suitable simple program in it, one which loops continuously for example, or one which lights a LED and halts. Then the rest of the circuit can be added and tested.

The main problem with testing a master device is starting. Once the system is working, programs can be written to help testing and debugging. Although a simple CRO can be used to get a system going, more advanced pieces of equipment can also be used to make testing easier.

6.4   Other test equipment

Storage oscilloscopes

For a CRO to show useful information, it must show the data repeatedly. However, if regular signals do not occur, for example, with the interrupt handler in the analog/digital board, a storage CRO can be useful in testing. Such a device is capable of storing information for a short period after some trigger event, and this information is then displayed continuously. For the analog/digital board the storage CRO could be triggered by the assertion of an interrupt (or the busy line from the ADC), and the values recorded being the interrupt line, the output of the 'vector fetch' comparator, etc.

Bus analysers

Another test device which can be useful is a bus analyser. This is capable of recording signals which travel along a bus over a particular period after some trigger event occurs. During this time all transfers along the bus are recorded and these are then presented to the user to help in debugging. Some analysers can recognise the signals from different microprocessors and so can tell that an instruction is being fetched and thus deduce what the instruction is: on some systems it is then possible to list these instructions in assembly language mnemonics. Such a device seems ideal, the only problem is that it provides a great deal of information, sometimes too much, which the user then has to process to extract the relevant data. Another problem is that these devices can be programmed to do a great variety of functions and working out which is the most appropriate, and how to program the device to do it, can be difficult.

In circuit emulators (ICE)

An ICE is a device which plugs into the socket of the microprocessor and simulates the action of the processor, as the EPROM simulator does for an EPROM. The ICE drives all the address, data and control signals of the processor, and so reads and obeys the program, thereby accessing memory and peripherals. In addition, the action of the program and the associated data are stored within the ICE so that the user can see what has happened over a period of time. The program can be run in parts, stopped at suitable moments, etc.

Unfortunately, ICEs are expensive pieces of test equipment. Also separate emulators or adaptors in 'universal' emulators are required for the different microprocessors, thereby increasing the cost of the device. However they can be very useful.

6.5   Monitor program

One of the most useful programs to assist in the testing of systems is a machine-code monitor. This program, which runs on the processor being tested, allows the user to examine the memory and peripheral devices in the system and to load, run and debug programs. In the course of operation, the monitor must be able to accept commands from the user and to display suitable messages. Thus it must have its own routines for reading the keyboard and writing to the VDU, and these routines (called *traps*) are often accessible by the user program. This would be useful, for example, in testing the ADC: the value read by the conversion routine could be displayed. For the tests described above, where very short programs are needed, these programs can be entered manually, but for longer programs it is best to use an editor to create a suitable source file, and to assemble or compile the program so that it can be loaded and run.

The monitor programs provided for a number of different microprocessors in the departmental bus systems used by the author have the same user interface irrespective of processor (except for processor specific details like the names of registers, the bus size, etc.). Philosophically this is nice: in a bus system the signals on the bus are made the same irrespective of the processor, with these monitors the software appears to the user to be the same. The monitors provide the following features:

Memory examination and modification: starting from a specified address the user is able to see the current contents of memory and is able to change the contents if required. Then the user can move on to the next location, back to the previous one, specify a new starting address, or stop.

Memory tabulation: the contents of a specified block of memory are displayed in tabular form in both hexadecimal and in ASCII.

Register examination and modification: the user is able to view the contents of the registers of the microprocessor and change them. This allows the user to set registers when the program under test is being run, or to examine their contents part way through the program.

Running a program: the user specifies the start of the program and is able to set an address where the program will stop. The latter address is called a *breakpoint*. It is useful to be able to test part of the program, so by setting a breakpoint the user is able to run the program until the breakpoint is encountered, then the program aborts and returns control to the monitor thereby allowing the user to check the state of the processor by examining registers or memory. Subsequently, the user can continue running the program from where it was until another breakpoint is found. It is also possible to single step through a program; that is, one instruction is obeyed, then the system halts and the user can examine its state, and then the next instruction can be obeyed.

Other facilities include being able to load programs from another computer (usually the output of an assembler or compiler), to disassemble the code into assembly language mnemonics, to be able to move an area of memory to another address, to be able to test peripherals, etc.

6.6 Software development

A monitor program is useful for testing the hardware and software, but other facilities are required to aid the generation of the software. Ideally a program should be written in a high level language as far as is possible, with assembly language being used for extremely time-critical operations or for functions which are very difficult (if not impossible) to specify in a high level language. To do this requires an editor for entering the program, compilers, assemblers, linkers and loaders and a suitable machine on which to do this, that is, one with disks and the available software. It is possible to connect a disk to an STE system and this can be used if suitable software is available. One way to do this is to use the IBM PC-compatible STE master board with the necessary other boards: this provides a system which will run the large quantity of DOS software. Similar systems are available for other processors and operating systems.

Software can also be developed using a system with a built-in BASIC or (better) FORTH interpreter stored in a ROM. Here the user can enter the code by hand, or from disk, and this is then interpreted by the code in the ROM. For slow applications this is possible but, in the author's opinion, a good high level language should be used!

An alternative scheme is develop the software on one machine and to download the program on to an STE system. The advantage of the latter scheme is that disks are not needed on the STE system, nor a keyboard and VDU, as these are provided on the 'development' machine (a PC for example). When a system is being developed where the final system does not require such facilities, it is a pity to have to add them just for development. Thus the scheme for developing programs is to write them using an editor, assemble or compile them on the PC, and then load the program down a suitable link to the STE system; then a program can be run on the PC to monitor the action of the STE system, by simulating a VDU and keyboard, for example.

This scheme has been adopted by the author and extended slightly. One problem with providing a system in which a number of different processors can be connected, is that a separate monitor program is required for each processor. To help with this the terminal emulator program which runs on the PC can be extended to include most of the monitor so that a small part only runs on the STE bus and that is the part which is written specifically for the particular microprocessor. One advantage of this strategy is that monitors for new processors can be developed very rapidly. It is also possible to provide an integrated package containing editor, assembler, terminal emulator and monitor.

This scheme can be implemented with a small set of commands between the PC and the STE system. These commands are:

read from or write to memory in STE system
read from STE input device or write to STE output device
read from or write to register in STE processor
instruct processor to run a program
service a 'trap' routine.

To load a program requires that data be written into memory. To run a program, the registers of the STE processor must be loaded (including the program counter which is given the start address of the program) and then the command is sent to run a program. When servicing a trap routine the contents of memory and registers contain any data (for example the character to be output to the VDU, or the character from the keyboard could be returned in a register), so these can be processed by the protocol. Thus this simple set of commands, which can be implemented with very little code in the STE system, can be used for implementing the monitor. This simple system provides a quick and powerful scheme for software development. If the editor, compiler/assembler and terminal emulator/monitor are part of an integrated package, it is possible for the monitor to access the source files and so determine that, for example, a breakpoint is associated with a particular statement in the original program.

Ideally one should write software in a high level language. One problem with this is that many compilers generate code which assumes a particular operating system for handling keyboard, VDU, disks, etc. In theory a language such as C or Modula-2 which does not include such routines as part of the language, but rather has them in libraries, should be ideal for the purpose; the user just needs to provide a suitable replacement library or part-library for handling the I/O for the application. The manuals provided with some compilers, however, do not give the user enough information on how to do this, or the code generated accesses the operating system directly and so prevents this scheme.

One solution to this is to buy in a system with a suitable operating system. Many are available, for example CP/M for 8080 or Z80, OS/9 for 6809 and 68000, CP/M68K for 68000, PCDOS or MSDOS for 8086, etc. These require disks, VDUs, etc., which will be needed in development, but which may not be required in the final version. When the program works, it must be blown into an EPROM together with those parts of the operating system which are needed. Such a system is available for MSDOS, but this requires a royalty payment to the author of MSDOS.

An alternative method is to simulate the operating system. This can be achieved by an extension to the scheme outlined above with the extended terminal emulator program running on a PC using MSDOS. This will be illustrated by reference to the CP/M operating system: an 8080 or Z80 is required in the STE system. CP/M uses memory as follows:

0..100H is used for the operating system. At address 0 there is a jump to BIOS (see below) at address 5 a jump to BDOS.
Between 100H and BDOS the user program operates.
Near the top of memory is BDOS, the disk operating system.
Above this is BIOS, the input/output system.

BDOS (amongst other things) contains the CP/M trap routines which process the data and call the BIOS routines. BIOS routines do the actual accessing of the VDU, disks, etc. Thus to be able to run a CP/M program, the BDOS and BIOS traps must be simulated. The MSDOS operating system grew from the CP/M system and most of the CP/M traps are equivalent to MSDOS traps, hence simulating BDOS traps can be achieved by calling MSDOS traps. The necessary data, that is, which trap and any appropriate parameters, are acquired by reading the registers of the processor and sometimes the memory in the STE system: this can be done using the scheme described above. After the MSDOS trap has been obeyed, appropriate data are written into the STE memory or registers and the STE program is set to continue running. A similar scheme is used for the BIOS traps.

Thus the simulation of the operating system is achieved in the STE system with the same routines as those provided with the monitor program. Only a very small amount of software is needed at the STE end, so BDOS and BIOS can be very near the top of memory: because both have to start at 256 byte page boundaries, BDOS can be at address 0FE00H and BIOS at address 0FF00H, thereby providing over 63K of user program area.

At the PC end a slightly more complicated program is required. Note that some of the CP/M traps require the movement of blocks of data (for example the trap which reads a sector from the disk), and that a serial link for transferring data between the PC and the STE system can be slow. A better solution is to use a link like that described in chapter 5.

Once the system is operating, any CP/M program (compiler, etc) can be used to generate code for the STE machine. A similar scheme can be used for simulating DOS, although there are further complications in that the DOS traps and many software interrupts have to be handled. A commercial system is available for DOS which uses this basic idea: in the STE bus there is a processor in the 8086 family with a ROM containing a version of DOS and this interfaces via a serial link to a PC which provides the disks, VDU and keyboard for the STE bus.

6.7 Conclusion

For testing and developing STE systems, suitable test equipment and software are required. Much development can be done using only a CRO and a simple monitor program, but bus analysers, in circuit emulators, etc., are useful. Then the software must be considered. Again, suitable software is needed for producing the code and for testing. Different methods are available on commercial STE systems for these purposes.

7 *Practical Considerations*

In this chapter various practical points will be discussed relating to the design of digital systems in general and the STE bus system in particular. There are many problems which can occur in digital systems which impair the performance of the system. Some of these problems are described briefly and simple solutions suggested. More detail on these problems can be found in *Microcomputer Buses and Links* by D Del Corso, H Kirrman and J Nicoud and in *Digital Hardware Design* by I Catt, D Walton and M Davidson. It is worth noting that some time ago a postgraduate in the department, who was having problems with a 9900-based computer system, spent a useful lunch time reading the second of these books, made a few changes to the system as a result and the system then began to work. Other references which might be useful are the STE specification from the IEEE and relevant the data books.

7.1 Logic elements

Characteristics of logic elements

When interfacing to the STE bus, circuits are designed which use chips from various logic families. Care is required in choosing these logic elements as there is a great variety of such chips with many different characteristics. The factors which need to be considered are as follows:

Logic levels: what constitutes a logic '0' and what a logic '1': these are usually voltages, but may be currents.
Type of output: whether totem-pole, open-collector or tristate.
Characteristics of inputs, whether there is any hysteresis for example.
Power consumption: the amount of power consumed by the element. This can vary depending on the state of the device.
The loading of a logic element. This includes the loading caused by the input of an element and the loading that an output can accept, in particular the number of devices which can be driven by one output (called *fan out*).

Propagation delay: the time taken for a change of input to reach and thus affect the output.

Transition time: the time taken for an output to change state (from a '0' to a '1', or from a '1' to a '0', or from a high impedance state to a '0' or '1', or from a '0' or '1' to a high impedance state). Note that on some logic devices the transition time from a '0' to a '1' is different from the '1' to '0' transition time.

Maximum clock frequency: the fastest changing signal that can be processed by the device.

Logic families

There are various families of logic elements the most common of which are CMOS, TTL and ECL for simple devices and NMOS or HMOS for more complicated devices like microprocessors, UARTs, memories, etc. The early CMOS devices consumed little power but were slow, ECL devices are very fast but consume much power, TTL devices are a compromise, but the high speed CMOS consume little power and are as fast as many TTL devices. There are many chips in the CMOS and TTL technologies, but less for ECL. There are a number of sub-families of TTL devices whose properties extend from those of CMOS devices to those of the ECL family. These sub-families include standard TTL, L (low power but slow: these devices have some similar characteristics to CMOS), LS (low power Schottky: a compromise between speed and power consumption), S (Schottky: faster than LS, but consuming more power), ALS (Advanced LS: improved LS, faster and also the '0' to '1' transition time is the same as for the '1' to '0' transition), AS (Advanced S) or F (fast). The high speed CMOS families are HC, HCT, AC and ACT. The HC family provides many chips functionally compatible with both the TTL families and the early CMOS devices. However, the HC and AC families do not have the same logic levels as TTL, so the HCT and ACT families are provided which are compatible with TTL. As regards STE, HC and AC devices cannot be used directly on the bus because of their logic levels, and HCT devices are not able to provide enough current to drive signals on to the bus, so ACT should be used.

In the following table a comparision is given of the characteristics of various logic families:

Family	CMOS	HC	TTL	LS	ACT	S	ALS	AS	ECL
Power dissipation static	0.001	2×10^{-7}	10	2	0.44	19	1	8.5	30
per gate (mW) @ 100 KHz	0.1	0.17	10	2	1.2	19	1	8.5	30
Propagation delay (ns)	105	8	10	10	8	3	4	1.5	1
Max clock frequency (MHz)	12	40	35	40	35	125	70	200	300
Fan out (No. of LS loads)	4	10	40	20	12	50	20	50	3

It should be noted that standard TTL is not recommended for new designs. Also, although CMOS gates can be connected to TTL, convertors are needed if ECL and TTL are to be connected together.

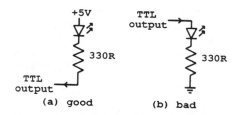

Figure 7.1 Driving a LED from a TTL gate

A TTL output can sink a greater current into its output than source a current from its output. Thus, for example, a circuit to drive a LED should be as in figure 7.1a, where when the LED is on, current flows through the LED, the voltage dropping resistor and into the TTL output, rather than the circuit in figure 7.1b. Thus the LED is lit when the output of the gate is a logic '0'. Note that some LEDs have a resistor in-built, and that resistors are available in dual-in-line and single-in-line packets.

The NMOS and HMOS technologies are used for very large scale integration devices (VLSI) where large numbers of gates are concentrated on to a small area. It is important that these devices do not get too hot, so the lower power MOS technologies are used instead of TTL. Thus these devices are often slower than TTL gates. As regards interfacing to these devices, there is no problem because they have TTL-compatible inputs and outputs. However, they are not able to drive significant loads, hence buffers are required when connecting these devices to the bus.

Electrical specifications on STE

The following section is a summary of part 7 of the STE specification and describes some requirements of circuits interfacing to the STE bus.

The types of output of the bus signals are as follows:

tristate:
    $A_{19}..A_0$, $D_7..D_0$, $CM_2..CM_0$, **ADRSTB***, **DATSTB***
open collector:
    DATACK*, **TFRERR***, **SYSRST***, $BUSRQ_1*$, $BUSRQ_0*$, $ATNRQ_7*..ATNRQ_0*$
totem pole:
    SYSCLK, $BUSAK_1*$, $BUSAK_0*$

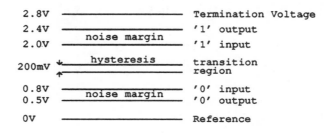

Figure 7.2 Logic levels on STE

The signal voltage levels on STE are as shown in figure 7.2. To summarise, a receiving device will accept a voltage greater than or equal to 2.0 V as a logic '1', and a voltage less than or equal to 0.8 V as a logic '0'. A device which drives the bus should output at least 2.4 V for a logic '1' and at most 0.5 V for a logic '0'. Thus there is a small noise margin between the levels for driving and receiving signals. These logic levels are compatible with most TTL gates, but not with HC TTL (for which a logic '1' is greater or equal to 2.8 V) so these cannot be used directly on the bus. ECL cannot be used for a similar reason.

Between these voltages *receivers* should exhibit Schmitt trigger characteristics with a hysteresis of at least 200 mV. This requirement is mandatory for the synchronisation signals **ADRSTB***, **DATSTB***, **DATACK***, **TFRERR*** and **SYSCLK**, and it is recommended for other devices to minimise the effects of noise.

The minimum sink capability of a driver should be 24 mA at 0.5 V, and it is recommended that the source capability be 24 mA at 2.4 V. The minimum rise and fall transition times of any line driver should be 5 ns when driving a capacitive load of 45 pF. When inactive no board should exhibit a load leakage on to a line greater than 50 μA at 2.4 V or greater than 200 μA at 0.5 V. Also, no board should present a capacitance greater than 20 pF for any signal line. The length of track from the bus connector to the on-board device should be less than 50 mm on a double-sided board and less than 25 mm on a multilayer board.

The STE specification does not state which form of digital technology should be used, instead it requires that the above criteria should be met. The LS logic family can be used, for example, but for new designs the high speed CMOS families are recommended because they consume less power. Some manufacturers produce boards containing only high-speed CMOS. Devices from the HC or AC families cannot be connected to the bus directly, but they can be used on STE boards if HCT or ACT components are used to provide an interface between the bus and the HC or AC devices. The HCT family can be used for receiving signals from the bus, but these cannot drive the bus directly as they do not have the necessary current drive capability, so the ACT family should be used instead.

7.2 Power supplies

A system will not work very well if the power supply does not provide a steady voltage. Modern switched-mode power supplies can form the basis of good systems, but these must be used properly. Some such supplies need a permanent load current, so a load resistor is needed: this gets warm so it should be placed in a suitable position where the heat can dissipate. For small systems, a linear power supply can be used.

Power supply requirements on STE

It is essential that the power supply of a system should be capable of supplying the necessary power. It should be remembered that a large current flows when the system is first switched on, so the supply should be able to handle this as well as the requirements during normal operation.

The main supply provided is +5 V which is passed through the system along four lines on the bus. No board in the system should require more than 4 A from this supply. As the maximum current through any pin on the bus connector is 1 A, boards which require more than 1 A should use all the four 5 V bus connections.

An auxiliary +/−12 V supply is also provided which is often used for serial communication and for analog signals. In practice this is sometimes not entirely suitable for analog signals for reasons explained in section 7.4. No board should require more than 1 A from these supplies.

A standby +5 V supply is also specified. This can be used for maintaining contents of memory, etc., when the main supply fails. In practice very few systems implement this feature. When it is used, no board should require more than 1 A. When not used, this supply should be derived from the main +5 V supply.

In the table below are given the recommendations for performance of the power supply. The power distribution on the bus interconnections (the backplane) must, however, be able to satisfy these requirements.

Supply	Nominal	Variation	pk-pk ripple (Below 10 MHz)	Maximum Current (Per board/per system)
+Vcc	+5 V	+5%, -2.5%	50 mV	4 A / 50 A
+AUX	+12 V	+/-5%	50 mV	1 A / 4 A
-AUX	-12 V	+/-5%	50 mV	1 A / 4 A
+VSTBY	+5 V	+/-5%	50 mV	1 A / 4 A
GND	0 V	ref	ref	- / -

Power failure

The STE specification also provides guidelines for handling power failure. If the system has an early indication of failure in the primary power supply and can do something appropriate, the attention request line ATNRQ_0* should be used to signal imminent power failure and the following protocol adopted:

For power down:

The DC output of the 5 V supply should remain within its specified tolerance for at least 4 mS after ATNRQ_0* is asserted.

The system controller should assert **SYSRST*** at least 2 ms after ATNRQ_0* is asserted.

SYSRST* should be asserted at least 50 μs before the 5 V supply falls below its minimum specified tolerance.

For power up:

SYSRST* should remain asserted for at least 200 ms after the 5 V supply reaches its minimum specified tolerance, and at least 200 ms after ATNRQ_0* is released.

Decoupling

In digital systems signals change rapidly, in a few nano seconds a change of current of a few milliamps can occur: often these changes happen on many lines at about the same time, when many address lines change state for example. The power supply must be able to handle such rapid current changes. This can be done by having many local reservoirs of current which can be tapped when required, rather than having to get the current directly from the actual supply which is physically distant. This can be achieved by connecting decoupling capacitors between the +5 V and 0 V rail near to the chips. Experience has shown that one tantalum bead capacitor of value about 2 µF is needed for every two TTL chips, and that 0.1 µF ceramic capacitors should be connected near each MOS device. Decoupling at the point where the power supply enters the board is also advisable. The +/-12 V supplies should also be decoupled near any device which uses them.

Earthing

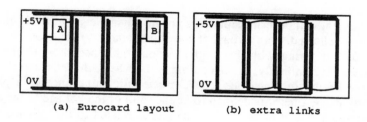

(a) Eurocard layout   (b) extra links

Figure 7.3 Earthing on eurocards

Currents flow in a complete circuit: thus when current flows from one device to another when the output of one device changes, there must be a return path to complete the circuit. It is best if this *return current* comes along the earth line rather than through the actual chips along the signal paths. To *encourage* the use of the earth line it should have as low an impedance as possible. Hence thick tracks should be used and they should be short. Unfortunately some eurocards are not very satisfactory: see figure 7.3a which shows the layout of the earth and the +5 V supply rails on one such board. Note the relatively long distance of the earth return between devices at points A and B. It is recommended that extra links should be made, as shown in figure 7.3b on both the earth and the +5V lines, to alleviate this problem. These links create earth loops which designers of analog circuits, particularly in audio systems, would want to avoid. However, such loops do not seem to cause any problems in digital systems. When designing the layout of a PCB, care is required as to the layout of earth wires: the principles described above should be applied.

In general, signal paths should be made as short as possible. This is emphasised by the requirement on STE, mentioned in section 7.1, of the maximum distances that a signal from the bus should travel into a board.

7.3   Buses

A bus has many wires along which signals travel. To analyse these the theory of transmission lines should be adopted. This is described in detail in the references cited at the start of the chapter and in *Transmission Lines for Communications* by Davidson, so some pertinent results only will be given here as well as those aspects which apply to STE. Also in this section other related problems will be discussed.

Termination

One problem with transmission lines occurs when a signal travels along the bus: it is reflected, that is, part of the signal starts flowing back along the bus thus interfering with the original signal. This occurs when the signal reaches a discontinuity. A discontinuity is where the *characteristic impedance* of the line changes (the characteristic impedance is a physical property of the line: it is defined to be the ratio of the voltage to the current of the signal travelling along the line and is related to the unit inductance and capacitance of the line). There is a discontinuity at the end of the bus and others can occur where there are sharp bends in a cable, for example, or at a joint on the line. To prevent a reflection, an impedance load should be connected at the end of the bus whose value is equal to the characteristic impedance of the line: the load is said to *match* the line. This load absorbs the energy of the signal as it reaches the end of the bus, so that no reflection occurs. This is called *termination*.

To calculate the parameters of the termination network it is necessary to know the characteristic impedance of the line. On STE it is defined that the unloaded characteristic impedance of a line should be 60 Ω +/–10% including the effects of plated-through holes and connectors. The line should have a constant width to maintain the characteristic impedance through its length. Termination networks are required at both ends of the bus except where there are at maximum 5 slots on the bus and its length is less than 100 mm when one network only is needed. The recommended termination networks are shown in figure 7.4. Figure 7.4a shows an active network, where each line is tied to 2.8 V +/–10% through a 270 Ω resistor. Figure 7.4b shows a passive network which has the appropriate impedance and where the termination voltage is derived from a resistor chain.

It is interesting to note that an unloaded STE bus line has a characteristic impedance of 60 Ω, and so the impedance of the loaded line is less than this, but the impedance of the termination networks are much larger. Thus matching is not achieved.

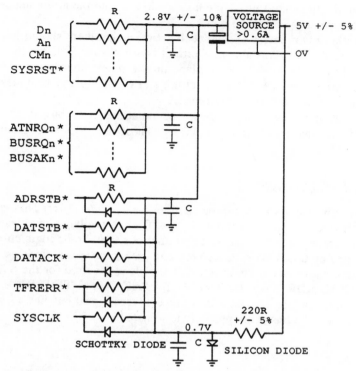

R = 270R +/- 5% C = 100nF mounted near the resistors

a) Active Termination Networks

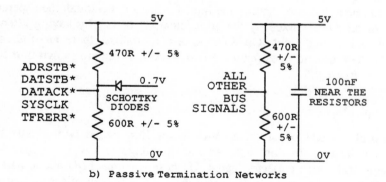

b) Passive Termination Networks

Figure 7.4 Termination networks on STE

Note that the maximum number of slots on the bus is 21, the maximum length of any signal line on the bus is 500 mm and the minimum separation between connectors is 20.3 mm.

Another requirement of the specification is that there should be a ground plane for the bus; thus a printed circuit board bus for STE has the tracks on one side and a complete earth plane on the other, interrupted only for the holes through which the connector passes. This plane provides 'a well defined transmission line enviroment'.

The easiest way to meet these specifications is to buy in the relevant backplane and termination networks. These are available from various sources.

Negative undershoot

Another problem which can occur is *negative undershoot*. This is where a signal, when it changes from a '1' to a '0', has a voltage level less than the 0 V reference before it settles to its final position. Some logic chips can be damaged by this. One form of protection is to connect a diode as shown in the termination networks in figure 7.4. This is required for the STE signals **SYSCLK, ADRSTB*, DATSTB*, DATACK*** and **TFRERR***. Negative undershoot should not occur in a properly terminated bus but, as was noted above, the STE bus is not properly terminated.

Crosstalk

Another problem which can occur when there are a number of wires in parallel, for example in a bus backplane, is that a signal in one wire can induce signals in the other. This mutual interference is called *crosstalk*. This can be reduced by having the lines further apart (though the separation of lines on STE is fixed by the connector) or, better, by having alternate signal and ground lines. On STE, as a compromise, there are four such intermediate ground lines (called guard tracks). These are shown in the bus layout in figure 7.5.

Wired-or glitch

This problem can occur on open-collector lines when two signals have asserted the line. In this case the signal voltage is low as current flows through both open-collector gates. If these are matched, about half the current flows through each. If one of these gates is then released, that gate no longer has current flowing through it. At that instant the other gate may not have enough current flowing through it for the output to remain at a logic '0'. Hence the output will go to a '1' for a short time until the effect

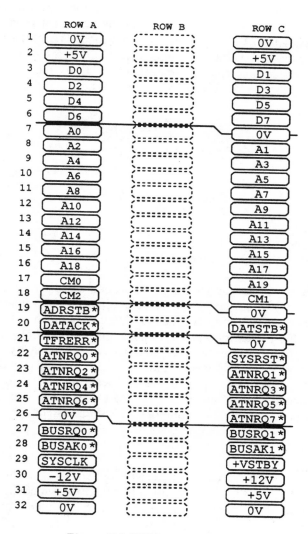

Figure 7.5 STE bus connections

of the change has propagated along the bus. The delay along the bus is approximately 3 ns/m.

On STE this is unlikely to be a problem as there are only two open-collector lines which may be asserted by many different devices at once. Attention request and bus request lines must be activated at one point only, as there is no way of determining which of many devices asserted the bus. **DATACK*** can be asserted only by the one board which is addressed. So only **TFRERR*** and **SYSRST*** may be asserted at the same time, of which **SYSRST*** is the most likely to cause problems, though it is rare for two devices to assert this reset signal at the same time. The glitch cannot be suppressed, so the best method is a simple RC filter, as shown in figure 7.6, whose time constant exceeds the propagation delay on the bus. This is a similar circuit to one used for debouncing switches.

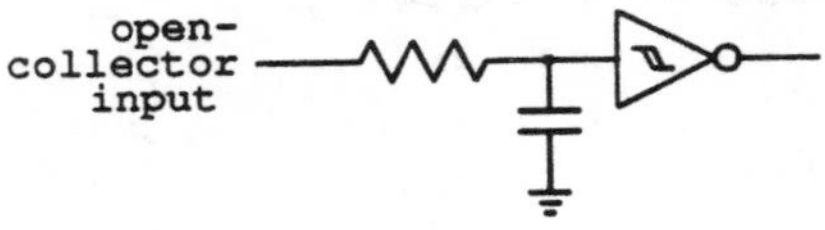

Figure 7.6 Glitch filter

7.4   Interfacing to the 'real world'

Digital systems provide an interface to the outside world at TTL levels. For some applications these ratings are sufficient, but they are inadequate for others. Hence extra buffering is required. Another problem is that devices connected to the digital system can induce signals back into the system which can prevent it from working. Isolation is required to try to prevent this. Furthermore, the requirements of the real world are often for continuous analog signals rather than discrete digital ones, and there are particular problems associated with the conversion between these forms. In this section these problems and their solutions will be discussed.

Buffering

The outputs from digital circuits provide an interface at TTL levels, typically 5 V d.c. and 24 mA max, which are often inadequate when connected to the outside world for driving motors, relays, etc. Buffering is therefore required to amplify the voltages or currents, or to change the d.c. level of the signal so that it is in the correct range. It is important to remember also that devices can break down, so they may then output signals far larger than those expected under normal operation: the system must be tolerant of such signals.

Buffering can be achieved by special buffer chips, for example, TTL chips with high current outputs, or line drivers like those used for serial communication. Higher currents can be achieved using transistors: the circuit shown in figure 7.7 allows the output of a gate to control a relay. Here the resistor is used as a voltage drop and the protection diode prevents

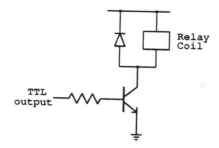

Figure 7.7 Transistor buffer circuit

overvoltage transients when the transistor current is turned off. Even higher currents can be generated using thyristors or power transistors.

The above provides on/off control only. Some applications require a varying voltage or current. This can be achieved using a digital-to-analog converter connected to a linear power amplifier, but in some circumstances a more economical solution is to use a form of pulse code modulation. In the simplest case this is achieved by outputting to an amplifier a signal of constant frequency but with variable mark-to-space ratio. The amplitude of the effective signal is determined by the amount of 'mark': if the signal is high for half the time, the amplitude is half full scale, if the signal is high a quarter of the time, the amplitude is a quarter full scale, etc.

Buffering is also required for input devices to ensure that the signal is in the right voltage and current range. In the simplest case a voltage drop can be a simple resistor potentiometer chain, though care is required to ensure that the impedance of the input device and the source of the signal do not affect the chain significantly. Comparators and Schmitt trigger circuits can also be used for this purpose.

Isolation

These buffer circuits provide the necessary power for the application, but unwanted signals may travel back along the signal connections from the external device and may affect the digital hardware. Therefore some form of isolation is often required. Two forms of isolation are often used, opto- and galvanic isolation; these are described below. Other electro-magnetic interference can also cause problems under certain conditions.

To reduce the effect of the interference, the system can be shielded by being enclosed in a continuous metal enclosure. Unfortunately, this does not allow any external connections, so holes are required in the shield through which these connections can pass, but so can the interference. Thus extra filtering is also recommended, particularly in power supplies, to remove transients caused by the interference. The mains supply itself can also cause some problems, but this interference can be reduced by a suitable filter on the power supply.

To reduce interference fed back along signal lines, opto-isolators can be used. These devices consist of a light-emitting diode and photo-transistor encased in transparent plastic within an opaque enclosure. The optical coupling between the two is good, so signal information is passed through, and the electrical isolation is very good, being able to withstand 2.5 kV signals typically. Unfortunately, these devices are not very linear, but they are suitable for transmitting digital information. To send analog information, where a linear transfer is required, voltage-frequency converters can be used: the data are transformed to a digital number before being passed through the isolator and then returned to analog form. Opto-isolation can also be achieved by sending information down optical fibres.

Galvanic isolation can be achieved using capacitors or inductors, a transformer for example. Here a voltage-to-frequency converter is used to process the signal to be sent, the output is fed to the primary of the transformer, the output is taken from the secondary coil, and then this is converted back to a usable signal. One advantage of using the transformer is that the choice of primary and secondary coils can ensure the appropriate signal size, impedance, etc., as well as providing the required isolation.

It is also possible, and sometimes desirable, to isolate physically the STE bus and the rest of the system, that is, to have the STE system in one box and other equipment separate but connected via a suitable link. In the separate system there can be suitable signal-conditioning circuitry. The outputs from the STE bus must, of course, be buffered suitably to be able to drive the link. A *de facto* standard exists for such links which has been adopted by many manufacturers of STE equipment.

Analog-digital conversion

When processing analog information the above points regarding buffering, isolation, power supplies, etc., still apply, but there are extra problems. First, with regard to power supplies, it is a good idea to separate digital and analog earth as far as possible and to connect them together at one point only. This is because the fast changing digital signals can interfere with analog signals, especially when these digital signals can be very much larger than the analog signals.

Switched mode power supplies are very suitable for digital signals, but for analog signals a linear supply is often preferable, so the auxilliary supply on STE is not necessarily the best to use. Also, for analog signals in the range +/−10 V, which is not uncommon, the +/−12 V supply is not large enough to support the amplifiers and other related chips. Amplifiers usually require that the power supply be 3 or 4 volts above the maximum signal voltage. For this reason some manufacturers of STE analog/digital boards allow the power supply for these boards to be derived from a source other than the auxiliary supply.

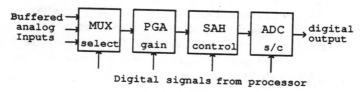

Figure 7.8 *Typical analog interface*

With analog-to-digital converters (ADCs), in addition to buffering it is often necessary to connect a sample-and-hold device (SAH) before the ADC so that the converter processes a constant signal. It must be ensured that the output of the SAH is stable before the ADC is told to start converting. For multiplexed ADCs, where there are many possible sources one of which is selected and then processed, the system must wait until the multiplexor has changed before conversion occurs. In a practical configuration, as shown in figure 7.8, the various buffered analog inputs are fed in through a multiplexor, then to a programmable gain amplifier (to scale the input to the required value) and then to a SAH whose output is passed to the ADC. Here the processor must wait for the multiplexor to settle, the signal to pass through the amplifier and the SAH to settle before conversion can begin. This can be a significant time. However, the time can be reduced by selecting the new input through the multiplexor just after telling the SAH to sample the signal.

Computers cannot process signals continually, only periodically: they *sample* signals. Hence sampling theory must be applied to the system. This is described, for example, in *Information Theory for Information Technologists* by M. Usher. One of the problems shown by sampling theory is *aliasing* where the sampled version of the signal appears to have a high frequency component which was not in the original signal. This problem can be overcome by connecting a low pass *anti-aliasing* filter which removes these components.

Another potential problem is that the outputs from digital-to-analog converters (DACs) may change too quickly in some applications where the device connected to the DAC may specify a maximum rise time. One cure for this is to arrange that large changes in the DAC output do not occur, instead, using software, these changes are done in a series of smaller steps. Alternatively, the operational amplifier following the DAC could contain a low pass filter to limit the slew rate.

A further problem that can occur is called *glitch feedthrough*. When a DAC converts a digital number there may be a glitch or spike on the output. This is caused by coupling between the output stages of the DAC and the analog switch drivers in the DAC and occurs particularly when many switches change: for bipolar operation, because of the offset binary coding used, this occurs at the 0 V level, so the glitch can be large relative to the signal. This problem can be reduced by low pass filtering, although this is unsuitable for high frequency applications, or an external buffer with in-built sample and hold which is enabled during the time when the potential glitch could occur. Glitches are difficult to remove because they have finite energy, and so filtering will not fully remove them.

7.5   Conclusion

Problems can occur in any digital system, but if the points described above are taken into account then these problems should be minimised. As an aid to the designer of such systems, the STE bus provides a good basis on which to build. The rigid requirements for the backplane, power supplies, etc., make the bus an excellent choice for various industrial applications, in research and in the teaching enviroment. In addition, the signals required on the STE bus make it very easy to interface devices to the bus, and many cards are available for a wide range of applications.

Appendix 1 Asynchronous Sequential Logic Design

In this appendix a design method for asynchronous sequential logic design will be described. This method can be used to solve the problem specified in section 3.3, but as this is complicated the technique will be explained first using a simpler example, and then used on the more complex problem. This simpler example is a logic problem involving dynamic RAMs. These RAMs can perform a normal memory cycle (where data are read or written) or a refresh cycle. The two address strobes, $\overline{RAS}$ and $\overline{CAS}$, determine which cycle is occurring, according to the following:

If $\overline{RAS}$ goes low and then $\overline{CAS}$ goes low, a normal memory cycle is instigated and continues while both strobes remain low.
If $\overline{CAS}$ goes low and then $\overline{RAS}$ goes low, a refresh cycle is instigated and continues while both strobes remain low.

A circuit is required which determines which cycle, if any, the RAM is operating. A suitable design technique for this problem is given below, though more detail can be found in *Design of Logic Systems* by D. Lewin.

A1.1 Sequential logic

A normal *combinational* logic circuit is one whose outputs are determined by its current inputs. The outputs of a *sequential* logic circuit are determined by the current *and* the past inputs to the circuit. Inherent, therefore, in a sequential logic circuit is memory. A block diagram of a sequential circuit or *machine* is shown in figure A1.1.

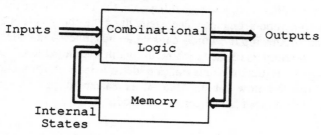

Figure A1.1 A sequential machine

191

There are two forms of sequential logic machines: synchronous and asynchronous. In a synchronous machine there is a timing signal, normally called a clock, which determines when the outputs of the machine change. Typically on, say, the rising edge of that clock, the state of the current and past inputs are processed and the outputs changed accordingly. At other times the inputs can change, but they have no effect on the outputs. An asynchronous sequential machine, however, is free running: any change in input is processed immediately and the outputs changed then.

Synchronous sequential machines are described in appendix 2; here we will concentrate on asynchronous machines.

When the inputs to an asynchronous machine are constant, the machine does not change: it is in a particular state. When an input changes, the machine is likely to change and so enter a different state. It is possible that the machine will pass through a number of intermediate states before reaching a stable state; this is reasonable. However, it is also possible to make the machine oscillate between two or more states, which is not good; but such problems should not occur if the following design method is used. Note that the inherent assumption in the method is that at most only one input can change at any one time.

A1.2   The design method

The first stage in the design is to manipulate the problem so that it is in a form which can be processed by the design algorithm. The object is to describe the problem in a tabular form. This *flow table* lists all the states that the machine can be in, the outputs of the machine when it is in each state, and the combinations of inputs which cause the machine to move to a different state. Sometimes the problem is sufficiently simple that the flow table can be written down immediately, but usually an intermediate stage is needed. This involves drawing a *timing diagram* or a *state diagram*, or both. Such diagrams for the dynamic RAM problem are given in figure A1.2.

The timing diagram shows what happens to the outputs of the machine as and when its inputs change. The state diagram shows all the states, the conditions of the inputs which cause the machine to transfer to another state, and the outputs of the machine in that new state. One advantage of the state diagram is that the information therein is in a form closer to that required for the flow table. Also, it is easier to see that all possible combinations of input have been considered.

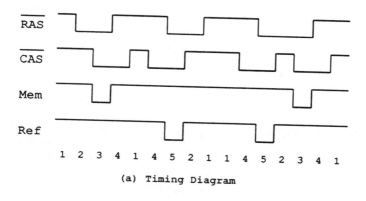

(a) Timing Diagram

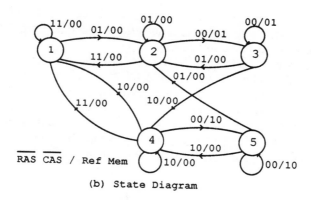

RAS CAS / Ref Mem

(b) State Diagram

Figure A1.2 Diagrams for dynamic RAM circuit

In this example there are two inputs, hence there are four possible combinations of input. The system remains in any state if the inputs have a particular value, for example, the system remains in state 1 while the inputs are both '1'. Given that only one input can change at any one time, there are two possible transitions from state 1: if $\overline{\text{RAS}}$ goes to '0', or if $\overline{\text{CAS}}$ goes to '0'. By examining the state diagram one can see that both transitions have been considered, hence the state diagram is a complete description of the machine. The numbers written on the timing diagram are the states.

The next stage is to transfer the information from the state diagram to the flow table. The resulting *primitive* flow table is shown below:

	Next State (Inputs $\overline{RAS}$ $\overline{CAS}$)				Outputs	
State	00	01	11	10	Ref	Mem
1	x	2	1	4	0	0
2	3	2	1	x	0	0
3	3	2	x	4	0	1
4	5	x	1	4	0	0
5	5	2	x	4	1	0

This shows for each state, the combinations of inputs that cause a transition to another state and the outputs of that state. An x in the next state columns indicates a *don't care* which means this combination of input cannot occur. For example in state 2, if the inputs are both '0', the machine will go to state 3, if the inputs are $\overline{RAS}$ = '0' and $\overline{CAS}$ = '1', the machine will stay in state 2, $\overline{RAS}$ = '1' and $\overline{CAS}$ = '0' cannot occur, etc.

The machine has five states, and this could be implemented directly in logic. However, it is possible to reduce the number of states. This is often a good idea as it can result in less logic circuitry.

The number of states can be reduced by *merging* two or more states together. This technique was developed by Hoffman. Two states can be merged if, in each of their next state columns, there is no contradiction (and *don't care* can mean anything). In this case, states 1 and 2 can be merged: 3 does not contradict x, 2 is the same as 2, 1 the same as 1 and 4 does not contradict x. However, states 3 and 4 cannot be merged: in their first column there is a 3 for state 3 and a 5 for state 4.

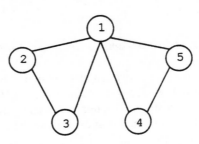

Figure A1.3 Merger diagram

So, each state is compared with each other state to see if they can be merged, and this information is put in a *merger diagram*. This consists of a series of nodes, one for each state, with lines drawn between those states which can be merged. The merger diagram for this problem is shown in figure A1.3. In order that two or more states can be merged, all of those states must be connected on the merger diagram. In this example, states 1, 2, 3 can be merged and states 1, 4, 5. As state 1 cannot be in both, it is arbitrarily assigned to the first group.

Hence the machine can be reduced to two states, A and B, where state A contains the states 1,2 and 3, and state B is made up of states 4 and 5. The reduced flow table is shown below:

	Next State ($\overline{RAS}$ $\overline{CAS}$)				Outputs Ref Mem ($\overline{RAS}$ $\overline{CAS}$)			
State	00	01	11	10	00	01	11	10
A	A	A	A	B	01	00	00	00
B	B	A	A	B	10	00	00	00

Note that as a result of the merge, different outputs are possible in each state. Hence the actual output depends both on the state that the machine is in and on the current inputs. In state A, the outputs are both 0 if the inputs are 01 and 11, but the outputs are 01 if the inputs are both 00. (When the input is 10, the machine will change to state B, so the output is undefined.) Thus, in this case, the reduced flow table has more columns than in the primitive flow table.

The machine has two states, and these could be represented by two bistables. However, one bistable can be used: if it is '0' then the machine is in state 'A', but if it is '1' the machine is in state 'B'. Let the bistable be called y.

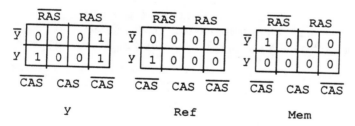

Figure A1.4 Karnaugh maps

The reduced flow table can now be relabelled and so become a Karnaugh Map (K-map). In fact it becomes three such maps, one for deciding the state and one for each output. These are shown in figure A1.4. Note that this requires just relabelling of the flow table (and splitting the outputs into separate tables) because the combinations of inputs have been written in the Gray code order 00 01 11 10, which is what is required for K-maps.

From these maps, the functions for y and the two outputs can be derived easily. Note that these functions should be *hazard free*. Thus:

$$y = y \ \overline{CAS} + RAS \ \overline{CAS}$$
$$Mem = \overline{RAS} \ \overline{CAS} \ y$$
$$Ref = \overline{RAS} \ \overline{CAS} \ \overline{y}$$

A circuit to implement these is shown in figure A1.5. Alternatively, they could be implemented directly in a PLA.

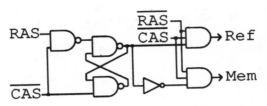

Figure A1.5 Final circuit diagram

A1.3   The DATACK* problem

Now that the method is known, the problem specified in section 3.3 can be solved. This requires a circuit with the following characteristics:

If SYSCLK is '0' when the signal e goes to '0', DATACK* should be asserted on the second rising edge of SYSCLK after e was asserted, and DATACK* should remain asserted until e is released.
If SYSCLK is '1' when the signal e goes to '0', DATACK* should be asserted on the second falling edge of SYSCLK after e was asserted, and DATACK* should remain asserted until e is released.

A timing diagram and a state diagram for this problem are shown in figure A1.6. From this the following primitive flow table can be derived:

State	Next State (for SYSCLK and e) 00	01	11	10	Output (DATACK*)
1	x	6	1	2	1
2	3	x	1	2	1
3	3	6	x	4	1
4	5	x	1	4	1
5	5	6	x	10	0
6	7	6	1	x	1
7	7	6	x	8	1
8	9	x	1	8	1
9	9	6	x	10	1
10	5	x	1	10	0

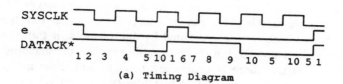

(a) Timing Diagram

(b) State Diagram   SYSCLK e / DATACK*

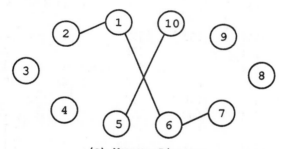

(c) Merger Diagram

Figure A1.6 Diagrams for DATACK problem

From this the merger diagram can be drawn: see figure A1.6c. The states which can be merged are 1 and 2, 1 and 6, 1 and 7, 6 and 7, 5 and 10. As 1 and 6 cannot be in two different states, 1 and 2, 6 and 7, 5 and 10 will be merged. Hence the reduced flow table is as shown below:

State	Next State (for SYSCLK and e)				Output (DATACK*)	Bistables		
	00	01	11	10		y_1	y_2	y_3
1	3	6	1	1	1	0	0	0
3	3	6	x	4	1	0	0	1
4	5	x	1	4	1	0	1	1
5	5	6	1	5	0	x	1	0
6	6	6	1	8	1	1	1	1
8	9	x	1	8	1	1	0	1
9	9	6	x	5	1	1	0	0

In this case there are 7 states, and one bistable could be assigned for each state. However, fewer bistables can be used. In the earlier example there were two states which were represented by one bistable: if this was a '1', the machine was in state B, but if the bistable was '0', the machine was in state A. For 7 states, three bistables are needed, and these are encoded suitably to represent the states. These bistables (y_1, y_2 and y_3) are shown in the flow table above. State 1 is where the bistables are 0 0 0, state 2 is where they are 0 0 1, etc. Note that there are 8 possible combinations of three bistables but only 7 states, so one state (5) is represented by two codes. The codes have been chosen to be in Gray code order (for ease of conversion to K-maps), though this is not necessarily the best choice: a different set might result in a circuit requiring less logic.

Note that the merging has resulted in groups of states where the output is the same irrespective of inputs while the machine remains in each state. Thus there is only one output column in the reduced flow table.

The next stage is to replace the state numbers in the table by the codes for those states. Hence:

State	Next State (for SYSCLK and e) 00	01	11	10	Output (DATACK*)	Bistables y_1 y_2 y_3
1	001	111	000	000	1	0 0 0
3	001	111	xxx	011	1	0 0 1
4	x10	xxx	000	011	1	0 1 1
5	x10	111	000	x10	0	0 1 0
5	x10	111	000	x10	0	1 1 0
6	111	111	000	101	1	1 1 1
8	100	xxx	000	101	1	1 0 1
9	100	111	xxx	x10	1	1 0 0

Note that in the above, in preparation for transforming the data into K maps, state 5 is duplicated. Thus the transformation consists of taking the first column in each group of three for the K map for y_1, the second column for y_2 and the third column for y_3. Hence the K maps for the bistables are as shown in figure A1.7. From these, the hazard-free logic functions for the bistables can be derived:

$$y_1 = \overline{\text{SYSCLK}}\ e + y_1\ \overline{\text{SYSCLK}} + y_1\ \overline{e}$$

$$y_2 = \overline{\text{SYSCLK}}\ e + y_2\ \overline{\text{SYSCLK}} + y_1\ \overline{y_3}\ \text{SYSCLK}\ \overline{e} + $$
$$y_2\ \overline{y_3}\ \overline{e} + \overline{y_1}\ y_2\ \overline{e} + \overline{y_1}\ y_3\ \text{SYSCLK}\ \overline{e}$$

$$y_3 = \overline{\text{SYSCLK}}\ e + y_3\ \text{SYSCLK}\ \overline{e} + \overline{y_1}\ \overline{y_2}\ \overline{\text{SYSCLK}} + $$
$$\overline{y_1}\ \overline{y_2}\ y_3 + y_1\ y_2\ y_3\ \overline{e} + y_1\ y_2\ y_3\ \overline{\text{SYSCLK}}$$

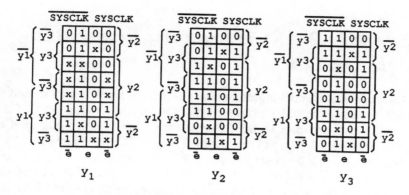

Figure A1.7 Karnaugh maps for DATACK problem

The output, DATACK*, is low only if the machine is in state 5, thus:

$$DATACK* = \overline{\overline{y_2}\,\overline{y_3}}$$

The above, rather complicated expressions, are probably best implemented using a PLA rather than in discrete logic.

Thus this asynchronous logic algorithm can be used to design sequential logic circuits. Given that there is an algorithm which could be implemented on a computer, such designs could be automated.

Appendix 2   Synchronous Sequential Logic Design

A synchronous sequential logic machine has a clock signal which is used to regulate when the machine changes state. On, say, the rising edge of the clock all inputs and past inputs (internal states) are sampled and used to generate the new outputs and new internal states. This can be realised by a machine whose form is shown in figure A2.1. The inputs to the machine and its internal states are processed by the combinational logic circuit the outputs of which are passed to an edge-triggered latch controlled by the clock. On the clock edge these signals are stored and passed to the outputs of the latch and thus the new machine outputs and the new internal states are generated. These internal states are then fed back to the combinational logic circuit. Assuming these signals propagate through the circuit and back to the latch before the signals are next sampled, hazards in the logic circuit can be ignored.

There are three examples in the book which require synchronous sequential logic circuits: the PLA of figure 3.8 in section 3.7, the controller for dynamic RAM in section 3.11, and the circuit to convert the signals from the 6809 into those for driving the STE bus in section 5.3. These circuits are relatively complicated, so the design algorithm will be described using a simpler example. More detail about this algorithm can be found in Lewin.

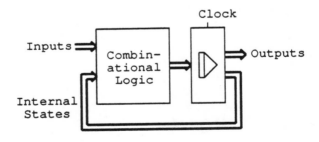

Figure A2.1 Synchronous sequential machine

A2.1 Synchronous sequential logic design method

The philosophy behind this problem is that the time a device takes to write data can be less than the time taken to read the data: this is true of many memories. The problem is to design a circuit which asserts DATACK* two clock cycles after a valid address is detected during a write cycle, but for a read cycle DATACK* should be generated after three clock cycles. DATACK* should be released at the end of the transfer cycle (when the valid address signal is removed). For the circuits given in this book, the valid address signal is the output of a comparator (see for example figure 3.3).

This is a synchronous sequential logic problem with SYSCLK as the clock and two inputs, V which is '0' when a valid address is detected, and CM_0 which specifies whether data are being read or written ('0' means write).

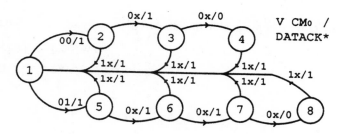

Figure A2.2 State diagram

The first stage is to process the problem so that it is in a form suitable for applying the design algorithm: as with asynchronous circuits a table is required and this is best generated by first drawing a *timing diagram* or a *state diagram*. Again a state diagram tends to be more useful. A suitable state diagram for this problem is shown in figure A2.2. Note that this is subtly different from the asynchronous case. The machine can change state only on the appropriate clock edge, it does not require a particular combination of inputs to stay in the current state, thus the diagram shows only the conditions for changing states. Also, because the machine can change only on the clock edge, many of the inputs could have changed between successive clock edges.

Referring to figure A2.2, the machine will stay in the inactive state (1) until V is asserted. Then either state 2 or state 5 is entered, the former if a write cycle is occuring, the latter if a read cycle has started. In a write cycle, on the following clock edge the machine moves to state 3 unless V is removed (when the transfer cycle has terminated). When the machine enters state 3 the cycle will have been in operation at least one clock period, hence DATACK* should be asserted on the following clock edge. This happens when the machine enters state 4. It remains in state 4 until V is released. For a read cycle, a similar sequence occurs, except that there is one extra state corresponding to the required extra clock period before DATACK* is asserted.

From this state diagram a *state table* should be drawn. This differs from a flow table in that it not only describes the next state that the machine will be in from the current state depending on the inputs; it also shows what the output(s) should be next, depending on the inputs, and not the current outputs. This is reasonable: consider the block diagram in figure A2.1. The design method will produce the combinational logic circuit. Some of the outputs of this will generate the actual outputs of the sequential machine after the next clock edge. Hence the combinational logic circuit should generate what these outputs should be in preparation for that clock edge. The state table thus must contain information as to what these outputs should be.

The state table for this problem is shown below:

State	Next State (Inputs V CM_0)				Next Output (V CM_0)			
	00	01	11	10	00	01	11	10
1	2	5	1	1	1	1	1	1
2	3	3	1	1	1	1	1	1
3	4	4	1	1	0	0	1	1
4	4	4	1	1	0	0	1	1
5	6	6	1	1	1	1	1	1
6	7	7	1	1	1	1	1	1
7	8	8	1	1	0	0	1	1
8	8	8	1	1	0	0	1	1

Thus the machine has 8 states but, as with asynchronous machines, it is often possible to reduce the number of states. With the earlier method merging could be used, but with synchronous circuits a different method is used: states are tested to see if they are *equivalent* and, if they are, they can be treated the same. Two states are *equivalent* if for all sequences of inputs, the machine produces the same outputs when it is started in either state. A necessary condition for two states to be equivalent, clearly, is that their *next outputs* must be identical. However, two states may be considered equivalent even if their *next states* are not identical, provided that it is possible to establish the equivalence of their unlike states.

In practice this is achieved by comparing each pair of states in turn. The first test is to check their next outputs: if these are different then the two states are not equivalent. If these are the same, however, then the next states are compared. Thus, in this example, states 1 and 2 could be equivalent as their next outputs are the same, but their next states are different; from state 1 the machine can change to state 2 or 5, but for the same inputs the machine will change from state 2 to state 3. Thus states 1 and 2 will be equivalent only if states 2 and 3 and states 5 and 3 are equivalent. Thus a check is needed on states 2 and 3. For these, their next outputs are different, hence states 2 and 3 are not equivalent and so states 1 and 2 are not equivalent.

This can become an involved process: it is possible to have a machine in which states A and B are equivalent if states C and D are equivalent, and that these are equivalent if states A and E are equivalent, etc. Hence a suitable method is needed for formalising the checks. This can be achieved using *implication charts*.

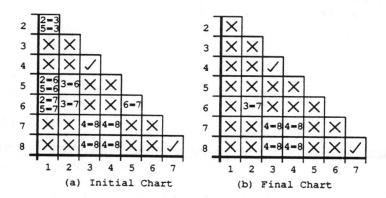

Figure A2.3 Implication charts

An implication chart for the current problem is shown in figure A2.3. The chart allows each state to be compared with each other state. Hence there are enough boxes for each pair of states. The box at the intersection of a particular row and column contains the conditions for equivalence (the *implications*) of the two states with that row number and that column number. The chart is first constructed as follows.

For all pairs of states, a cross is put in the appropriate box if their next outputs are different, that is that the two states are not equivalent. A tick is put in the box if the states are identical (and hence equivalent). Otherwise the conditions for equivalence are put in the box. Here states 1 and 2 are equivalent if states 2 and 3 and states 5 and 3 are equivalent, so '2=3' and '5=3' are put in the first box, etc. The initial chart is in figure A2.3a).

The chart is now examined systematically until a cross is found. There is a cross in row 2 column 3, which indicates that states 2 and 3 are not equivalent. The chart is then examined to see if there is a box in which '2=3' is written: in this case there is, in row 2 column 1 which means that states 2 and 1 are equivalent if states 2 and 3 are equivalent. But states 2 and 3 are not equivalent, so states 1 and 2 are not equivalent, thus a cross should be written in row 2 column 1.

This process is repeated until all the chart has been examined. The chart is then examined again and all those boxes with new crosses are checked in the same way. This continues until the chart is scanned and no new crosses are written. For the current problem the final chart is in figure A2.3b.

The next stage is to examine the result. Any boxes without crosses indicate equivalent states. Thus, in this case the equivalent states are 2 and 6, 3 and 4, 3 and 7, 3 and 8, 4 and 7, 4 and 8, and 7 and 8. Hence states 2 and 6 can be combined as can states 3, 4, 7 and 8. Hence the machine can be represented by four states: 1, 2 (and 6), 3 (and 4, 7, 8) and 5.

From this the reduced state table can be drawn:

State	Next State (Inputs $\vee$ CM_0)				Next Output ($\vee$ CM_0)				Bistables
	00	01	11	10	00	01	11	10	b_1 b_2
1	2	5	1	1	1	1	1	1	0 0
2	3	3	1	1	1	1	1	1	0 1
3	3	3	1	1	0	0	1	1	1 1
5	2	2	1	1	1	1	1	1	1 0

Again separate bistables can be assigned to each state, but fewer bistables are needed if suitable encoding is done. In the above table, two bistables have been used, b_1 and b_2, and codes assigned: state 1 is where both bistables are '0', etc. The states in the table can now be replaced by their codes, thus:

State	Next State (Inputs $\vee$ CM_0)				Next Output ($\vee$ CM_0)				Bistables
	00	01	11	10	00	01	11	10	b_1 b_2
1	01	10	00	00	1	1	1	1	0 0
2	11	11	00	00	1	1	1	1	0 1
3	11	11	00	00	0	0	1	1	1 1
5	01	01	00	00	1	1	1	1	1 0

This shows how the bistables should be set or reset depending on the current state and inputs, so suitable K-maps can be produced by separating the two columns of digits (as was done in the asynchronous method), and a map for each output should also be drawn. These K-maps are shown in figure A2.4.

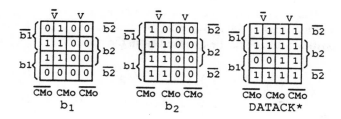

Figure A2.4 Karnaugh maps

From the K-maps, the appropriate functions can be derived:

$$b_1 = \overline{V} \, b_2 + \overline{V} \, \overline{b}_1 \, CM_0$$
$$b_2 = \overline{V} \, b_1 + \overline{V} \, b_2 + \overline{V} \, \overline{CM}_0$$
$$DATACK* = V + \overline{b}_1 + \overline{b}_2$$

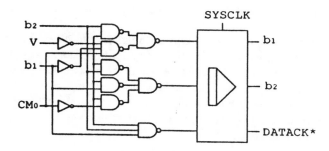

Figure A2.5 Final implementation

These can be implemented by a circuit like that shown in figure A2.5, or in a registered PLA. Note that in implementing the circuit checks should be made that the set-up and hold times for the latch are met.

A2.2   PLA in keypad and displays circuit

This circuit is introduced in section 3.7, where the circuit and informal state diagram are shown in figure 3.8. The state diagram is reproduced more formally in figure A2.6. In this circuit there are 4 inputs (**VALID***, A_1, A_0 and CM_0) and 6 outputs (the 4 clock signals for the latches $CP_0..CP_3$, the enable of the buffer **OE**, and the acknowledge signal **DATACK**). For this problem, the state diagram as drawn already has some minimisation in-built: for example, in state 2 there are five different outputs. Thus four states are needed in this machine, and this number cannot be reduced, so there is no great reason for producing a state table. Instead the logic functions for the problem will be deduced from the state diagram directly.

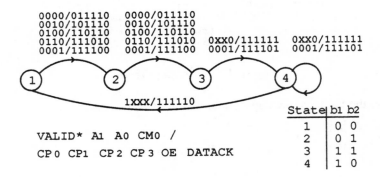

State	b1	b2
1	0	0
2	0	1
3	1	1
4	1	0

Figure A2.6 State diagram for keyboard and display circuit

The four states are encoded by two bistables b_1 and b_2 as shown in figure A2.6. From this figure the conditions for setting these bistables can be deduced directly. Bistable b_2 must be set if the next state is state 2 or 3. Similarly, b_1 should be set if the next state is state 3 or 4. When implementing these conditions the transitions to the state and when the machine stays in a state should *both* be considered. Thus the conditions for setting b_2 on the next clock cycle are:

$$\overline{b}_1 \, \overline{b}_2 \, (\overline{\text{VALID*}} \, \overline{A}_1 \, \overline{A}_0 \, \overline{CM}_0 + \overline{\text{VALID*}} \, \overline{A}_1 \, A_0 \, \overline{CM}_0 +$$
$$\overline{\text{VALID*}} \, A_1 \, \overline{A}_0 \, \overline{CM}_0 + \overline{\text{VALID*}} \, A_1 \, A_0 \, \overline{CM}_0 + \overline{\text{VALID*}} \, \overline{A}_1 \, \overline{A}_0 \, CM_0)$$
$$+ \, \overline{b}_1 \, b_2 \, (\overline{\text{VALID*}} \, \overline{A}_1 \, \overline{A}_0 \, \overline{CM}_0 + \overline{\text{VALID*}} \, \overline{A}_1 \, A_0 \, \overline{CM}_0 +$$
$$\overline{\text{VALID*}} \, A_1 \, \overline{A}_0 \, \overline{CM}_0 + \overline{\text{VALID*}} \, A_1 \, A_0 \, \overline{CM}_0 + \overline{\text{VALID*}} \, \overline{A}_1 \, \overline{A}_0 \, CM_0)$$

Simplified, the expression for b_2 is:

$$b_2 = \overline{b}_1 \, \overline{\text{VALID*}} \, (\, \overline{CM}_0 + \overline{A}_1 \, \overline{A}_0 \,)$$

Similarly, the expression for b_1 is:

$$b_1 = (\, b_2 + b_1 \,) \, \overline{\text{VALID*}} \, (\, \overline{CM}_0 + \overline{A}_1 \, \overline{A}_0 \,)$$

CP_0 should be low if the machine will be in state 2 or 3 next, and the inputs are correct, thus:

$$\overline{CP}_0 = \overline{b}_1 \, \overline{b}_2 \, \overline{\text{VALID*}} \, \overline{A}_1 \, \overline{A}_0 \, \overline{CM}_0 + \overline{b}_2 \, b_2 \, \overline{\text{VALID*}} \, \overline{A}_1 \, \overline{A}_0 \, \overline{CM}_0$$
$$= \overline{b}_1 \, \overline{\text{VALID*}} \, \overline{A}_1 \, \overline{A}_0 \, \overline{CM}_0$$

Similarly,

$$\overline{CP_1} = \overline{b}_1 \ \overline{VALID^*} \ \overline{A}_1 \ A_0 \ \overline{CM_0}$$
$$\overline{CP_2} = \overline{b}_1 \ \overline{VALID^*} \ A_1 \ \overline{A}_0 \ \overline{CM_0}$$
$$\overline{CP_3} = \overline{b}_1 \ \overline{VALID^*} \ A_1 \ A_0 \ \overline{CM_0}$$

The output enable on the buffer is

$$\begin{aligned}
\overline{OE} &= \overline{b}_1 \ \overline{b}_2 \ \overline{VALID} \ \overline{A}_1 \ \overline{A}_0 \ CM_0 \ + \ \overline{b}_1 \ b_2 \ \overline{VALID} \ \overline{A}_1 \ \overline{A}_0 \ CM_0 \\
&\quad\ b_1 \ \overline{b}_2 \ \overline{VALID} \ \overline{A}_1 \ \overline{A}_0 \ CM_0 \ + \ b_1 \ b_2 \ \overline{VALID} \ \overline{A}_1 \ \overline{A}_0 \ CM_0 \\
&= \overline{VALID} \ \overline{A}_1 \ \overline{A}_0 \ CM_0
\end{aligned}$$

Finally, the acknowledge signal should be on if the next state is state 4:

$$DATACK = b_1 \ \overline{VALID^*} \ (\ \overline{CM_0} \ + \ \overline{A}_1 \ \overline{A}_0 \ )$$

These expressions should be installed in a registered PLA to provide the requisite control for the circuit.

A2.3   6809 interface circuit

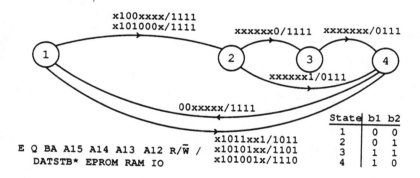

Figure A2.7 State diagram for 6809 circuit

This problem is introduced in section 5.3, where an appropriate state diagram is shown in figure 5.5. This is reproduced more formally in figure A2.7. As can be seen from this diagram, there are eight inputs to the circuit (E Q BA A_{15} A_{14} A_{13} A_{12} R/$\overline{W}$) and four outputs (DATSTB*, and enables for the EPROM, the RAM and the I/O circuit). Although it would be possible to construct the state diagram for this problem, it would require 256 lines and generally be unmanageable (unless done by computer). Also, one reason for producing the state diagram is to allow the number of states to be reduced. By inspection of the state diagram it is clear that the next outputs from each state will differ, thus the minimum number of states for the machine is four. Hence the design procedure can continue from just the state diagram.

As shown in figure A2.7, two bistables are encoded to represent the four different states. The next stage is to deduce the expressions which determine when these bistables are set. For the simpler example described in section A2.1, K-maps were drawn, but this is impractical for eight inputs. Instead the following argument is used:

Bistable b_1 should be set if the next state is state 3 or state 4. Bistable b_2 should be set if the next state is state 2 or state 3. Again, the transitions to the state and when the machine stays in the state should *both* be considered. Thus, in words, b1 will be set if:

state 3 is entered from state 2, i.e. in state 2 $R/\overline{W}$ is '0'
or state 4 is entered from state 1, i.e. in state 1 a non STE cycle starts
or state 4 is entered from state 2, i.e. in state 2 $R/\overline{W}$ is '1'
or state 4 is entered from state 3, i.e. the machine is in state 3
or the machine remains in state 4, i.e in state 4 either E or Q is '1'.
Hence the expression for setting b_1 is:

$$b_1 = \overline{b}_1\, b_2\, R/\overline{W} + $$
$$\overline{b}_1\, \overline{b}_2\, Q\, \overline{BA}\, (\, A_{15}\, A_{14}\, R/\overline{W} + A_{15}\, \overline{A}_{14}\, A_{13} + A_{15}\, \overline{A}_{14}\, \overline{A}_{13}\, A_{12}) + $$
$$\overline{b}_1\, b_2\, R/\overline{W} + b_1\, b_2 + b_1\, \overline{b}_2\, E + b_1\, \overline{b}_2\, Q$$

which simplifies to:

$$b_1 = b_2 + b_1\, E + b_1\, Q$$
$$+ \overline{b}_1\, Q\, \overline{BA}\, A_{15}\, (\, A_{14}\, R/\overline{W} + \overline{A}_{14}\, A_{13} + \overline{A}_{14}\, A_{12})$$

Similarly, b_2 should be set if state 2 is entered from state 1 or state 3 is entered from state 2, that is

$$b_2 = \overline{b}_1\, \overline{b}_2\, Q\, \overline{BA}\, \overline{A}_{15} + \overline{b}_1\, \overline{b}_2\, Q\, \overline{BA}\, A_{15}\, \overline{A}_{14}\, \overline{A}_{13}\, \overline{A}_{12} + \overline{b}_1\, b_2\, \overline{R/\overline{W}}$$
$$= \overline{b}_1\, \overline{b}_2\, Q\, \overline{BA}\, (\overline{A}_{15} + \overline{A}_{14}\, \overline{A}_{13}\, \overline{A}_{12}) + \overline{b}_1\, b_2\, \overline{R/\overline{W}}$$

As regards the outputs, these are only active (low) when the machine is in state 4. Each output is asserted when state 4 is entered, and remains asserted while the machine is in state 4. Thus, for example, DATSTB* should be '0' if state 4 is entered from states 2 or 3, or if the machine will remain in state 4 and DATSTB* is currently '0'. Hence,

$$\overline{DATSTB^*} = b_1\, b_2 + b_2\, R/\overline{W} + b_1\, \overline{b}_2\, (E + Q)\, \overline{DATSTB^*}$$

and similarly,

$$\overline{EPROM} = \overline{b}_1\, \overline{b}_2\, Q\, \overline{BA}\, A_{15}\, A_{14}\, R/\overline{W} + b_1\, \overline{b}_2\, (E + Q)\, \overline{EPROM}$$

$$\overline{\text{RAM}} = \overline{b}_1\ \overline{b}_2\ Q\ \overline{BA}\ A_{15}\ \overline{A}_{14}\ A_{13} \quad + \quad b_1\ \overline{b}_2\ (E\ +\ Q)\ \overline{\text{RAM}}$$
$$\overline{\text{IO}} = \overline{b}_1\ \overline{b}_2\ Q\ \overline{BA}\ A_{15}\ A_{14}\ \overline{A}_{13}\ A_{12} \quad + \quad b_1\ \overline{b}_2\ (E\ +\ Q)\ \overline{\text{IO}}$$

A2.4 Dynamic RAM controller

The synchronous dynamic RAM controller introduced in section 3.11 is a more complicated example still. A block diagram showing the requirement for the controller is shown in figure 3.15 and the timing diagram for the circuit is shown in figure 3.16. The circuit processes three inputs, **Valid*** (which indicates that a valid STE memory cycle is in operation), CM_0 (which distinguishes between a read and a write cycle), and **RfREQ** (which is asserted when the next row in the memory should be refreshed). The outputs are the address strobes for the RAM **RAS** and **CAS** , the signal to select the row or column address **SEL**, the bus acknowledge signal **DATACK***, the write signal on the RAM **WE**, the output enable on the data buffer **OE**, and the signal to clear the refresh request **RfCLR**.

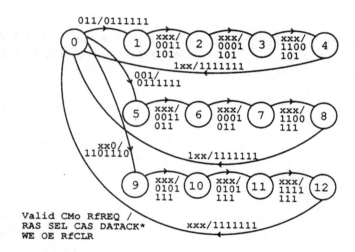

Figure A2.8 State diagram of dynamic RAM controller

The state diagram, shown in figure A2.8, is derived from the timing diagram. Again the problem is over complicated for a state table to be useful if the design algorithm is implemented manually. Also, by inspection, no two states have the same next outputs, so no reduction of states is possible. Thus the design method is to assign bistables and then implement the functions. In this case there are 13 states, so four bistables will be needed, suitably encoded, and three codes will be unused. The final circuit is often simplified if these extra codes are used by, say, allocating four codes to one state. This is done here; the bistables are coded as follows:

State	b_1	b_2	b_3	b_4
0	0	0	x	x
1	0	1	1	0
2	0	1	1	1
3	0	1	0	1
4	0	1	0	0
5	1	1	0	0
6	1	1	0	1
7	1	1	1	1
8	1	1	1	0
9	1	0	1	0
10	1	0	1	1
11	1	0	0	1
12	1	0	0	0

Using the table, b_1 should be set if the next state is one of states 5, 6, 7, 8, 9, 10, 11 and 12, etc. Thus, by referring to the state diagram, the following expressions can be derived:

$$
\begin{aligned}
b_1 \;=\; &\overline{b_1}\,\overline{b_2}\,\overline{\text{Valid}}\,\overline{\text{CM}_0}\,\text{RfReq} \;+ &&\{\text{next state is } 5\} \\
&b_1\,b_2\,\overline{b_3}\,\overline{b_4} \;+ &&\{\text{next state is } 6\} \\
&b_1\,b_2\,\overline{b_3}\,b_4 \;+ &&\{\text{next state is } 7\} \\
&b_1\,b_2\,\overline{b_3}\,b_4 \;+\; b_1\,b_2\,b_3\,\overline{b_4}\,\overline{\text{Valid}} &&\{\text{next state is } 8\} \\
&\overline{b_1}\,\overline{b_2}\,\overline{\text{RfREQ}} \;+ &&\{\text{next state is } 9\} \\
&b_1\,\overline{b_2}\,b_3\,\overline{b_4} \;+ &&\{\text{next state is } 10\} \\
&b_1\,\overline{b_2}\,\overline{b_3}\,b_4 \;+ &&\{\text{next state is } 11\} \\
&b_1\,\overline{b_2}\,\overline{b_3}\,b_4 &&\{\text{next state is } 12\} \\
b_2 \;=\; &\overline{b_1}\,\overline{b_2}\,\overline{\text{Valid}}\,\text{CM}_0\,\text{RfReq} \;+ &&\{\text{next state is } 1\} \\
&\overline{b_1}\,b_2\,b_3\,\overline{b_4} \;+ &&\{\text{next state is } 2\} \\
&\overline{b_1}\,b_2\,b_3\,b_4 \;+ &&\{\text{next state is } 3\} \\
&\overline{b_1}\,b_2\,\overline{b_3}\,b_4 \;+\; \overline{b_1}\,b_2\,\overline{b_3}\,\overline{b_4}\,\overline{\text{Valid}} &&\{\text{next state is } 4\} \\
&\overline{b_1}\,\overline{b_2}\,\overline{\text{Valid}}\,\overline{\text{CM}_0}\,\text{RfReq} \;+ &&\{\text{next state is } 5\} \\
&b_1\,b_2\,\overline{b_3}\,\overline{b_4} \;+ &&\{\text{next state is } 6\} \\
&b_1\,b_2\,\overline{b_3}\,b_4 \;+ &&\{\text{next state is } 7\} \\
&b_1\,b_2\,\overline{b_3}\,b_4 \;+\; b_1\,b_2\,b_3\,\overline{b_4}\,\overline{\text{Valid}} &&\{\text{next state is } 8\} \\
b_3 \;=\; &\overline{b_1}\,\overline{b_2}\,\overline{\text{Valid}}\,\text{CM}_0\,\text{RfReq} \;+ &&\{\text{next state is } 1\} \\
&\overline{b_1}\,b_2\,b_3\,\overline{b_4} \;+ &&\{\text{next state is } 2\} \\
&b_1\,b_2\,\overline{b_3}\,b_4 \;+ &&\{\text{next state is } 7\} \\
&b_1\,b_2\,b_3\,b_4 \;+\; b_1\,b_2\,b_3\,\overline{b_4}\,\overline{\text{Valid}} &&\{\text{next state is } 8\}
\end{aligned}
$$

$$\overline{b_1}\ \overline{b_2}\ \overline{RfREQ}\ + \qquad \{\text{next state is 9}\}$$
$$b_1\ \overline{b_2}\ b_3\ \overline{b_4} \qquad \{\text{next state is 10}\}$$
$$b_4\ =\ \overline{b_1}\ b_2\ b_3\ \overline{b_4}\ + \qquad \{\text{next state is 2}\}$$
$$\overline{b_1}\ b_2\ \overline{b_3}\ b_4\ + \qquad \{\text{next state is 3}\}$$
$$b_1\ b_2\ \overline{b_3}\ b_4\ + \qquad \{\text{next state is 6}\}$$
$$b_1\ \overline{b_2}\ b_3\ b_4\ + \qquad \{\text{next state is 7}\}$$
$$b_1\ \overline{b_2}\ b_3\ \overline{b_4}\ + \qquad \{\text{next state is 10}\}$$
$$b_1\ \overline{b_2}\ b_3\ b_4 \qquad \{\text{next state is 11}\}$$

These expressions should be simplified. For the outputs a similar process is needed. For example, RAS should be asserted (low) if

  from state 0, Valid is '0', CM_0 is '1' and RfREQ is '1'

or if the machine is in states 1 or 2

or from state 0, Valid is '0', CM_0 is '0' and RfREQ is '1'

or if the machine is in states 5, 6, 9 or 10.

Thus,

$$\overline{RAS}\ =\ \overline{b_1}\ \overline{b_2}\ \overline{Valid}\ CM_0\ RfREQ\ +\ \overline{b_1}\ b_2\ b_3\ \overline{b_4}\ +\ \overline{b_1}\ b_2\ b_3\ b_4\ +$$
$$\overline{b_1}\ \overline{b_2}\ \overline{Valid}\ CM_0\ RfREQ\ +\ b_1\ b_2\ \overline{b_3}\ b_4\ +\ b_1\ \overline{b_2}\ b_3\ b_4\ +$$
$$b_1\ \overline{b_2}\ b_3\ \overline{b_4}\ +\ b_1\ \overline{b_2}\ b_3\ b_4$$

$$\overline{SEL}\ =\ \overline{b_1}\ b_2\ b_3\ \overline{b_4}\ +\ \overline{b_1}\ b_2\ b_3\ b_4\ +\ b_1\ b_2\ \overline{b_3}\ \overline{b_4}\ +\ b_1\ b_2\ \overline{b_3}\ b_4$$

$$\overline{CAS}\ =\ \overline{b_1}\ b_2\ b_3\ b_4\ +\ \overline{b_1}\ b_2\ \overline{b_3}\ b_4\ +\ \overline{b_1}\ b_2\ b_3\ \overline{b_4}\ \overline{Valid}\ +$$
$$b_1\ b_2\ \overline{b_3}\ \overline{b_4}\ +\ b_1\ b_2\ b_3\ b_4\ +\ b_1\ b_2\ b_3\ \overline{b_4}\ \overline{Valid}\ +$$
$$\overline{b_1}\ \overline{b_2}\ \overline{RfREQ}\ +\ b_1\ \overline{b_2}\ b_3\ \overline{b_4}\ +\ b_1\ \overline{b_2}\ b_3\ b_4$$

$$DATACK^*\ =\ \overline{b_1}\ b_2\ \overline{b_3}\ b_4\ +\ \overline{b_1}\ b_2\ b_3\ \overline{b_4}\ Valid\ +$$
$$b_1\ b_2\ \overline{b_3}\ b_4\ +\ b_1\ b_2\ b_3\ \overline{b_4}\ Valid$$

$$\overline{WE}\ =\ \overline{b_1}\ b_2\ b_3\ \overline{b_4}\ +\ b_1\ b_2\ \overline{b_3}\ b_4$$

$$\overline{OE}\ =\ \overline{b_1}\ b_2\ b_3\ \overline{b_4}\ +\ \overline{b_1}\ b_2\ b_3\ b_4\ +\ \overline{b_1}\ b_2\ \overline{b_3}\ b_4\ +$$
$$b_1\ b_2\ b_3\ \overline{b_4}\ Valid$$

$$\overline{RfCLR}\ =\ \overline{b_1}\ \overline{b_2}\ \overline{RfREQ}$$

Again these expressions should be simplified. Then they should be implemented in a PLA to provide the required dynamic RAM controller.

A2.5 Automatic design

The synchronous sequential logic techniques described here provide a method for designing synchronous sequential machines. Clearly, these problems can become quite complicated and so are prone to error when implemented manually. However, as the method provides an algorithm for designing these machines, it must therefore be possible to implement that algorithm on a computer.

Also, in the above, the codes for the bistables were assigned arbitrarily.

A computer could try different codes to find which produced the best solution.

In the public domain PLA programming package used by the author, the user is allowed to enter the requirements for the machine in terms of states, and the package processes the data to generate the appropriate code for the PLA. Also, and most important, the package provides a simulation of the PLA so that the user can verify that the machine will work as required. The user supplies a set of test data for the inputs and specifies what the outputs should do given these data. The simulation package then verifies that this happens. Note that the simulation only verifies that the machine will work on the given test data and not necessarily in all circumstances. These test data are also used for verifying that the PLA has been programmed correctly, as they provide suitable signals to inject into the chip and also the signals which should be output.

Bibliography

The literature on the subject of computing is very large. Listed here are some of the books and articles that the author has found useful in the preparation of this book and as general background reading. The list is not exhaustive. In addition, when designing circuits like those given in this book, the reader should consult the data sheets on the appropriate devices.

Introductory material

B.S.Walker *Understanding Microprocessors* Macmillan Education London 1982

J.C.Cluley *Interfacing to Microprocessors* Macmillan Education London 1984

B.R.Bannister and D.G.Whitehead *Fundamentals of Modern Digital Systems* Macmillan Education London 1987

N.W.Heap and G.S.Martin *Introductory Digital Electronics* The Open University Press Milton Keynes 1982

D. Lewin *Design of Logic Systems* Van Nostrand 1985

A.E.A Almaini *Electronic Logic Systems* Prentice-Hall 1986

Bus systems

D. Del Corso, H. Kirrman and J.D. Nicoud *Microcomputer Buses and Links* Academic Press 1988

J.D. Nicoud *MUBUS STANDARD* MicroScope Vol 1 No 8. 1977

Elmer C Poe and James C Goodwin *The S-100 & other MICRO BUSES* Howard Sams & Co Inc USA 1979

High Technology Electronics Ltd *The VMEbus Specification* HTE Southampton 1985

SYNTEL *G64 Specifications Manual* SYNTEL MICROSYSTEMS Huddersfield 1984 J. Barthmaier *MULTIBUS Interfacing* Intel Corp. 1979

Paul Borrill *IEEE 896.1 the Futurebus* Electronics & Power Oct 1987 IEE

IEEE *STEbus SPECIFICATION IEEE 1000* IEEE 1987

Communications, disks and graphics

Ian Cullimore *Communicating with Microcomputers* Sigma Press England 1977

A.S. Tanenbaum *Computer Networks* Prentice-Hall 1981

M.R. Tolhurst (Editor) *Open Systems Interconnection* Macmillan Education 1988

Dimitri Bertsekas and Robert Gallager *Data Networks* Prentice-Hall 1987

Harold S. Stone *Microcomputer Interfacing* Addison-Wesley Massachusetts 1982

J.D. Foley and A. Van Dam *Fundamentals of Interactive Computer Graphics* Addison-Wesley 1982

W.M. Newman and R.F. Sproull *Principles of Interactive Computer Graphics* McGraw-Hill 1979

Donald Hearn and M.Pauline Baker *Computer Graphics* Prentice-Hall 1986

Different microprocessors

Lance A. Leventhal *6809 Assembly Language Programming* Osborne/McGraw-Hill California 1981

Russell Rector and George Alexy *The 8086 Book* Osborne/McGraw-Hill California 1980

Roger Hutty *Z80 Assembly Language Programming for Students* Macmillan Education 1982

Patrick Jaulent *The 68000 - Hardware and Software* Macmillan Education 1986

P. Jaulent, L.Baticle and P.Pillot *68020 68030 Microprocessors and their Coprocessors* Macmillan Education 1988

J.P. Royer *Handbook of software & hardware interfacing for IBM PCs* Prentice-Hall 1987

Zilog *Z8 Microcomputer Technical Manual* Zilog Inc 1984

Practical considerations

Ivor Catt, David Walton and Malcolm Davidson *Digital Hardware Design* Macmillan Education 1979

M.J. Usher *Information Theory for Information Technologists* Macmillan Education 1984

Roger J Kemp *A Guide to Analog Input and Output with STEbus* presented at STE Applications Seminar – 1988, STEMUG

C.W. Davidson *Transmission Lines for Communications, second edition* Macmillan Education London 1989

D.R.J.White *E M I Control in the design of PCBs and backplanes* White Consultants, Virginia

Harold S. Stone *Microcomputer Interfacing* Addison-Wesley Massachusetts 1982

Index

64180 127
68000, 68008 28, 29, 127
68020, 68030, 68040 11, 133
6809 28, 113
74 series logic families 176
8080, 8085 23, 28
8086, 8088, 80286, 80386 28, 135

access time 53
acknowledge (see also DATACK*) 9, 16
address 3
address bus, $A_{19}..A_0$ 3, 36
address strobe, ADRSTB* 37
aliasing 66, 109
analog-to-digital converter (ADC) 63, 188
arbiter 27, 108
arbitration 11
ASCII 87
asynchronous bus protocol 7, 9
asynchronous sequential logic 43, 191
asynchronous serial communication 86
attention requests ($ATNRQ_7..ATNRQ_0$) 68

back porch 101
baud rate 87
bipolar operation of ADC, DAC 63
BISYNC 91
bit shifting 99
black level clamp 106

block (or burst) transfer 20, 83
breakpoint 171
buffer 13, 186
burst mode (of DMA) 149
bus 2
bus acknowledges ($BUSAK_1$*, $BUSAK_0$*) 109
bus analyser 26, 169
bus connections on STE 185
bus requests ($BUSRQ_1$*, $BUSRQ_0$*) 109
bus LAN 92
bus System 2

cache memory 20, 31
cache coherency problem 31
Cambridge Ring 92
CCAS before RAS refresh 59
central processing unit (CPU) 1, 13, 15
characteristic impedance 182
clock (see also SYSCLK) 14
CMOS 176
coaxial cable 94
column address strobe, CAS 57
command lines, $CM_2..CM_0$ 37
comparator 40
computer-aided design (CAD) 162
control bus 4
coprocessor 133
CP/M 121, 173
CP/M 68K 173
CRO (Oscilloscope) 163

crosstalk 184
CRT 100
crystal oscillator 14, 90, 111
current loop 89
CYBUS 25
cycle 3
cycle stealing (for DMA) 149
cyclic redundancy check (CRC)
  90, 94

daisy chain prioritisation 12, 13, 17
data 4
data acknowledge, **DATACK*** 37
data bus, $D_7..D_0$ 4, 14, 18, 37
data strobe, **DATSTB*** 37
data transfer protocol 5, 7–11
decoder 48, 71
decoupling capacitors 180
default master 108
delay line 43
diode pump 66
digital-to-analog converter (DAC)
  63, 188
direct memory access (DMA) 6,
  11, 14–15, 18, 68, 148
DIN 41612 connector 22
disk 2, 97
disk controller 99
DMA controller 18, 148
DOS 172
dual port memory 20
dynamic RAM 56, 191, 209

earthing 181
ECL 176
EPROM 52
EPROM simulator 163, 167
equivalent state 202
Ethernet 92, 148
eurocard 27, 43, 181
explicit response (to vector fetch)
  69
extender card 164

fan out 175
fibre optic 94
flash converter 106
flow table 192
formatting a disk 99
FM coding on disk 98
frame store 106
front porch 101
full duplex 85
Futurebus 20, 31

G64, G96 28
geographical addressing 3, 30
glitch feedthrough 190
graphics 100
graphics display controller, GDC
  104

half duplex 85
handshake 10
hardware handshake 87
HDLC 91
HMOS 176
hold time 35

IBM PC 137, 172
IEEE 488, instrument bus (GPIB)
  22, 32, 96
implication chart 203
implicit response (to vector fetch)
  69
in circuit emulator (ICE) 170
input/output (I/O) 1, 13, 15
intelligent slave 19, 153
interface 13
interlace 101
interrupt 5, 11, 67
interrupt controller 74
interrupt cycle 20, 30
interrupt service routine 5
isolation 187

JEDEC standard 52

Kermit 88
key bounce & debounce 36
keypad 34

latch 4, 15, 35
LCD 35
LED 35, 175
local action response (to vector
  fetch) 69
local area network (LAN) 91, 151
lock (on bus) 20
logic families 176
logic levels 175, 178

master 3
memory 1, 13, 15
memory mapped I/O 3
merger diagram 194
MFM coding on disk 98
MIDI 95
MODEM 88
monitor program 170
monostable 42
MOSFET 49
MUBUS 24
Multibus I 24
Multibus II 30
multiplexed address/data bus 4
multi-processor system 19
multi-way (ribbon) cable 94

negative undershoot 184
NMOS 176
non-maskable interrupt (NMI) 5, 15
non volatile memory 5–6
NRZ coding on disk 98

open-collector/drain 17
open systems interconnect, OSI 93
operating system 172

optical disk 100
OS/9 173

packet 90
page mode access of D-RAM 59
parallel communication 95
parallel processing 19
parity check 30
persistence 101
phased locked loop, PLL 100
PIA, PIO 96
polling 5, 13, 67
power failure 180
power supplies 179
precharge time on D-RAM 57
printed circuit board (PCB) 162
printer, plotter 2
priority encoder 123
processor independent buses 22
programmable logic array (PLA)
  43, 51, 60, 78
propagation delay 49, 176

RAS only refresh 59
raster scan graphics 101
read cycle 7
read modify write (RMW) cycle
  20, 59, 82, 154
refresh of D-RAM 24, 57
RESET (see also **SYSRST***) 14
round-robin prioritisation 11
row addess strobe, RAS 57
RS232, RS422, RS423, RS449
  88–89
run length coding 95
run length limited, RLL 98

S-100 23
sample and hold (SAH) 66, 107,
  189
sampling theory 189
schmitt trigger input 39, 178

sector on disk 97
semi-synchronous bus protocol 7–9, 51
serial communication 85
set-up time 35
seven segment display 34
shadow mask 101
shared memory 82
shift register 42
simplex 85
slave 3
software 162, 170
state diagram 51, 62, 117, 192, 201
state table 202
static RAM 55
start bit 87
STD 26
STE 11, 27–8, etc
stop bit 87
storage CRO 169
synchronous bus protocol 7–8
synchronous sequential logic 51, 60, 117, 192, 200
synchronous serial communication 90
system clock, SYSCLK 37
system controller 27, 108
system reset, SYSRST* 37

termination 182
testing 162
timer 67, 73
to-down approach 162
track on disk 97
transfer error, TFRERR* 37

transition time 176
transmission lines 182
tristate output/buffer 13, 36
TTL 176
twisted pair 94

UART 67, 87, 90, 152
unipolar operation of ADC, DAC 63

VDU 2, 104
vector (for interrupts) 12, 15, 17, 68
vector fetch cycle 12, 68
vector graphics 101
video dynamic RAM 59, 103
VME 27, 29

wait state 8, 11, 16
wired-or glitch 184
WORM optical disk 100
write cycle 7

XON/XOFF 87

Z8 110, 141, 161
Z80 121, 148
Z8000 148